Executing Justice

The Moral Meaning of the Death Penalty

Lloyd Steffen

The Pilgrim Press
Cleveland, Ohio

To Joe Ingle

" . . . as for knowledge it will pass away. For our knowledge is imperfect."
—*St. Paul*

"It's an educated person who can be moved by statistics."
—*paraphrase of a quote attributed to Mark Twain*

The Pilgrim Press, Cleveland, Ohio 44115
© 1998 by Lloyd Steffen

Biblical quotations are from the New Revised Standard Version of the Bible, © 1989 by the
Division of Christian Education of the National Council of the Churches of Christ in the
U.S.A., and are used by permission.

03 02 01 00 99 98   5 4 3 2 1

Library of Congress Cataloging-in-Publication Data

Steffen, Lloyd H., 1951–
    Executing justice : the moral meaning of the death penalty / Lloyd
Steffen.
        p.   cm.
    Includes bibliographical references and index.
    ISBN 0-8298-1219-9 (paper : alk. paper)
    1. Capital punishment.   2. Capital punishment—United States.
I. Title.
HV8698.S74   1998
364.66'0973—dc21   98-36236
                                                           CIP

Contents

Preface   v

1 Popular Support for the Death Penalty   1

2 Who Was Willie Darden?   9

3 Just Means and Ends, or "Just Killing"?   19

4 The Right to Life, Liberty, and Security   31

5 A Service to the Greater Good   49

6 A Just Retribution for Murder   69

7 A Theory of Just Execution   88

8 Just Execution: Testing Practice against Theory   112

9 Symbol, Power, and the Death of God   142

   Notes   171

   Index   181

Preface

This book confronts the assumption widely held in American society that the death penalty is—and can be—morally justified. What the death penalty is and what it can be are, from a moral point of view, two different questions. Both questions beg investigation into the actual practice of execution.

This book treats execution as a social practice, something people do to other people in community. American law has sanctioned the death penalty and continues to widen the opportunities for its application. Because the practice of execution is directed by a system of justice administration, this inquiry confronts that system as well, although it is the moral meaning rather than the detail of death penalty litigation that is my focus. The 1972 Supreme Court decision *Furman v. Georgia,* for instance, the decision that imposed a moratorium on executions and, incidentally, declared that all legal executions in this country prior to 1972—all 18,000 of them—were unconstitutional, is mentioned along with other court cases at relevant points. But I am an ethicist in this project, not a legal scholar.

The resulting ethical critique yields a conclusion inconsonant with the widespread assumption that the death penalty is so clearly justifiable that it can withstand any challenge. I conclude, in contrast, that the death penalty can be loosened from its usual moral moorings. The execution practice is nothing less than an "unnecessary evil." That phrase captures the moral challenge—and the heart of the moral meaning question—investigated in these pages.

My introduction to the death penalty was legal. As an undergraduate enrolled in a seminar on the Supreme Court and criminal justice, I received from Professor Anthony Amsterdam, then of Stanford Law School, a copy of the *Furman v. Georgia* briefs that were scheduled to go before the Supreme Court and which convinced five of nine justices that the death penalty—as practiced at the time—was unconstitutional. Even though my reflection on the death penalty has veered from law into moral and theological issues, I have continued conversations about legal issues in various forums.

I would particularly like to thank a graduate student at Lehigh University, Eric Williams, for all he has done to keep me abreast of legal developments, help stimulate critical conversation on campus, and comment on a draft of this book.

My colleagues in the Religion Studies Department at Lehigh are to be thanked for their patience and forbearance while I worked on this book, especially Professor Michael Raposa, who first suggested this project and then graciously provided a critical reading.

Many friends and conversation partners deserve a special mention, and I mention them not to spread blame for my shortcomings but because by engaging with me—even in disagreement—they contributed to what strengths this book can claim. So I thank Professor Thomas P. Kasulis of Ohio State University for all he did to keep the clarity and power of Kant's position before my eyes, and William Hamilton, who insisted that I come clean on Jesus when doing theological exploration. Professor Frank Davis of Lehigh's Political Science Department is the source of the Orrin Hatch quote in chapter 7. Richard Brown, formerly of Pilgrim Press, encouraged me to undertake the project, and Timothy G. Staveteig, my present editor at Pilgrim, gave me time to complete it.

I am also grateful for the opportunity afforded me by an NEH Institute in 1995 to stay at the East-West Center in Honolulu. Much of the research I did for this book was begun during the study time that Institute afforded.

I wish also to thank those many students in my ethics classes at Lehigh who have scrutinized this issue with me. I have been stimulated by their insights, challenges, and disagreements—and made hopeful by their willingness to listen and reflect on the question of capital punishment's moral meaning.

One of the rare privileges of my life, occasioned by work on this issue, has been coming to know the Reverend Joe Ingle of the Neighborhood Justice Center in Nashville, Tennessee. Tireless in seeking abolition of the death penalty, Joe has spent over twenty years as a minister to death row prisoners throughout the South and has done as much as anyone to keep the issues of race and poverty at the forefront of the death penalty debate. His insistence that death row prisoners be given faces, that their stories be told as human stories that are a part of our story in moral community, is, in my view, the most important moral work that has been done to date on the death penalty. The dedication of this book is but a small indication of my gratitude for all Joe is and makes possible.

Finally, thanks to Em Finney, my patient but not interminably patient spouse, for all her love, support, and encouragement as this project sought room for attention amid the many demands of our lives, especially the joyous ones: Nathan, Sam, and Will.

1

Popular Support for the Death Penalty

Albert Camus contends in "Reflections on the Guillotine" that any society that sanctions the death penalty is foundationally unjust. The sentiment in contemporary U.S. society is quite the reverse. A majority of U.S. citizens find nothing morally objectionable about state-sponsored execution. Approval ratings for the death penalty hover at 75 percent, up from the 50 percent mark of twenty-five years ago; and a recent poll in Texas, which leads the nation in numbers of executions, pegs support in that state for the death penalty at 87 percent.[1]

Camus had in view the violence done to the executed; U.S. citizens see only the violence done to the victims of crime. Use of a death penalty power constitutes a forceful political response to the impotence many citizens feel in the face of such crime. Supporting the death penalty constitutes a symbolic act of resistance to crime and its threat to individual and societal safety. The death penalty transfers the experience of impotence from an anxiety-ridden public fearful for its safety to the individual criminal offender facing loss of life by execution.

No candidate for public office can afford to ignore the power of the death penalty symbol. Support for the death penalty has become a political necessity for any candidate who wants to be associated with taking crime seriously and acting effectively to protect law-abiding citizens. Surely Camus would find it difficult currently to garner campaign funds. Yet Camus was raising a question not about popular sentiment, but about moral meaning. Rarely does the moral question arise in public forums, because everyone whose opinion counts knows that of course the death penalty is morally justified, of course it serves justice. Those executed have earned their punishment, the argument goes; the state obviously

1

has the right to execute. Indeed more executions will undoubtedly affect in a positive way the social goals the death penalty is thought to serve, namely, punishing the guilty and protecting the innocent; enhancing respect for human life and reducing the number of homicides. Let heads roll.

Yet notice how of all the life-and-death issues besetting us today—abortion, euthanasia, and assisted suicide—the death penalty enjoys a rare consensus of political justification. Such a consensus can be inferred from a variety of public policy developments, including that thirty-nine states currently authorize capital punishment, that recent federal crime legislation has expanded to sixty the number of crimes for which the government may seek the death penalty, that Congress without public outcry has acted to limit the number of habeas corpus appeals of death row prisoners to a single federal eligibility review, and that federal funding for resource centers to defend people on death row has been eliminated. Debate over the death penalty is likely to concern not the question of moral meaning but the issue of appeals and the slow pace at which convicted capital criminals are put to death.

Notice that whereas execution policy in contemporary China garners attention and reminds us of the kinds of uses for which the death penalty has typically been used throughout history, the morality of state-sponsored executions is not questioned. (Executions are being carried out today for political crimes and, in the new market economy developing in China, the organs of executed prisoners are being sold for transplantation.[2]) Moral meaning is assumed; and the moral meaning assumed is that the death penalty is a nonproblematic justified killing— and obviously so.

In such a climate, can we dare to follow Camus's lead and raise the specter of moral meaning? So strong is the present political support that those who voice opposition to the death penalty risk being marginalized. Opposition is taken to mean "more concern for the criminal than the victim of crime." Opponents of capital punishment are commonly viewed as weak, squeamish, "soft on crime." To supporters of the death penalty, they seem to lack some fundamental sense of retributive justice, essential, or so the argument goes, if society is to survive and thrive under the rule of law.

Popular Support Is Not Moral Meaning

It is against this backdrop of widespread support for the death penalty that I propose to reexamine the moral meaning of the death penalty. That most Americans support the death penalty is a political fact, not a moral justification. The moral meaning needs to be constructed independently of popular support.

Determining moral meaning by appealing to polling data is to define morality in terms of the power of the majority. This would reduce ethics to the study of a "might makes right" morality. This book rejects such a notion of ethics as unworthy of our deepest moral sentiments and aspirations. That a majority of Americans support the death penalty is in itself no measure of the moral defensibility or permissibility of the killing that takes place when the state puts an individual citizen to death.

Executions do not proceed in a moral vacuum. Any investigation into the moral meaning of the death penalty needs also to attend to the background of ideas that have traditionally provided moral justification for state-sanctioned execution. These ideas will be discussed in the pages ahead.

Moral meaning, however, is not simply a question about the strength of an argument. Moral meaning must be derived from attending to the moral life in all its complexity, in its social context as well as in its expression in individual lives. Moral meaning must be derived from the complexity of all that is human. To extract it we need to reach into the depths of individual lives and attend to the communities of which those lives are inextricably a part. We must listen to their stories. Moral meaning will emerge from the encounter we have with persons and their communities, so that the first question we ought to ask in an inquiry into the moral meaning of the death penalty is not why someone is being executed but who that person is.

Structure of Moral Inquiry

This moral inquiry begins by meeting a death row prisoner whose life was judged unworthy of being continued. Introducing this story raises some of the critical issues, particularly those concerning race and class, that surround the death penalty. It also prompts a confrontation with the prominent arguments employed to justify the death penalty. Many still find these to be persuasive moral arguments today.

In particular, two arguments will be examined in detail: first, that the death penalty is justified because it deters crime; and second, that retributive justice—the eye-for-an-eye perspective—demands that whoever kills ought also be killed. I have chosen to confront these arguments in their classic formulations by thinkers I consider clear, thorough, and powerful. John Stuart Mill will be confronted on the deterrence question, and Immanuel Kant on the retributive justice issue. I will also consider the human rights perspective that protection from loss of life is a fundamental and inviolable human right, questioning how or whether this right can become eligible for forfeiture.

Theory of Just Execution

In examining these positions, I have applied a moral critique to the death penalty as practiced in the United States today. I not only find the arguments for deterrence and retribution wanting, but I suggest that the advocates of these arguments for the death penalty, Mill and Kant in particular, would not be supporters of the death penalty were they participating in the contemporary debate over moral meaning. From this critical perspective, I suggest that there is a theory of "just execution" that can be gleaned from the American practice of execution today, and I will articulate that theory. I will connect that theory to the evolution of the death penalty in American law, which I believe implicitly appeals to it. But then, having articulated that theory, I will argue that even this theory will not provide the moral warrants to justify execution as it is practiced today. The theory of just execution accepts the possibility that execution may be morally justified, but it imposes a standard of justice that the execution practice does not satisfy.

This book, then, is an inquiry into the moral meaning of the death penalty, and I will argue that the execution practice that appeals to just execution for moral legitimation acknowledges the moral presumption, widely held, that the state, even though it ought not to kill its citizens, can, in certain circumstances, use lethal force to protect society. I will critically examine how the American appeal to a theory of just execution creates the possibility of morally justified execution, then fails to meet the requirements of that theory in practice—empirically. My aim will be to show how we have devised a death penalty system to conform to action guides that can be traced to a coherent "just execution" theory, my argument being that in light of that theory the practice has gone astray.

Once articulated, it becomes apparent that the just execution approach to moral meaning has yielded one obvious benefit to society: the achievement of a general consensus on the moral acceptability of restricted execution. This consensus over moral meaning has not emerged on, say, the abortion issue, and society has experienced deep fractures, even outbreaks of violence, because of that lack of consensus. Capital punishment, however, has so clearly appealed to a commonly accepted understanding of moral meaning that the form of killing it sanctions has been exempted from contemporary culture war skirmishes, and there is no tearing at the fabric of society because of anguished moral debate on the issue.

I do not deny the power of this societal benefit. I come to the capital punishment issue having actually defended in a previous book on the abortion issue this kind of moral theory, which I termed in that study a *theory of just abortion*. I argued that a just abortion approach would allow for a broader consensus over moral meaning to be built on that terribly divisive issue, and that society would benefit from that effort.[3] Capital punishment enjoys just such a consensus and does so because our execution practice has implicitly appealed to a just execution theory. It shows that such a consensus can be built and that benefits to society can result.

Just execution is a theory structurally continuous with just abortion and the paradigmatic case of just war. It requires that a moral presumption be established against the state executing its citizens. This presumption is in place. As a moral community we are generally opposed to the state killing its citizens, even for heinous crimes. Out of nearly twenty-three thousand homicides per year, fewer than three hundred persons are sentenced to death, with only a small fraction of that number actually executed. Death sentences are imposed relatively rarely, involving less than 1 percent of all reported homicides. The requirement that a moral presumption against the state killing its citizens is being observed, as just execution requires.

But just execution is a nonabsolutist theory; that is, it considers exceptions to our presumption against citizen killing by the state. By examining the practicalities of the death penalty through a just execution theory, the possibility that the death penalty is a morally authorized exception arises. We restrict the crimes for which the death penalty can apply, then impose all kinds of safeguards to prevent a miscarriage of justice, including a sentencing phase in which juries consider guiding criteria in individual cases to determine the appropriateness of the death sentence. A follow-up appellate review process is even mandated by law to ensure that so serious a matter as the taking of a life is not done casually, frequently, or without due regard to the demands of law and justice.

Given the relatively small numbers of executions and the safeguards the legal system attaches to prevent error, it seems unmistakable that a theory of just execution can be gleaned from the American practice of state-sponsored execution, and that this theory is functioning not only legally but as a matter of moral consensus. In view of a theory of just abortion and the way just execution seems logically to extend this ethical approach and argument, such a theory of just execution would be exactly the kind of argument I should be willing, as a matter of moral commitment and philosophical consistency, to defend.

Yet I am not willing to defend such an argument. Not on this issue. I will specify the details of just execution and consider its theoretical strengths. But I will not ignore the gap between the theory and its practical application. Instead I will make a case that given certain problems inherent in the imposition of the death penalty, this kind of nonabsolutist theory will not meet the standards of justice required for any state-sponsored execution. Furthermore, I will argue that for all the restrictions and safeguards imposed to render executions just, a deeper problem lies in the status of the presumption against executions. A deeper analysis reveals that the death penalty is imposed not in accordance with a moral presumption *against* execution (for which any actual execution is an exception) but in relation to a more fundamental presumption that the state has a right to defend itself by using lethal force, even against its own citizens. I will defend that presumption as reasonable. But I will not defend execution as a just—or morally justifiable—means of putting that presumption into practice. Execution, rather, will be presented as a practice that does not satisfy the requirements for lifting the moral presumption against the state killing one of its own citizens. And it will fail in the same way that in my just abortion theory the idea of aborting a fetus for the reason of gender preference fails—and always fails—to satisfy the requirements for a just abortion.

Capital punishment appeals to a moral and epistemological absolutism that any state must necessarily presume in order to actually proceed to kill one of its citizens. An executed person is delivered an absolute justice in the sense that once executed, the person is beyond the reach of justice—and irretrievably so. I will oppose this absolutism as it emerges in the practice of imposing the death penalty, showing that just execution—being ostensibly a theory that some executions are justifiable and others are not—inevitably invokes the very absolutism it claims to oppose.

So this book articulates a theory of just execution but then uses that theory to oppose capital punishment. For just execution will establish a framework for establishing moral meaning that the death penalty as a legal and social practice fails to meet. Capital punishment, I will argue, is not about just execution, but about executing justice. In the end, I will return to the place Camus began—with the observation that a society that employs the death penalty is foundationally unjust. I shall argue that moral justifications for the death penalty are never compelling—even if theoretically defensible—and are always problematic. This states the conclusion to be derived from the moral analysis offered in the book.

Power as the Symbolic Meaning

In the final section of this book the death penalty is considered as symbol, thus returning to the starting place. That no necessary connection can be established between the death penalty and justice challenges the conventional wisdom concerning the death penalty symbol. The death penalty is a symbol of power, not justice. That justice is the primary and core meaning of the death penalty symbol is a view maintained at best because of ignorance of the nature of the death penalty system and at worst through individual and corporate acts of self-deception.

The death penalty as symbol is religiously significant. I will present a case for considering the theological morality (or moral theology) that attaches to state execution. In the last chapter, I lay out a theo-moral argument about the death penalty that I think merits consideration by persons committed to the tenets of Christian faith.

This book is therefore offered primarily as a work in moral philosophy and "applied ethics." The moral analysis I offer will critically engage major arguments and classic positions that even today make their way into the debate over the morality of capital punishment. The book is, in its final chapter, also an exercise in constructive theological reflection and, I hope, faith education, but I will be suggestive rather than dogmatic, my tentativeness coming from a deeply held suspicion that there is, in the Christian interpretation of the cross as symbol of salvation, a profoundly imaginative act of theological sublimation to be discerned. That act of sublimation, which shows itself in the theological justification of the cross as a positive symbol of universal salvation, has pushed from theological consciousness not only the moral horror of that execution, but, more significantly, the guilt of Jesus before the authorities who in exercise of their legal authority put him to death. I want to reclaim the guilty Jesus to remind Christians that we ought not so blithely support the practice of killing the undesirables amongst us, of whom Jesus in his day and time proved to be a curious example. If the cross is a death penalty symbol, I argue that as Christians we need to reclaim its meaning. My suggestion is that by standing together against the executions to which we have all become party, we who are Christians might awaken from the anesthetizing effects of the violence and injustice that so infect modern life and encounter the Jesus who stands before us, not innocent but guilty, and whose death still stands as an accusation against our pretense to absolute power and infallibility. But more on Jesus and the problem of theological sublimation later.

Moral conversation has broken down in our culture today with the too-easy assumption of moral certainty on complex life-and-death issues like abortion, euthanasia, and, yes, even the death penalty. And what has infected our moral debate is the sense that moral certitude is easily accessible and easily applicable to social policy decisions. But staking out a claim to such certitude is to participate in an absolutism that is destructive of moral thinking grounded in goods of life, in relationships, and in an appreciation of the need to recognize the complexity of moral meaning. Restoring nonabsolutist complexity to public debate over moral issues has become a difficult task, especially in the abortion debate where the pitting of pro-life against pro-choice perspectives in a social policy debate covers up the assumption of moral certainty expressed in the public policy debate— and on both sides. Difficult as it may be to show that the abortion debate has suffered because of an implicit appeal to opposing absolutist perspectives, the attempt to pry loose and expose the moral absolutism that undergirds support of capital punishment is perhaps an even more difficult chore. For the moral problematic involved in the death penalty is even more deeply hidden from view. It is obscured by a societal consensus that capital punishment is free from moral taint, and that the moral meaning of the death penalty is easily discernible, so that social policy on capital punishment is easily defensible.

Camus argued that state-sponsored execution was, not only as event but also as symbol, the great moral issue of our time. While such a judgment may seem out of step, even preposterous, today—at least in light of the high percentage of support capital punishment has received—that is an understanding I share and a position I will argue for in these pages.

2

Who Was Willie Darden?

In a 1990 article published in *The New American* entitled "Deserving to Die," Robert W. Lee advanced a spirited defense of the death penalty.[1] The core of Lee's argument is the familiar "just deserts" position: the death penalty, because it is directed against those who have taken a life and thus offended against society's most cherished values, is a punishment deserved by those who receive it.

One story Lee tells is meant to illustrate the old adage "Justice delayed is justice denied." Lee is concerned about the present system of capital case review by appellate courts and the danger this system poses to justice. Justice is imperiled, he argues, because of the time that elapses between the imposition of a death sentence and actual execution. And Lee broaches this issue in the course of addressing another issue—the high cost of executions. For Lee notes—quite rightly— a fact that many who are unfamiliar with the details of capital punishment often find surprising, namely, that it is much more expensive in our current system to execute an individual than to impose a sentence of lifetime incarceration. (Studies Lee does not cite indicate that death penalty cases in Texas cost on average $2.3 million, three times the cost of imprisoning for forty years; Florida averages $3.2 million per execution; and California death penalty costs are $90 million per year beyond the ordinary costs of the justice system.[2]) The high cost of capital punishment is, like the delays, a function of the appeals process. Lee levels a stout criticism at the legal system that spawns "redundant appeals, time-consuming delays, bizarre court rulings, and legal histrionics by defense lawyers."[3] And just to show how absurd the process can get, Lee asks his reader to consider the case of Willie Darden.

Lee could not have chosen a better example. For Willie Darden sat on death row for fifteen years. In that time, Darden faced seven death warrants and secured six stays of execution. He came within hours of death several times. Before he died, Darden had compiled a record of stays and delays that had not, and still has not, been equaled.

Lee asks his reader to look at Willie Darden, consider his story, then join Lee in asking, in the interests of justice, even reform, that the capital case review machinery be overhauled and streamlined. And given what Lee presents of the Willie Darden story, one would be hard pressed to disagree. Here is the story Lee actually tells about Willie Darden:

> Willie Darden, who had already survived three death warrants, was scheduled to die in Florida's electric chair on September 4, 1985, for a murder he had committed in 1973. Darden's lawyer made a last-minute emergency appeal to the Supreme Court, which voted against postponing the execution until a formal appeal could be filed. So the attorney (in what he later described as a "last-minute ingenuity") then requested that the emergency appeal be technically transformed into a formal appeal. Four justices agreed (enough to force the full court to review the appeal) and the execution was stayed. After additional years of delay and expense, Darden was eventually put out of *our* misery on March 15, 1988.[4]

In Lee's account of the particulars of Willie Darden's story, there is no doubt that Darden was guilty of the crime for which he was convicted and no doubt that justice was served when he was finally executed. Darden, then, serves Lee's broader moral argument in defense of the death penalty, for in Lee's retelling of the story, Darden illustrates an individual who merited forfeiture of his own life by his criminal killing. His execution, as a just desert, restored the balance of justice grievously upset when the murder occurred. It is in the context of this bigger issue about the justice of the death penalty—and Lee assumes Willie Darden was justly executed—that Lee advances the critical point that justice is ill served by a system that permits the kinds of delays and expenses we see in this case.

Even a critic of Lee's position must concede that Lee is raising important issues when he questions the system that administers justice in capital cases. Inquiry into the moral meaning of capital punishment must, after all, attend to the practical issue of how consistently and fairly justice is administered.

But Lee's general argument about just deserts and his criticism of the capital case review process ought not to be accepted too quickly, however, at least not because of an invocation of Willie Darden. For how much does one really know about Darden from Lee's account? When I read Lee's description of Willie Darden, I could not help wondering, is there more to the Willie Darden story? Critical inquiry begins not by simply opposing Lee's argument about the moral justifiability of the death penalty, but with questions. The first question that jumped out at me was in one sense Lee's own question: Why the delay in executing Darden? Why did Willie Darden—and his attorneys—work so hard to prevent his execution? Were his attorneys simply doing their job as assigned, or were they using Darden to advance their principled objection to the death penalty? Were there some justice issues—issues beyond those of delay and expense, of legal histrionics and bizarre court rulings—at stake? Why were the courts that heard Darden's appeals apparently willing to grant stay after stay?

Those were my critical questions, and in order to answer them beyond Lee's narrative scan I undertook some research. Given that Darden's case was widely reported in the news because of the record delays involved, news accounts and background stories on Darden were not hard to come by. To get more of a feel for who Willie Darden was, I even talked with one of his death row spiritual counselors. On the basis of the information I received from publicly available sources, I have reconstructed a story that I believe answers some of the "whys" about Willie Darden. The conclusions I reached are to me morally disconcerting, even terrible in what they bode about the bigger question Lee does not consider, namely, the moral legitimacy of the death penalty itself. In seeking answers to all these questions, I found myself getting closer to that most important question, the question Lee failed to ask, much less answer: Who was Willie Darden?

The Story Robert Lee Did Not Tell

Willie Darden, the man who Lee said "put us out of our misery" when he was put to death by the State of Florida, was a black man who died at the age of forty-four. He was born in 1933 in rural North Carolina, where blacks were sharecroppers. He entered the segregated world of the Depression-era South where economic opportunity for blacks was limited and bleak. In that world, vigilantism and lynching of black men were common.

Darden's fifteen-year-old mother died in childbirth two years after Willie's birth, and Willie went to live with his maternal grandfather. He worked the farm and helped raise his cousins, going to a local school for "colored" folks. Willie had native ability, for in a place and at a time when the average black adult advanced no further than the second grade, Willie completed the eighth grade. An aunt described Willie as a solid and responsible young person, but his life changed dramatically when his grandfather died and his stepmother deserted the family. Willie Darden went into foster care.

When his foster parents demanded work of him but gave him no money, Willie began to steal to get food and clothing. At the age of sixteen, after being caught stealing from a mailbox, he was sent to the National School for Boys, a segregated juvenile facility. When released, he took odd jobs to support himself, and for the rest of his life, odd jobs would be his only source of income. He was married in 1955 after a two-year courtship. In January 1956, Darden was arrested for trying to cash a $48 forged check and received a four-year prison sentence. His ex-wife later said, "It broke my heart that they put him away so long because I knew that he had done it to buy us some food."[5]

Willie Darden compiled a lengthy criminal record for a variety of offenses. In the late summer of 1973, he was arrested on the charge that would take him to death row. In Lakeland, Florida, Darden was accused of killing a white man while robbing a furniture store. He denied the charges and consistently maintained his innocence. When he faced a jury trial on murder charges in January 1974, he was represented by a white court-appointed attorney from the community and tried before a white judge and an all-white jury. He was convicted of the murder and, on January 23, 1974, sentenced to death.

This tells more of the story of Willie Darden, but not all. The murder with which Darden was charged occurred late in the afternoon of September 8, 1973. The actual time of the shooting is important for understanding Darden's claim of innocence, so I will present what is publicly available with respect to what is—and is not—known about when the shooting took place.

The scene of the crime was Carl's Furniture and Refurnishing Store, in Lakeland, owned by James Turman. According to the first information she gave to police, Helen Turman, wife of the murder victim, was closing her store at the usual closing time, 5:30 P.M., when a black man appeared and demanded the money in the register. When the owner of the store, James Turman, entered the room, Mrs. Turman tried to warn him away. The assailant shot Turman between the eyes. He then sexually assaulted Mrs. Turman, while her husband lay dying nearby. The scene was then interrupted by a sixteen-year-old boy who came in to help. The assailant shot the boy three times, then fled with the contents of the cash register—$15.00. The boy, though seriously wounded, survived the shooting. The police responded to a call for help, but no record of the call was kept and no official report about the time of the shooting was entered into the official court record.

Willie Darden was in Lakeland on the afternoon of September 8, the day of the killing, and at 4:00 his car broke down in a white neighborhood eight miles from the Turman store. Darden walked up to the front door of the closest house, the residence of Christine Bass, a secretary in Lakeland, and asked for help. She agreed to call a tow truck for Darden. She informed Darden that the truck would be at least forty-five minutes to an hour in arriving. Darden went back to his car to await help. A police cruiser patrolling the area spotted Darden's disabled vehicle, and two officers helped Darden reposition his car. After they left, a neighbor of Bass's who came out to see if he could be of help reattached a loose battery connection. Then able to start his car, Darden proceeded to drive away. According to Christine Bass, Darden had been in front of her home from 4:00 to 5:30 P.M.

In a sworn affidavit, Bass noted Darden's departure as 5:30 P.M. Darden then drove to a local filling station where the station owner, Bob Brazen, repaired a loose muffler on the car. Brazen would later report to police that Darden left his filling station at closing time—around 6:00 P.M.

After leaving the filling station, Darden lost control of his car and crashed into a telephone pole. At this point he was three miles from the crime scene. When a witness to Darden's accident, John Stone, stopped, Darden asked him to call for a tow truck. On his way to a phone, Stone passed the furniture store where the murder had been committed, and he noted the time as being around 6:00. Stone recalled seeing flashing lights and a police presence at the furniture store by the time he passed it. Meantime, Darden had been able to contact a wrecker with information about the whereabouts of his car, then got a ride to his girlfriend's home in Tampa. From there, he called the sheriff's office to report his disabled car, informing the authorities of his intention to come by the next day to take care of the car. The authorities found Darden's car and impounded it before the wrecker got to it. Mrs. Turman gave a report of the killing to police, and because Darden was in the vicinity of the crime and fit some of the general characteristics of the assailant, Darden came under immediate suspicion. Police tracked him to East Tampa, where he was staying at his girlfriend's house, and charged him with the murder of the furniture store owner.

Christine Bass was a critical witness in establishing the whereabouts of Willie Darden at the time of the Turman killing, yet she was never called to testify for the defense. She saw Willie Darden outside her home as late as 5:30 P.M.; another witness, filling station owner Bob Brazen, accounted for Darden's time immediately after leaving Bass's home and up to around 6:00. Bob Brazen and the police officers who helped move Darden's car were never called by Darden's defense team to testify.

Bass's testimony, had it come into court, might have led to Darden's acquittal. For if the shooting occurred at the 5:30 closing time of the store—Mrs. Turman certainly knew when the store usually closed and 5:30 was her first report to police of the time of the shooting—Darden was in front of Christine Bass's home and had a clear alibi. Given the distance from Bass's home to the furniture store and the stop at the filling station for a repair, there was insufficient time for Darden to have driven to the furniture store and committed the murder. Christine Bass went to the court house and waited four days to be called to the stand. Again, Darden's attorneys never called her to testify, and even though through her own efforts she succeeded in getting her statement into a posttrial hearing record five years after Darden's sentencing, it was deemed not useful because it was not corroborated.

Darden's defense team was appointed by the court. The team consisted of two local attorneys who had never tried a capital case, and they called no witnesses except Darden. They conducted no investigation and raised no questions about possible innocence for use in the appeals process. They did not press Mrs. Turman on her original claim that the shooting of her husband occurred at closing time, 5:30 P.M., when Willie Darden had witnesses as to his whereabouts. They did not contest the coroner's office report when it established the time of James Turman's death as 6:00 P.M., or object when the prosecution, aware that even this later time was not sufficient to build the strong case needed to convict Darden, accepted an unsubstantiated police finding that the killing occurred as late as 6:30. There were no official records to support this time as the time of the killing, and eyewitness testimony was available to challenge, even rebut it. But Darden's defense did not challenge it, much less rebut it. With the prosecution working from a 6:30 time of death for James Turman, the prosecution was able to argue—coherently—that Darden clearly had time to commit the robbery and shooting. Darden was convicted.

An interesting twist in the Darden story occurred eleven years after the Turman murder. New evidence to establish the time of the crime as 5:30 P.M. came to light, and it provided the corroboration for Christine Bass's original story that Darden was in front of her house at 5:30.

In 1984, a clergy friend of Christine Bass's who knew of her involvement in the Darden case put her in contact with Rev. Sam Sparks, a minister in the area who had also been involved in the Turman killing. Sparks was the clergyperson called in to be of assistance to Mrs. Turman immediately after the police arrived at the furniture store and began to secure the crime scene. Bass and Sparks met to share with each other their independent recollections of the events of that afternoon and evening.

Sparks clearly remembered arriving at the crime scene to be with Mrs. Turman at 5:55 P.M. What makes this significant is that Sparks needed thirty minutes to travel from his home, where he received the call notifying him of the emergency, to the furniture store. If Sparks arrived at the scene at 5:55, having received the call thirty minutes before, this can only mean one thing: the crime itself had to have occurred at or before 5:30, a time when Willie Darden was visible outside the home of Christine Bass.

Before his meeting with Christine Bass, Sparks was not aware of any other information about Darden's 5:30 P.M. whereabouts. Moreover, he had not thought to come forward prior to his meeting with Bass because he was not aware that Darden was protesting his innocence. Only after meeting with Christine Bass did he grasp the significance of his own information about the time of the killing.

Sparks offered a sworn affidavit to accompany Bass's account of the time sequence, corroborating Bass's story about Darden's whereabouts, and supporting

Mrs. Turman's first report of the time of the crime. These statements effectively established Willie Darden's alibi, thus exonerating him of possible guilt.

Darden, however, was not exonerated. He was convicted, sentenced to death, and finally executed. What brought about Darden's conviction was not a preponderance of evidence, for no physical evidence linking him to the crime was ever introduced or established. What made it possible to convict Darden was a time frame that created opportunity for Darden's involvement—and eyewitness testimony. The eyewitness testimony, however, was at least as suspect as the time frame issue. The victim's widow, Mrs. Turman, after initially telling police she could not remember what the black assailant looked like or what he was wearing, identified Darden. She did not pick Darden out of a line-up. The day after her husband's funeral she was led into a small courtroom where Darden sat. He was the only black man in the room. She was asked if Darden was the man who had shot her husband. The one thing she did remember about the assailant was that he was black. She picked him out.

Another eyewitness, the sixteen-year-old boy who had been shot while trying to help the Turmans, was recuperating from his gunshot wounds when police showed him pictures of possible suspects. Of the six photographs he was shown, only Darden's carried a label beneath it: "Sheriff's Department, Bartow, Florida." This witness, too, picked out Darden.

Both eyewitnesses agreed the assailant was "colored." Independently of one another, however, they disagreed about his height, the color and type of clothing he was wearing, and even whether he had facial hair. This is the testimony that was sufficient for a jury to convict Darden.

Some of the events that occurred at Darden's trial are worth mentioning as well. When the case came to trial before an all-white jury, the prosecutor, C. Ray McDaniels, treated Darden contemptuously, as if he were subhuman. He used inflammatory language several times in his remarks before the jury. At one point, McDaniels described Darden as an "animal who should be placed on a leash" and, in summation, shared his wish that he could "see [Darden] sitting here with no face, blown away by a shotgun."[6] Darden received no better from the bench. The white judge in the case referred to Darden as "vicious." And Darden's defense team offered no resistance to such prosecutorial misconduct. Dardens' two defense attorneys later testified that at mid-trial, a one-day postponement in the proceedings had been necessary because the senior partner of the team got drunk the night before while carousing with prosecution witnesses. The next day he was in no shape to appear in court.

This was the general tenor of the court proceeding that convicted Darden of murder and sentenced him to death. In 1991, a federal magistrate overturned Darden's conviction on the grounds of prosecutorial misconduct, but that decision was itself overturned. When, in 1986, Florida Governor Bob Martinez was informed of the Sparks and Bass evidence, he refused to meet with the two of them and continued to sign Darden death warrants in the tradition of his predecessor, Governor Bob Graham, who had twice signed Darden warrants and who had in political speeches accused the courts of interfering with the death penalty itself. The Supreme Court accepted Darden's petition and agreed to hear his case, but his final review lost by one vote. Darden's appellate attorneys continually petitioned the courts to protest gross violations of fair procedure and due process in Darden's trial, as well as to try to reintroduce the new Sparks-Bass evidence.

Darden's pleas did not ultimately win him a new trial, but neither did they fall completely on deaf ears. Darden lost appeal after appeal by the slimmest of margins, and even at the level of the U.S. Supreme Court, Darden's case was sufficient to shock. Supreme Court Justice Harry Blackmun, a Nixon appointee, wrote a blistering dissent when the Supreme Court denied Darden's final appeal, concerning himself simply with the issues of procedural fairness:

> Thus, at bottom, this case rests on the jury's determination of the credibility of three witnesses. . . . I cannot conclude that McDaniel's sustained assault on Darden's very humanity did not affect the jury's ability to judge the credibility question on the real evidence before it. Because I believe that he did not have a trial that was fair, I would reverse Darden's conviction; I would not allow him to go to his death until he has been convicted at a fair trial. I believe this Court must do more than wring its hands when a state uses improper legal standards to select juries in capital cases and permits prosecutors to pervert the adversary process. I therefore dissent.[7]

At the time of his retirement from the Supreme Court, Justice Blackmun spoke out against the death penalty, going so far as to express doubts that the constitutional protections of due process and equal protection could ever be satisfied in capital cases. Undoubtedly the Willie Darden review was a factor in Blackmun's evolution to this position. In a rare public comment on a case the Court had reviewed, Blackmun had said in a speech before the Eighth Circuit Court of Appeals: "If ever a man received an unfair trial, Darden did. He may be guilty, I don't know, but he got a runaround in that courtroom."[8]

Darden's case attracted national as well as international attention. Pleas for clemency came by the thousands from around the world, and the pope and Nobel Peace Prize recipient Andrei Sakharov were among the petitioners of conscience. But to no avail. When Darden's appeals ran out, the delays finally came to an end. In accordance with his original sentence, the State of Florida directed that a 2000-volt current be passed through his body for two minutes. Before he died, Willie Darden was asked if he had any final statement. From his seat in the electric chair, Darden said this:

> I tell you I am not guilty of the charge for which I am about to be executed. I bear no guilt or ill will for any of you. I am at peace with myself, with the world, with each of you. I say to my friends and supporters around the world, I love each and every one of you. Your love and support have been a great comfort to me in my struggle for justice and freedom.[9]

It cost the state of Florida $101,250 to imprison Darden for fifteen years, and over one million dollars to pursue the legal effort to execute him. The anonymous person who was brought into the Stark County prison to throw the switch that killed Darden was paid a state executioner's fee of $150.

Willie Darden in Narrative Depth

The story of Willie Darden I have just told is the story Robert Lee did not tell. The appeals seem not so frivolous now: they are, rather, the reasonable actions of a reasonable man demanding fair treatment while trying to prevent a gross injustice. Told with attention to the particularities of the case, the story explains why Darden and his defense team worked so long and hard to prevent his execution. Darden claimed to be innocent, and there was evidence to support that claim.

Why did those who worked with Darden after his conviction pursue his appeals with such persistence and vigor? I think the reason need extend no further than this: they believed an innocent man was being unjustly sentenced to death. And why was Darden convicted and sentenced to death? My conclusion is that Willie Darden was convicted, sentenced to death, and finally executed because he was a black caught up in the racial realities of his time and place, and because he was poor and unable to secure even minimally adequate counsel. Furthermore, those whose job it was to defend him did not defend him, nor did they seek out the truth of the killing. Darden did not receive a fair trial, and those who turned down his appeals and refused to allow information vital to his case be heard compounded the original injustice. From arrest to indictment through trial to conviction and sentencing, the system of justice Willie Darden encountered failed to offer him a reasonable chance to defend himself. He stood without resource and went to his death because he had been rendered powerless in that system.

The Moral Issues to Be Investigated

Robert Lee opened up the issue of system failure in the case of Willie Darden, but the moral conclusion to be drawn from his case extends beyond Darden. For if the legal system failed to deliver justice to Darden, it fails all of us. Of course the system can make mistakes, but if Darden is dead, it cannot correct those mistakes. Only if Darden were alive today, either a free man exonerated of the Turman killing or a felon convicted in a new trial that was fairly conducted and in which the showing of new, potentially exculpatory evidence was convincingly rebutted, could we conclude that the system had not failed. Mistakes are one thing; closing off the possibility of correcting them is a catastrophic and arrogant failure of justice itself.

There are over three thousand human beings on death row in the United States at the moment I write this—three thousand individuals, each with a story, most of whom will never receive the kind of attention Willie Darden received. This book will not tell those stories, but by beginning where I have—with a story—we are reminded that attached to each of those individuals condemned to death is a fundamental humanity that we cannot deny.

The Willie Darden story raises questions about justice, not only whether Darden himself received justice in the procedural sense of fair treatment but also whether justice was in any sense served by his execution. Investigating the moral meaning of the death penalty requires that both of these senses of justice be considered and explicated. That issue is the concern of chapter 3.

3

Just Means and Ends, or "Just Killing"?

The Willie Darden case raises two justice questions. The first question is whether execution killing, as a form of killing, serves the end of justice. Ordinarily, execution killing would be presumed morally prohibited on the grounds that life is itself a fundamental good and as such should be honored, protected, and even promoted by persons in moral community. Practical reason would hold that destroying the good of human life violates our obligation to promote this good and protect it from lethal assault and destruction. Yet capital punishment is asserted to be morally just. How is moral meaning to be reconfigured and reconstructed so that the direct and intentional killing of a human person is transformed into what might be termed a "just killing"? This is the big question at stake in the death penalty debate: How can the intentional killing of a human person unable to offer resistance or defense be rendered morally permissible?

If the first justice question pertains to the moral ends which it is believed execution serves, the second issue addresses the means employed to seek that end. Assuming for the moment that capital punishment can be rendered morally justifiable, the issue of means allows us to ask, What does morality require of us in pursuit of this end?

Given that a life is at stake in a capital case, rules and procedures must be observed both as a matter of law and as a matter of morality to ensure that so foundational a good as the good of life is not wrenched from a condemned person unfairly or wrongly. Failure to deliver an individual to the execution chamber by means of fair and just procedures threatens the person facing execution with the prospect of morally wrongful death, and in that failure the claim that an execution is morally justified is denied. Procedural fairness affects how the ends of justice are served. These two questions—the justice of means in service to the end of justice—intertwine and affect how moral meaning is to be determined.

It is appropriate at this point to consider more explicitly what we mean by justice so that we can then identify those points on which both supporters and opponents of the death penalty would find themselves in agreement.

The Concept of Justice

Justice as a concept of fairness pertaining not only to ends but also to the means we use to pursue those ends is familiar to all of us. We know that it's not fair, not just, when someone receives preferential treatment based on race or sex or economic status. We know that someone who secretly uses a calculator on an exam where calculators are not allowed acts unjustly towards others and advances at others' expense. Even if the end sought by the cheating is intrinsically worthy, say, getting into medical school and becoming a physician and thereby helping humanity, the cheater treats others disrespectfully and pursues that end unjustly, so that whatever good was sought is compromised and the cheater becomes unworthy of enjoying the good of the end.

This common way of thinking about fairness and the moral relation of means to ends applies to the death penalty as well. A person put to death after being denied procedural justice is cheated of a great good, the good of life, and the end sought by society by means of the condemned's death cannot—ought not—be enjoyed.

But, to be fair, justice means more than fairness. We broaden the concept of justice to take into account other kinds of concerns and contexts of relationship. Beyond a focus on the individual, many of our ordinary appeals to the concept of justice extend to the social, corporate, and collective dimensions of our lives. It is in the moral domain of our relations with others that other notions of justice come into play. Those notions include the justice that governs exchanges between people (commutative justice), the justice that governs the apportioning of community goods (distributive justice), and social justice itself, the justice that refers to the obligation to participate actively in the life of society, with society having a duty to enable such participation.[1]

Justice as a concern of moral meaning comes to involve what philosopher Robert Solomon has identified as "collective fellow feeling and responsibility."[2] When we extend our concern for justice into the realm of self-other relations and concern ourselves with collective fellow feeling as well as the responsibilities we owe others and what they owe us, we provoke inquiry into the question of what constitutes a just society. This is a broad question, but I contend that the particular issue of state-sponsored execution cannot help but provoke it. For we must ask whether the death penalty is a practice compatible with justice considered in this corporate sense, and whether a social order sanctioning the death penalty serves the end of justice. Does the death penalty in some way enhance collective fellow feeling and promote justice corporately by engendering a deeper sense of responsibility of each for all, and all for each one?

Justice never stands alone, unrelated to human emotion and volition and involvement with the care of others. Justice is a relational concept that extends to a variety of other concepts. Mercy, for example, is a concept we relate to justice in our ordinary linguistic usages and in our everyday reflection. The connection between justice and merciful compassion led the ancient Greeks to hold that failure to provide for widows and orphans was not so much a failure of compassion as a failure of justice.[3] In that kind of connection, we see that justice is a dynamic concept that extends into all aspects of human relations, expressive of our ideals of civility, caring, and compassion.

Unfairness and the Subversion of Justice

There are some simple things we can say about justice that are not controversial. We associate justice with fairness and with the idea of rendering to each what is their due. We also say that justice governs fairness in our relations and transactions, and that justice is itself promoted by fairness. Conversely, unfairness subverts justice. Justice as fairness is promoted in capital cases procedurally when we demand that trials be fair; that witnesses, judges, and jurors be unbiased; that evidence be presented without taint; that guilt be established on the merits of the evidence and beyond a reasonable doubt; that sentencing be guided by criteria that are applied evenhandedly. If the requirements of fairness are not observed in these matters, justice is not served; and if justice is not served, even a legal execution presumed to be morally justifiable will be transformed into an morally unjust killing. The Darden case illustrates, in its details and particularities, how an execution killing can obstruct, even pervert, the end of justice by failures of fairness along the way.

If one of the common meanings we share about justice is that justice entails a notion of fairness and that the death penalty requires, if it is to be just, fairness in its distribution and application, then the details of Darden's story should give us pause. Not only opponents of the death penalty, but even—especially— supporters who appeal to the death penalty as a just exception to our ordinary prohibitions on the killing of human beings should be concerned with problems that cast doubt on whether justice was served: Were Darden's trial, conviction, and sentencing free of racist taint? Was his economic status no barrier in his ability to secure adequate counsel? Did those who tried Darden conduct themselves dispassionately, fully disclosing all the available evidence in the case and communicating it without inflammatory rhetoric? Did the appellate review process ensure that all reasonable efforts were made to avoid mistakes and errors, including the demand that potentially exculpatory evidence was properly introduced and weighed by a jury? And did the criminal justice system in what turned out to be a high-profile case demonstrate that it could not be influenced in the pursuit of justice by public servants seeking an execution for political advantage?

I do not know with absolute certitude that Willie Darden was innocent of the crime for which he was executed. Although I believe him to be, disagreement may persist over certain factual matters in the Darden case. This much, however, is clear: the demand of justice that an accused person be fairly tried and put at no undue disadvantage when so valued and cherished a good of life as life itself weighs in the balance was not obviously satisfied in this case. No rational person, death penalty supporter or opponent, would argue that the direct and deliberate killing of a human being is morally justified if the killing is not exempted from our ordinary moral prohibitions against such killings. Exemption for capital punishment is claimed on the grounds that the forfeiture of the condemned's life is a fitting redress of injury, a just punishment demanded in retribution for wrongdoing by justice itself. Execution killings that fail the test of procedural fairness will fail to meet the standards for exempting a particular killing from our ordinary prohibitions against such killing. Such executions are not morally permissible and cannot be morally sanctioned, even in the name of justice.

The questions of procedural fairness raised by the Darden case surface before we even get to the more abstract—and more usual—issues about the death penalty as justifiable on grounds of deterrence or just retribution. Particular fairness issues in particular cases, however, are not usually topics for heated public debate. They do not provoke widespread public reaction because citizens assume that fairness standards are met in the criminal justice process, and the impression is widespread that the lengthy delay in appeals actually gives too much attention to such questions. Furthermore, the death penalty has passed moral muster in society and is perceived to lack any moral taint as a means of delivering or distributing justice. This means that fairness issues pertaining to how the death penalty is applied are relegated to second-order issues, often characterized as trivial disputes over legal "technicalities." Those who offer such characterizations are especially likely to do so when the procedural flaw at issue seems not to impinge directly on the essential soundness of a finding of guilt.

Yet in a social and political environment where an unbridgeable divide separates opponents and supporters of the death penalty on the big question of the moral legitimacy of the execution practice, procedural justice issues fashion the only hope of a meeting place for the two sides. And as a stratagem for keeping moral debate alive, death penalty opponents will often raise procedural issues trusting that death penalty supporters will object to any execution that fails to satisfy the moral requirements of justice. Procedural issues, then, may provide common ground for a moral debate, since procedural injustice in any particular capital case undermines the claim that an execution killing can be justified. Any such killing ought, from a moral point of view, to be prohibited; on that issue both death penalty supporters and opponents ought to agree.

It falls to supporters of the death penalty, then, not opponents, to demonstrate convincingly that in a particular case justice has been served with respect to procedural fairness. Death penalty opponents may locate their opposition elsewhere than in procedural questions, but procedural questions are the only justice obstacles supporters face. Supporters are the ones seeking to exempt capital punishment from our ordinary prohibitions on the direct and intended killing of human beings, so they necessarily take on the burden of proving that the test of procedural justice has been met. Historically, this is precisely the position that death penalty supporters have taken. One prominent death penalty supporter, John Stuart Mill,[4] argued in the nineteenth century that there is less likelihood of injustice and error in capital cases than in any other, for with a life at stake, "juries and Judges [will be] more careful in forming their opinion, and more jealous in their scrutiny of the evidence."[5] Whether history bears out such a claim is certainly arguable, but philosophically, it is clear that no person convinced of the essential moral justifiability of capital punishment should confuse support for execution in general with support for any particular execution, especially when the demands of justice are in question or clearly have not been satisfied. The death penalty opponent realizes this and pushes the question of justice at precisely those procedural points in specific cases where lies the only hope that the death penalty supporter will become in a particular case a death penalty opponent.

No incoherence attaches to a death penalty supporter opposing an execution in such a circumstance. In fact, just the opposite holds true. For a death penalty supporter to maintain support for execution in the face of evidence of procedural unfairness would be to claim that the death penalty serves the end of justice even when it does so by unjust means. This is to say that a killing imposed unjustly can still serve the end of justice. But that would be to advance the contradictory notion that an unjust killing is a just killing; and even the death penalty supporter recognizes the incoherence of that description.

Citizens respectful not only of law but of morality will, of course, require that trials and sentencing procedures be fair in capital cases, and it is clear that

citizen confidence is high that when a death sentence is imposed and administered it is done justly. Raising questions about how justice might be affected by
race, poverty, and adequacy of legal counsel has come to seem out of place in contemporary public debate,[6] for given what is at stake in capital cases—the potential forfeiture of life—it is reasonable to assume that protections and safeguards
are more, rather than less, strictly observed. It can furthermore be assumed that
given the mandatory and thorough—if also byzantine and sometimes exceedingly lengthy—review process designed to prevent error, it is more likely that justice will be served in capital cases than in any other.

These assumptions, however, are challengeable. The Darden story demonstrates how they fail to stand up under close scrutiny in one particular case. So it
is ironic and paradoxical, if not actually self-deceptive, that in a political environment and social atmosphere of suspicion concerning the ability of the American criminal justice system to deliver justice,[7] public confidence is actually high
that in capital cases the system works and justice is delivered. We often hear it
said that the justice system is flawed, arbitrary, and subject to abuse, yet this
general suspicion is not transferred to the disposition of capital cases. Americans
who readily admit that mistakes in our justice system are all too commonplace
when death is not at issue assume almost blithely that mistakes are nonexistent
in capital cases, where all kinds of inflammatory factors—the heinousness of a
crime, a defendant's ineffective defense, prosecutorial passion, public sentiment
for revenge—may affect process and deliberation. In capital cases, the well-
documented suspicion Americans have that the criminal justice system is imperfect and flawed seems mysteriously to drop away. Lots of things may account for
this, including the fact—and it is a fact—that many—most—of those convicted
in capital cases are indeed guilty, and the crimes at issue can be heinous and bru-
tal. But if we assume that a fallible criminal justice system does not suddenly become infallible when the system veers toward the death penalty, only one logical
conclusion can be drawn: that mistakes are possible in capital cases and some of
these mistakes pertain to issues of procedural fairness (in legal language, "due
process" or "equality before the law").

But raising questions of procedural fairness does not attract the attention of
the death penalty supporters. As argued above, they would find in such issues the
only basis for a moral objection to execution. That the demands of procedural
justice have been met is assumed, and raising questions about the manner in
which a death sentence is imposed not only fails to arouse public interest and suspicion, but, to the contrary, actually aggravates a sense of public impatience, since
the process whereby procedural justice issues are reviewed simply delays executions. Appellate review of capital cases has evolved into a lengthy process, but
what is not widely appreciated is the fact that these appeals have evolved as they

have precisely because the system itself assumes mistakes can occur. Review is designed to prevent and rectify any procedural mistakes which, if not addressed and corrected, would collapse the moral support of a justified execution and render an execution a morally unjust killing.

The review process is lengthy: the average time between sentencing to death and execution is over eleven years.[8] Execution delays are frustrating to many observers, and the issues that give rise to the delays—the effects of racism, inadequate counsel, and the poverty of defendants—have likewise proved to be tiresome. Critics of the appeals process have met with a receptive public audience, and there has been no outcry as the number of executions has increased. If there is a general criticism of the death penalty today, it is not that the death penalty is immoral, or cruel and unusual, or unfairly imposed, but that too much time passes between sentencing and actual execution. The justice question at issue for many focuses on the unfairness, not only to families of victims but to the condemned themselves, of dragging out the appeals process and delaying execution—and the execution of justice.

Citizens are rarely given reason to stir from a complacent acceptance of current execution policy. Only when something happens to add a wrinkle to a news wire story is there even a possibility of arousing interest in an execution—perhaps the ghoulish suggestion of a botched procedure, like that involving convicted mass murderer John Wayne Gacey,[9] or a malfunctioning Florida electric chair.[10] Another attention-getter is the unusual execution practice. Arkansas, for instance, has a penchant for serial executions. In early 1997, the State of Arkansas executed by lethal injections three prisoners in one execution session. The tandem executions were justified by a concern for reducing the stress on execution teams and saving money. (Arkansas auditors should note that each of the condemned received a new needle as well as an alcohol swab, a truly frivolous expense that might, now that it has been pointed out, lead to even more stringent economies in the future.) The point is that unless the unusual or bizarre is attached to a particular execution, the news concerning an execution will no longer make the front page. Reports of execution are now kept before the public as regional, even local, rather than national, news.

With the loss of public attention, interest in raising questions about the moral meaning of the death penalty also wanes. Moral controversy can still arise in an occasional outcry over executing a person who committed a crime while a legal minor or a person known to be mentally defective, or when the suspicion of cruelty is raised by reports of a messy or botched execution. But in general the question of moral meaning is difficult to raise in the contemporary cultural and political environment. Only one issue remains so fraught with drama that it is still capable of attracting attention and engendering doubt about the morality of state-sponsored execution. And that is the problem—even in some cases the prospect—of wrongful execution.

The idea that an individual condemned to die is in all likelihood not the person who committed the offense still has sufficient power to prick the moral imagination and awaken conscience to the possibility of injustice. The prospect of a wrongful execution can still shock and arouse moral horror, even moving people to action in particular cases and generating media attention as celebrities, human rights groups, and moral and religious authorities get involved.[11]

Wrongful execution provokes questions about the fundamental morality of the death penalty. But wrongful execution is not ordinarily considered a broadside attack on the morality of the death penalty itself. Wrongful execution is a fair application issue.

Wrongful execution provokes the question of procedural justice, for if a person has been wrongfully executed, the system has failed to deliver justice and the particular execution in question is rendered unjust. It is the prospect of a wrongful execution that I would suspect most heavily weighs on the minds of those readers who attended to the details of the Darden story recounted earlier in these pages. The reason procedural questions are so critical as we investigate the question of moral meaning is this: Procedural failures reveal a flawed justice system that makes errors. Execution, however, imposes an absolute sentence that not only eliminates a human person but also eliminates the possibility of addressing an error or correcting it, which justice would also demand. Execution exacts an absolute penalty through a system that, as the appeals process reveals, doubts its own capacity to achieve certainty or the kind of perfection that carrying out an absolute, uncorrectable act would seem to require. Confronting the jarring realization that an innocent person might be wrongly executed still has power to provoke the moral imagination. And well it should. If an innocent person can be executed, then persons in the class of innocent person are susceptible to such a miscarriage of justice. And even if this susceptibility is only theoretical, a functioning moral imagination can direct attention very quickly to one member of that class of innocent persons—me. Those who are able to say to themselves, "It could happen to me," not only show themselves capable of exercising moral imagination—they are the individuals who confront the issue of procedural injustice.

That people make this kind of imaginative move may account for the fact that in a national poll conducted in 1993, 58 percent of voters indicated that the prospect of wrongful execution was the reason most likely to produce reservations about continued use of the death penalty.[12] This reaction by voters was not based on evidence that in a given year or decade there were so many known wrongful executions reported. In fact, those who responded probably could not have cited with confidence any particular instance of a wrongfully executed person. The reservations emerged from the moral queasiness generated by considering the prospect of an innocent person being put to death.

I have cautioned against making assumptions. I have advanced the perception that many Americans do not trust that the criminal justice system actually delivers justice, then offered the view that that distrust of the system seems not to extend to capital cases. The assumption of error-free adjudication of capital cases seems to me worthy of our skepticism, but only because of another assumption I am willing to make and which seems reasonable to make, namely, that the death penalty system makes errors and can be assumed to make errors. Why is this assumption justifiable?

It seems clear to me that an ordinary citizen confronted with evidence of a wrongful execution could easily acknowledge the system as error-prone and in the wake of that admission generate reservations about the death penalty itself. But such evidence is hard to come by. What if an individual asked to consider the moral meaning of the death penalty knows of no such instance? What if the individual considers the lengthy appeals process and responds by saying that the system checks itself to identify and correct errors, thus accounting for the more than fifteen hundred reversals of death sentences since 1973?[13] Given this involved check to ensure justice, is it really reasonable to assume that wrongful executions occur and that innocent persons are—or have been—actually executed?

My first response to this important question is to make a logical and philosophical response rather than seek out empirical data to support a claim one way or the other. A reasonable person queried about wrongful execution could reasonably assume that wrongful executions are possible, even probable, if that assumption is tied to a belief, also reasonable to hold, that the American criminal justice system is fallible and imperfect. The belief that wrongful executions occur rests on a more foundational belief, namely, a belief that fallible human beings and their fallible systems of justice administration can make mistakes, and that these mistakes may persist despite appellate safeguards, despite all that might be done procedurally to ferret out errors and prevent mistakes from happening.

Respondents to that 1993 polling survey would not have to form an opinion based upon personal knowledge of a particular case where beyond doubt it has been established that a condemned person was put to death for a crime he or she did not commit. All that would be necessary would be a deep acquaintance with human imperfection and skepticism regarding the perfection of any human endeavor. A belief that no human project is infallible or free of potential error is all that is needed to build a foundation of support for the reasonable inference that some executions will be mistakes.

But this may seem too simple a response. Logical inference based on a belief in human fallibility is not proof of any wrongful execution in particular. Some empirical data would be helpful in clarifying the degree to which this logical possibility is an actual, empirical reality, and, fortunately, research on the phenomenon of wrongful execution has been conducted in recent years. In a widely read and discussed 1992 book, *In Spite of Innocence: Erroneous Convictions in Capital Cases*, Michael Radelet, Hugo Adam Bedau, and Constance Putnam reported the results of their investigation into numerous capital cases where significant evidence of innocence was available. As a result of revisiting the records of problematic capital cases, they concluded that in the United States since 1900, 416 persons were wrongfully convicted of capital crimes. Of that number, 23 were actually put to death.[14]

As one might expect, determining that already executed individuals were in fact not guilty of the crimes for which juries found sufficient grounds to convict them, and appellate courts found sufficient reason to deny their appeals, is not uncontroversial. The Radelet, Bedau, and Putnam study is certainly not without detractors, as is the phenomenon of wrongful execution itself. Arguments have been made that wrongful execution does, in fact, constitute a practical impossibility.[15] But even without going through the controversial process of retrying cases in an academic research study, one can find another kind of empirical grounding to support the claim that mistakes are made in capital cases. Where I have looked for evidence of system fallibility is in those cases where persons convicted in capital cases and sentenced to death were actually released from prison because they were exonerated of guilt.[16] Since 1970, fifty-nine people have been released from America's death rows because of the finding that they had been wrongfully convicted.[17]

I do not doubt the basic thrust of the Radelet, Bedau, and Putnam study, nor am I prepared to dispute their findings regarding particular cases. I do, however, acknowledge the methodological problems that attach to any reassessment of fundamental guilt or innocence in a historical investigation of the kind undertaken in their study. But the fact that we know of fifty-nine people who were released from death row upon findings of wrongful conviction and sentencing does not suffer from such methodological problems. That fifty-nine individuals in the past thirty years went through the process of capital conviction and sentencing to death, then were exonerated because of evidence of innocence is, to my mind, sufficient to make an empirical case that individuals are mistakenly convicted in capital cases and unjustly sentenced to death. These fifty-nine persons erroneously sent to death row were released as the result of a fallible system of justice administration reviewing itself to see if it had adequately met its own test of fairness, then establishing through its own review process that it had made a mistake—fifty-nine potentially lethal and uncorrectable mistakes. If fifty-nine citizens can be mistakenly convicted in a fallible criminal justice system and sentenced to death only to be later released upon a finding of wrongful and mistaken conviction, it takes no extraordinary leap of imagination to infer that these fifty-nine condemned individuals do not possibly exhaust the possible number of wrongfully convicted persons. Reason allows the assumption that in a fallible system, not all the injustices would be corrected and that others besides these fifty-nine were also mistakenly and unjustly sentenced to death. And from this inference it likewise stands to reason—and demands no huge leap of imagination to infer—that from this unfortunate number of those wrongly convicted, certain individuals were not so lucky as to avoid actual punishment. Some wrongfully convicted individuals had to have been unable to establish their innocence and thus were executed—wrongfully executed. To deny this possibility is to believe that the system of trial, conviction, sentencing, and appeal is capable of achieving absolute certainty of guilt in every case. And it is the prospect of such epistemological certainty that those 58 percent of respondents greeted with skepticism.

If the system that places persons on death row and threatens them with execution is fallible and capable of error, supporting capital punishment in the face of that recognition entails support for a system that will on occasion kill a person as punishment for a crime he or she did not commit. How often this happens will remain uncertain, despite our best research efforts. How often it happens is, in some ethical views, irrelevant so long as it can happen to even one individual. That it can happen, has happened, and will happen in the future is certain so long as the system that subjects persons to state execution is fallible and liable to error. It is this reality—and this prospect—that will prove critical for our consideration of the moral meaning of the death penalty.

Procedural issues of fairness, then, are critical to constructing a moral meaning for the death penalty, and I have indicated that these kinds of issues, while not widely debated publicly, are—or should be—crucial to death penalty supporters, who must bear the burden of justifying particular executions even in the face of their more general philosophical position in support of the death penalty. It is worthwhile to remember what I said before: even though death penalty opponents will engage the questions of procedural fairness to expose injustice, death penalty opponents in general object to the death penalty before it even gets to issues of procedure and application. So this discussion is directed to death penalty supporters. It is the supporter of the death penalty who cannot reasonably maintain in the face of a demonstration of injustice that a state-sponsored execution can turn the trick of becoming a morally justifiable killing. The moral warrants— assumed to be in place for the death penalty supporter—drop away in the face of procedural injustice so that even the supporter of the death penalty is confronted with the prospect of an unjust killing. However one might feel in general about the justifiability of a particular form of killing, it is not morally controversial to claim that an unjust killing ought to receive no moral endorsement.

Procedural unfairness renders the process leading up to execution unjust. If there is common ground for supporters and opponents of the death penalty, it rests in the shared understanding that no execution that has failed to serve justice procedurally and with respect to issues of fairness ought to be considered on moral grounds a just killing. Again, supporters and opponents ought to agree that no execution tainted by injustice should proceed, and where these questions arise common moral ground can be staked out for moral agreement.

But what if justice has been served procedurally? What if fairness issues are not in debate? What if we know with certainty that a particular individual committed a capital crime and was, in accordance with a legal system of justice, duly sentenced to death, with no obvious specter of unjust procedure infecting the disposition of the case or suspicion of moral taint in the justice delivery system? Then what?

At this point we engage the question about the moral meaning of the death penalty at the level of the first question we asked as we opened this chapter. Does the death penalty serve the end of justice? Is a death delivered to a person by state-sponsored execution a just killing? It is not a procedural question we ask at this point, but a question about whether the moral warrants of the death penalty are sufficiently strong to justify the claim that the death penalty is moral, and that the killing it entails is, in moral review, a killing transformed into a justified killing.

I wish to engage this question by offering a review of critical philosophical views that address it. It is the moral assessment of the killing that occurs in the death penalty—and possible modes of justification through well-known ethical theories—to which our attention now turns.

4

The Right to Life, Liberty, and Security

The practice of execution may be as old as political society itself. That it is as old as recorded history is an indisputable fact. In the West, the Code of Hammurabi (c. 1750 B.C.E.) specified execution for twenty-five offenses, including theft, certain sexual offenses (adultery, a son's incest with his mother), robbery, theft of public property, neglect of public duty, malfeasance in office, and defiance of legal authority, which included a death sentence for innkeepers (almost always women) who cheated customers by shortchanging them on an agreed-upon amount of grain or alcohol.[1] Section 1 of the code specified punishment by death for those who falsely accuse another of murder; and section 153 directed that a woman who kills her husband to marry another be impaled. Curiously, these are the only two of the 282 laws in the Hammurabi Code that require execution in response to the commission of murder.[2] This lack of attention to lethal punishment for murder ought not to be viewed as an expression of societal forbearance or leniency toward murderers. Near Eastern scholar Edwin Good concludes that execution for murder was probably so commonplace in the Babylon of the eighteenth century B.C.E. that it was not perceived as requiring explicit legislative formulation.

Death as a punishment for offense is commonplace in early legal codes. Egyptian and Assyrian laws (c. 1500 B.C.E.) and the Hittite legal code (c. 1300 B.C.E.) all sanctioned death as a legitimate punishment for crimes against the state. The Hittite Code distinguished manslaughter from murder, but, in another curiosity, it called for compensatory payment rather than death in such cases. Compensation rather than death was also called for in cases of kidnapping, which was regarded a more serious crime than murder, exacting from such offenders forfeiture of their entire estate and the relinquishing of more slaves than was required in cases of murder.[3] The Hebrew Bible, which includes the Code of the Covenant (Exod. 20:22–23:19), the Code of Deuteronomy (Deut. 12:1–26:19), and the Priestly

31

Code (Exodus, Numbers, and Leviticus, with Leviticus 17–26 being a sixth-century exilic "Holiness Code"), identifies nineteen capital offenses, including homosexuality, sorcery and witchcraft, and cursing a parent.[4] Ancient Athens included the defacing of coins and pickpocketing as capital crimes, and under the Roman Empire, public execution by burning, decapitation, or crucifixion was commonly employed to preserve order in the state and deter crime.

The history of state-sponsored execution in the West is both bloody—it is estimated that during the thirty-six-year reign of Henry VIII over seventy-two thousand people were put to death—and commonplace: by 1769 England had identified over 160 capital crimes.[5] Significant leadership in the Christian church—including Aquinas, Luther, and Calvin—upheld the authority of the state to inflict death as a punishment for crime.

But the history of state-sponsored execution is marked by moments of significant protest and controversy.[6] Voices of opposition to execution have never been lacking, even in the church. The early church fathers Tertullian (*De Idololatria*, ch. 17), Origen (*Contra Celsum*, iii.7), Cyprian, Lactantius (*Divinae Institutiones*, VI. xx, 15–17), and, inconsistently and with reservations, even Augustine (*Epistles* 133, 152–4), expressed opposition to the execution of criminals;[7] and Pope Leo I (fifth century) and Pope Nicholas I spoke against church involvement in the death penalty. Both the Council of Toledo (675) and the Fourth Lateran Council (1215) forbade the clergy to participate in judicial trials where the death penalty was under consideration.

Given that by 1860, death penalty opponents in England were able to eliminate 190 crimes from the category of capital crimes, spurred in part by the 1833 hanging of a nine-year-old boy who had stolen some children's paints from a London shop,[8] it is clear that advocates of capital punishment reform have effected change in the practice and application of the death penalty. During the Enlightenment era, strong voices were raised in opposition to the death penalty. In addition to Cesare Beccaria, author of the influential essay "On Crimes and Punishments" (1764), other important voices opposing the death penalty included intellectuals of the stature of Voltaire, Rousseau, Karl Marx, David Hume, and Jeremy Bentham in Europe, and, in America, Benjamin Franklin and Thomas Paine.

Since the first execution in the Virginia Colony in 1622—Daniell Frank was hanged for stealing Sir George Yerdley's calf [9]—up through the most recent of the over eighteen thousand legal executions carried out in America, many changes have taken place in how law and society regard the death penalty. Recounting the history of the death penalty sometimes serves those who wish to argue that the changes that have occurred over time demonstrate that American standards of decency have evolved, especially in light of the movement toward restricting the kinds and numbers of crimes warranting death and the use of more humane techniques for performing the actual killing.

Appeal to an "evolving standard of decency" principle, however, has not yet led to a societal consensus that the death penalty is, as a matter of justice and morality, fundamentally flawed, or that imposing death is inherently cruel or contrary to an American standard of decency. In America, death penalty abolitionists began organizing in the nineteenth century to effect legal change, establishing the Society for the Abolition of Capital Punishment in 1845; and the abolitionist movement, being one expression of the reform impulse more dramatically apparent in the antislavery movement, did have a discernible impact on societal attitudes, and even on the law itself. It was during the mid-nineteenth-century reform era that the death penalty was abolished in certain jurisdictions. The territory of Michigan outlawed execution in 1846 for every crime except treason, with Rhode Island following in 1852 and Wisconsin in 1853.[10]

The history of the death penalty in America reveals that at least twenty-three states have eliminated capital punishment at one time or another, with twelve states having restored it after abolition.[11] But American society has never been convinced—in general, as a society—that the death penalty lacks moral warrants. A presumption of moral justification exists, and this presumption is—and has been—widely accepted throughout American society from pre-Colonial times to the present.

The history of America's use of the death penalty is worthy of study in its own right, but that history is not the present focus, even though that history will necessarily impinge on our effort at clarifying moral meaning. One important insight that historical study produces is that the state's imposition of an irrevocable and absolute punishment—absolute at least as far as the condemned is concerned—is itself not action based on absolute epistemic certainty, as if so serious an act as killing a citizen were beyond the pale of possible error, dispute over facts, and debate over moral meaning.

The fact is that execution policy and practice have, historically, been subject to the contingencies of social, historical, and political context, which is clear from the way race, gender, and class have over the centuries been factored into decision-making about criminal justice in general. One need only consider such startling statistics as those presented by Charshee C. Lawrence-McIntyre, author of *Criminalizing a Race: Free Blacks during Slavery*, to see the point of these contingencies. Lawrence-McIntyre writes that in 1820 Virginia, 100 percent of the female inmate population in that commonwealth was black: "In other words, according to the records that year in Virginia, no white women committed prisonable crimes."[12] It requires no boldness to claim that the criminal justice system does not operate in an environment of value neutrality. The dispensation of justice is affected by a variety of cultural contingencies, which can be exposed and addressed, and ultimately changed, even from within the system itself; and to make this simple admission is to note that execution policy has likewise been affected by the influence of contingent factors that fail the ideal of impartial justice.

Recognizing the contingency of racial attitudes and a racist environment led the U.S. Supreme Court in the 1972 *Furman* case to acknowledge that the death penalty for rape in southern states fell so heavily and disproportionately on black males in relation to white males that execution policy for this crime violated any reasonable standard of fairness and amounted to cruel and unusual punishment. As a result of this recognition of contingency, the death penalty for rape was summarily disallowed. Race is a primary factor—a culturally contingent factor—affecting the criminal justice system in general and execution policy in particular. Blacks are executed for murder at over five times the rate of execution for whites, and blacks have been executed for rape at about nine times the rate of execution for whites. Noting that race, class, and gender have long attended the debate over how the death penalty is imposed and on whom is a historical as well as a sociological issue. The data revealed by examining such factors lends itself to moral interpretation, and the moral force of these issues persists, even if the law has wearied of trying to address them.[13]

But alongside these questions about fairness, there is the broader moral question involved in the very idea of the state taking direct and intentional action to kill one of its citizens. The death results not simply because a person assigned by the state has thrown a switch, sprung a trapdoor, pulled a trigger, or started a flow of lethal drugs. Executioners are part of a complex system of act and symbol, and their personal responsibility for bringing about a death is, in this complex system, no more significant than the responsibility that could be said to attach to any other citizen; for the responsibility for intentionally taking a life by execution is authorized by a peculiar—even unique—act of societal legitimation. All are responsible. All act symbolically through the executioner to deprive a person of life.

Execution is never simply about a death, but it is always about a killing. Killing human beings is the most serious matter that moral reflection can consider; and because it is a killing—and not simply a death—that is at issue when executions are performed, moral reflection will demand an answer to the central moral question at stake in this or any other killing: Can the killing be justified?

The question of justification, as I have already noted, assumes center stage in any inquiry into the moral meaning of the death penalty. A moral issue is provoked, as in other life-and-death issues, not because executions are legal or because they enjoy, and have historically enjoyed, popular support, but because execution involves an intentional killing. Morality does not in general permit or sanction the intentional killing of human beings, though certain killings and even types of killings, such as killing in self-defense against unprovoked aggression, can withstand the scrutiny of moral analysis and be deemed defensible.

But in moral community, we ordinarily seek to protect ourselves and one another from the intentional harm that a killing necessarily delivers; and morally speaking, the loss of life that results from a killing, whether in self-defense or as punishment for crime, is to be recognized by reasonable persons as the most harmful outcome that can be visited upon a person. Accordingly, the act of intentionally killing a member of the moral community—a person—is a most grave act: the hurdle of justification is set higher for intentional killing than for any other moral issue, and few killings cross the bar. The claim that we observe a moral presumption against the death penalty is derived from the fact that execution is an act of intentional killing not ordinarily considered justifiable in moral community. In fact, the language of rights may be invoked at this point to articulate the claim of persons—their right, even their natural right—to be free of the threat of this most serious form of harm.

So why does the idea of state-sponsored execution not present itself to us as a wrenching moral problem? What has allowed us to achieve widespread societal agreement that this form of killing is not particularly problematic, but that it is justifiable? Which arguments or moral positions have proved so persuasive that we have found ourselves able, as a society, to preserve and even extend capital punishment? What kind of moral thinking justifies state-sponsored killing, especially in the face of a moral presumption that the state ought not to kill its citizens?

The purpose of this book is to question the death penalty as a practice that presumes moral meaning of a certain sort. That practice, and the moral warrants for it, has a history that certainly predates formulation in the Code of Hammurabi. What the history of the death penalty reveals is that the execution practice has been a primary means by which societies have exhibited their most cherished values. The death penalty identifies those offenses that a society most detests, a negative expression, if you will, of those values a society holds most dear. Justification for the death penalty—moral arguments and perspectives—are generated in relation to this societal valuation.

How has the death penalty been—or how could it be—evaluated in light of what we might term modern or Enlightenment moral perspectives?[14] My view is that modern Americans hold the particular views they do about the death penalty because they have interpreted the killing that takes place in execution as action morally justified, and that moral justification expresses itself in arguments and positions and appeals to justice that are themselves related to a broader vision of goodness. How that vision of goodness is to be interpreted and how justifications for particular actions accord with values, assumptions, and philosophical underpinnings that vary over time is, of course, relevant to interpretations of moral meaning.

In our ethical reflection today, we continue to live under the influence of Enlightenment modes of moral interpretation. We still refer, for instance, to the ideals of the natural equality of all persons and of natural—even human—rights to life, liberty, and the pursuit of happiness. This language surfaces continually in our political and moral debates over contentious public policy issues like abortion. We still attempt to operate a utilitarian calculus to anticipate consequences and weigh benefits and burdens in all our everyday decision-making. And the idea that we are, as human beings, endowed with a capacity for moral insight and knowledge and that what is required for moral action is to conform to the duties morality imposes is another Enlightenment-inspired ethical position still widely heard today.

These modes of access to moral meaning are all heard in death penalty debate—and on both sides. The first ethical perspective we shall consider is human rights, and we begin by considering the moral position of Amnesty International, which opposes the death penalty as a violation of a basic human right to life.

Human Rights and the Case of Amnesty International

Amnesty International is an organization that investigates human rights abuses worldwide. Dedicated to the release of prisoners of conscience—defined as those who have not used or advocated violence but have been detained by governments (or opposition groups) for their beliefs, color, sex, ethnic origin, language, or religion—the organization has gone on record as opposing the death penalty categorically, that is, "in all cases and without reservation." Justification for this position is grounded in what may be termed a "human rights" ethic.

In its official statement of purpose, Amnesty International states that "everyone has the right to life, liberty and security of person," and this direct quote from Article 3 of the 1948 UN Charter *Universal Declaration of Human Rights* is itself grounded in Article 1, which states, "All human beings are born free and equal in dignity and rights. They are endowed with reason and conscience and should act toward one another in a spirit of brotherhood."[15] Amnesty International holds that the use of the death penalty is incompatible with humanitarian standards because of its irreversibility, its use for political repression, and its arbitrary and unjust imposition through error-prone systems of justice administration.

Amnesty International—and the UN Charter *Universal Declaration of Human Rights*—is not without controversy in the moral appeal it makes. That appeal is to universal moral norms. As the UN Charter states repeatedly, the rights enumerated in the document are universal, applying to "everyone" and "no one," as in "Everyone has the right to recognition everywhere as a person before the law" (Article 6), and "No one shall be subjected to arbitrary arrest, detention or exile (Article 9)."[16]

The idea of a "human rights" ethic that avows universal rights has its detractors, for the question can—and should—be asked, "Are the rights advanced by the UN Charter and Amnesty International truly universal and applicable outside the contingencies of time and place?" It is worth noting that the American Association of Anthropology condemned the original UN Charter by calling it "a statement of rights conceived only in terms of the values prevalent in Western Europe and America."[17] The heart of this criticism is that such claims to universal rights, having originated in the West, are "ethnocentric" and thus insensitive to the complexities of cultural contingencies and site-specific moral norms. This critique of Western bias and the inherent ethical imperialism of "universal" human rights advocates has often been made, one of the major sources of this criticism being social scientists who encounter other cultures, study them, and seek not to impose moral judgments in the course of their study. These are the advocates of moral relativism, the perspective that right and wrong, and conceptions of moral good and evil, are purely social constructions contingent to time and place. Despite the prominence of some of the advocates of such a relativistic perspective—anthropologist Ruth Benedict was well known for articulating such an ethic[18]—moral relativism amounts to doing away with moral standards, moral progress, and, ultimately, any kind of appeal to moral meaning beyond egoism or its communal counterpart, the ethnocentric ethic of those who decide and evaluate moral meaning by appeal to majority rule. When ethics arrives at this end, what is right and what is wrong are determined by sheer force and the exercise of power. Power, and ultimately domination, then become the foundation for the construction of moral reality.

Clearly, the Amnesty International (and UN Charter) ethic opposes such moral relativism. The "human rights" ethic appeals to universal moral norms that are not influenced by the contingencies of time and place and cultural situation. I support the human rights perspective and endorse the universalism that underlies it, but the critical question put to human rights ethicists by relativists—the question of bias, particularly Western bias—strikes me as a valid question deserving attention and response. Bias must be acknowledged, since the human rights ethic has beyond any question been a peculiarly Western development historically.

Locating the origins of the ethic in the West, however, ought not to be a reason for discrediting the ethic out of hand. Human rights advocates can, it seems to me, construct a "human rights" ethic that can successfully resist the challenge of relativism and expose its incoherence. But given the background of such an ethic in the West, watchfulness and continued critique are in order. This is the position advocated by Preston Williams, whose work on the problem of human rights in developing African nation states has contributed to clarifying many of the issues at stake here. Williams acknowledges that values and moral norms are shaped by culture and the contingencies of cultural differences. Yet having taken cultural difference into account, Williams supports the moral push, so well established in Western ethics and moral reflection, to address the *universal* struggle of individuals and groups to secure justice.[19]

A human rights ethical perspective seeks to identify, articulate, and envision universal action guides derived from moral relations and through moral communities. Amnesty International thus asserts a claim to moral meaning that condemns any state that resorts to the death penalty on the grounds that execution violates a basic and inviolable human right of persons to possess and enjoy life. The *Universal Declaration of Human Rights* puts the issue negatively, noting that no "state, group or person [has] any right to engage in any activity or to perform any act aimed at the destruction of any of the rights" the document sets forth. A state that resorts to use of the death penalty necessarily violates these fundamental or basic human rights.

Amnesty International appeals explicitly to the universal human rights issue that use of the death penalty provokes, and it criticizes the violation of human rights wherever it occurs, regardless of culture or form of government, regardless of the moral or legal or political justifications a state might offer in support of its use of the death penalty.

Amnesty International monitors and reports on human rights abuses wherever they arise. In a 1995 report Amnesty International criticized Japan for being one of the few industrialized countries in the world to maintain a death penalty. Attention was drawn to the twenty-eight-year death row experience of seventy-seven-year-old Tsuneyoshi Tomiyama, whose long imprisonment was evaluated as exacerbating the "already cruel, inhuman and degrading experience of being under sentence of death." The report then went on to make its explicit human rights appeal: the "death penalty," the report stated, "is a denial of the fundamental right to life."[20]

Expressing in its own charter documents a condemnation of the death penalty, Amnesty International interprets execution as an inevitable tool of political repression, saying, "No matter what reason a government gives for executing prisoners and what method of execution is used, the death penalty cannot be separated from the issue of human rights." Amnesty International holds that the death penalty has been used historically not only to punish for a crime such as murder, but for crimes against the state, which may include various forms of political opposition. Given how particular states are constructed with respect to law and power, execution policy may be devised to protect the state from political opposition, which may be treated in a particular political-legal system as seditious or treasonable and thus a grave or extreme threat to the existing social order. (That the state may impose a death sentence in cases of extreme gravity is a widely cherished notion, one that even the Roman Catholic Church in its catechetical teachings continues to endorse even though the church in general opposes use of the death penalty.[21]) The point, however, is that for the human rights advocate, execution of a human being violates a fundamental human right to life no person ought to relinquish in the face of state force; and any such attempt to destroy life through the violence of state-enforced execution constitutes immoral action that violates the rights all persons possess by virtue of their fundamental humanity to be free of such violation. This moral assessment holds even in the face of legal procedures that would legally impose such a penalty for offenses in a particular state.

Locke's Natural Rights Justification

The human rights ethic to which I have referred has a historical pedigree, and one of the most significant voices raised on behalf of the view that certain rights attach by virtue of an individual's simple humanity was that of the seventeenth-century English political philosopher John Locke (1632–1704). In his influential *Second Treatise on Civil Government*,[22] Locke advanced the view, grounded in a Protestant theism, that human persons possess *by nature* the foundational human rights to life, liberty, and property generated by their own labor. These human rights—natural rights in Locke's language—were gifts of God, applying to all. Locke held that these rights were inviolable and not subject to relinquishment, either voluntarily or by the act of another.

Grounding his political theory in these foundational natural rights, Locke argued that governments could only wield power legitimately upon express "consent of the governed." Locke is therefore to be joined with political theorists of the "social contract" school, although Locke himself never used this phrase. In his formulation of the civic state, Locke located sovereignty in the people, each of whom was the equal of every other and each of whom possessed individual power to protect natural rights to life, liberty, and property. "The State of Nature," Locke wrote, "has a law of Nature to govern it, which obliges everyone: And Reason, which is that Law, teaches all Mankind, who will but consult it, that being all equal and independent, no one ought to harm another in his Life, Health, Liberty or Possessions" (II, 6, p. 289).

For those who transgress against the law of nature, which is to offend against the rule of reason itself, punishment is to be meted out inasmuch as such offense is dangerous to others who have a natural right to be free from injury and violence. Such offenders may be dealt with by lawfully harming them proportionate to their offense for purposes of reparation and restraint. Locke claims that it is lawful in the state of nature to "bring such evil on anyone, who has transgressed that Law (of Nature), as may make him repent the doing of it," adding this utilitarian justification, "and thereby deter him, and by his Example others, from doing like mischief." Murder is a particular crime for which death may be deemed an appropriate punishment, lawful by reason of utilitarian deterrence, retribution, and self-defense. Locke writes:

> And thus it is that every Man in the State of Nature, has the power to kill a Murderer, both to deter others from doing the like Injury [deterrence], which no Reparation can compensate [retribution] . . . and also to secure Men from the attempts of a Criminal, who having renounced reason, hath . . . declared War against all Mankind and therefore may be destroyed as a *Lyon* or a *Tyger* [self-defense]. (II, 11, p. 292)

Concluding his remarks on the right to punish in a state of nature, Locke postulates, "every *Man hath a Right to punish the Offender, and be Executioner of the Law of Nature*" (II, 8, p. 290). In the state of nature, then, every individual, possessed of natural rights, claims individual power to assume the role of judge and executioner of nature's law, understood by reason to be God's law.

We can see from this brief extract of Locke's thought that in the state of nature, the power to use lethal force in protection of one's fundamental and basic human rights to life, liberty, and property is clearly defended. The power to kill to protect these rights is authorized by reason, which appeals for authorization to nature, and nature to God—it is God who sanctions in the state of nature an execution power. But Locke's execution power theory as it applies to a state of nature must undergo reconsideration as human beings pass from the state of nature and enter civil society.

By consent and voluntary action human beings form communities "for their comfortable, safe, and peaceable living one amongst another, in a secure Enjoyment of their Properties, and a greater Security" (VIII, 95, p. 349). They leave the state of nature and join the commonwealth, thereby transferring their individual power to the state. "Where-ever therefore any number of Men are so united into one Society, as to quit every one of his Executive Power of the Law of Nature, and to resign it to the publick, there and there only is a *Political, or Civil Society*" (VII, 89, p. 343). In entering civil society, individuals authorize the society itself to make and execute laws for "the publick good," agreeing to resign the individual power held in a state of nature—including the execution power. In entering civil society, the individual accepts an obligation or compact "to everyone of that Society, to submit to determination of the *majority*" and set up a particular form of government" (XIII, 97, p. 350).

Locke conceived the state as governing by consent of each for the benefit of all. The conduct of governmental affairs was to be determined by the rule of law; and a civil society's laws were to be written and codified to conform to reason and nature's God. In Locke's view magistrates and officials hold power legitimately only so long as they remain responsible to the people and their well-being. When they fail in their duties, the people have the right—and the duty—to redirect the state and revolt, for a compact of trust can dissolve in the face of transgressions against the people. The dissolution of the people's trust and consent constitutes a forfeiture of governmental power, which "devolves to the People, who have a Right to resume their original Liberty" (*Second Treatise*, XIX, 222, p. 430). Locke upheld in the name of the fundamental rights to life, liberty and property various political rights possessed by persons in the state, including the citizen right of revolution.

As a Enlightenment figure who held high regard for the individual and for the capacity of reason, Locke endorsed a view that what is moral is what conduces naturally to happiness and pleasure. Grounding ethical norms in natural rights which themselves conform with natural and divine law, Locke held that persons should be free to pursue their happiness. They possess as human creatures a fundamental right not to be interfered with, rights being conceived as entitlements that prevent others from meddling in one's life. Those who advocate human rights make an unmistakable Lockean appeal in claiming that status as a person is sufficient to protect a person from the undue interference of others.

Given this understanding of a human rights ethic, what might Locke—a natural rights political philosopher—have said about capital punishment? Would he support the Amnesty International call for abolition of the death penalty on the grounds that such action by the state interferes with a fundamental human right of which no person should be deprived?

Locke did address the issue of the death penalty. While I acknowledge that there is serious scholarly debate over the specifics of Locke's position, a plain reading of relevant texts will support the view that Locke endorsed rather than opposed the death penalty. His support of the death penalty and the governmental power to impose such a punishment was advanced as consistent with his commitment to a human rights ethical perspective.

At the end of the opening chapter of the *Second Treatise of Government*, Locke declares that "*Political Power* then I take to be *a Right* of making Laws with Penalties of Death, and consequently all less penalties, for the regulating and Preserving of Property, and of Employing the force of the Community, in the Execution of such Laws, and in the defence of the Common-wealth from Foreign Injury, and all this only for the Publick Good" (I, 3, p. 268). Given what I have said above about Locke's general philosophical view, the transfer of individual power to the state requires giving up the power "of doing whatsoever [individuals] thought fit for the preservation of [themselves]" (IX, 129, p. 370) and, secondly, "the *Power of punishing* [they] wholly *give up*" (IX, 130, p. 371) to the state.

In Locke's view, the state, acting for the common good, holds the right to impose the death penalty as that right is derived from the natural rights which all persons possess in their natural state. In Locke's formulation, a lawbreaker not only transgresses against the laws of nature but departs from the rule of reason itself. Other members of society have a right to protect themselves from such a transgressor, and the right to self-protection, which issues from the natural human right to life itself, includes the right to kill a transgressor. As sovereignty rests in the people, when the people empower the state to act for their collective benefit and welfare, the people act through the state to protect their own natural rights: "For *by the Fundamental Law of Nature, Man being to be preserved,* as much as possible, when all cannot be preserv'd, the safety of the Innocent is to be preferred. And one may destroy a Man who makes War upon him, or has discovered an Enmity to his being" (III, 16, pp. 296–97). To those who threaten to deprive individuals of their natural right to liberty or life itself Locke says, "it is lawful for me to treat him, as one who has put *himself into a State of War* with me, i.e., kill him if I can; for to that hazard does he justly expose himself, whoever introduces a State of War, and is aggressor in it" (III, 18, p. 298).

Locke is saying, then, that self-defense, even lethal self-defense, is a lawful and justified response to such aggression. But how does this justify state action to impose death as a penalty for crime? Locke's response is this: Given that every person is equally entitled in civil society to enjoy natural rights and to protect them "against the Injuries and Attempts of other Men," it follows from the natural law of reason that such actions should be punished as "the Offence deserves, even with Death itself, in Crimes where the heinousness of the Fact . . . requires it" (*Second Treatise,* VII, 87, pp. 341–42). So this supports the case that Locke views capital punishment as a legitimate means of retributive punishment for those who commit what are viewed as "heinous" offenses. Criminal acts harm society itself, and the law will determine which deeds constitute offenses against society deserving punishment. Moreover, the law will establish in a commonwealth a rule of proportional punishment, with the worst crimes—those fitting the category of heinousness—deserving the most serious punishment, death. Locke nowhere claims that it is the duty of a commonwealth to impose a death penalty. Locke, rather, deems a death penalty a justifiable punishment option in civil society. Commonwealths may choose to use it, but its use will necessarily conform to the rule of law and observe the rule of proportionality.

Locke's willingness to endorse the right of a commonwealth to put a death penalty into law seems unambiguous. All persons have a natural right to preserve themselves and ought not "unless it be to do Justice on an Offender, take away or impair the life . . . of another" (II, 6, p. 89). Locke, then, supports the death penalty while not requiring it. He justifies its use as a means whereby society protects itself from those who would war upon it in defiance of reason and nature's laws. He justifies it as a deterrent to potential offenders. And he finally makes reference to it as a way of delivering justice to an offender, this remark being related perhaps to the retribution perspective quoted earlier, namely, the idea that a murderer commits an injury that "no reparation can compensate." Locke does seem to transfer to civil society from a state of nature "the power to kill" as a means of serving a notion of justice. For Locke, a state-sponsored execution as punishment for a heinous crime imposes, in the end, a just—and justifiable—societal sanction on those who by unjust slaughter and violence have declared war on humankind.

Extracting Issues from Human and Natural Rights

Having connected the language of a human rights ethics perspective to the natural rights political philosophy of John Locke, with its attendant ethical supports, we have positioned ourselves to raise critical issues about the moral meaning of the death penalty. For all that separates the human rights appeal of Amnesty International from a Lockean natural law ethic, both perspectives examine the moral legitimacy of the death penalty in an affirmation of a fundamental human right of persons to life, a right possessed universally by virtue of being human, or, as Locke would put, by nature. Amnesty International avows a human rights ethic that conforms to the Lockean claim that individual persons possess natural human rights to life and liberty. By appropriating this claim and absolutizing it to cover—and protect—all persons from the potentially lethal use of political power, the organization upholds the value of life as inviolate, nonrelinquishable, and exempt from lethal state force. The human rights ethic Amnesty International endorses does more than signal opposition to all manner of infringements on human rights. It identifies the death penalty as an illegitimate and immoral use of force whatever standing such a penalty has in law, and so constructs the moral meaning of the death penalty that it is disallowed as an inevitable and absolute human rights violation. Morally speaking, state-sponsored execution is inherently unjust.

Locke did not draw this conclusion, although he also articulated a universal right to life. In his political philosophy, Locke located authorization for the death penalty in the sovereign will of the people, who transferred a right of punishment and self-defense to the state in the original compact whereby individuals left the state of nature and formed political society. Locke seemed not to doubt that the death penalty was a means that a state could lawfully employ as a legitimate use of collective power. In the state of nature, individuals possessed the power to defend their natural rights to life, liberty, and property. This power could be lethal, and it was potentially extensive. While this power to kill in self-defense is maintained in the face of an immediate threat of destruction, the compact of civil society in general transfers the power of punishment to the legislature and the rule of law, and it is to the law, in its "unbiased application," that justice is to be served.

Locke was a proportionalist when it came to employing the death penalty as a legitimate use of force within civil society, restricting its use to heinous crimes (i.e., murder). The death penalty in civil society was directed—and restricted— as a punishment for offenses that threatened the well-being of all. A death penalty, then, could, in Locke's view, serve justice, but only conditionally. Imposing a death sentence constituted a use of force, and Locke articulated strong opposition to the "use of Force without Right" (XIX, 232, p. 437). This view would obviously demand an "unbiased application" of the law "to protect and redress the innocent" so that the death penalty would be imposed fairly and not fall unjustly on the innocent.

In considering Locke's understanding of moral and legal warrants for the death penalty, it is important to consider that he nowhere articulated a view that states have a duty to impose death as a punishment for crime. The only exception to this is the state where the people, in an exercise of sovereign power, through legislation, demand such a penalty. One could infer that this legal requirement would be only for specific "heinous" crimes that threaten the well-being of all. What moral duty there is pertains not to execution but to the preservation of one's own life, which allows for the use of lethal force when the threat to life from an aggressor is immediate, the potential victim faces the irreparable loss of life, and "I could not have *time to appeal* to the Law" (XVIII, 207, p. 422).

Locke held open the possibility that the guilty are to be spared, as earlier cited, "where it can prove no prejudice to the innocent." Since his moral commitment to the idea that "all the Members of Society are to be preserved" as much as possible and that account ought to be taken of those situations where "a strict and rigid observation of the Laws may do harm" (XIV, 159, p. 393), Locke justified a pardoning of offenders, and may have even believed that offenders could reform. Civil society, which creates the political environment for these new ways of understanding punishment options, is clearly not the state of nature.

Having surveyed how a "human rights ethic" could be applied in two quite different ways to assess the moral meaning of the death penalty, I wish now to extract some points from this discussion that will be relevant as we proceed with this moral inquiry.

1. The first and most obvious point to glean from this discussion is this: An appeal to "human rights" or "natural rights" does not yield an uncontroversial moral perspective on capital punishment, neither Locke's position allowing it conditionally nor the absolute prohibition advocated by Amnesty International.

2. Locke defends the possible use of the death penalty in civil society, but he is restrictive in holding that it be reserved for heinous acts. Even then, he defends pardoning power on the grounds that the law applied in certain situations may simply be too harsh. Locke appeals to deterrence and nonreparation as justification for the death penalty when murder has been committed, but seems strongest in arguing for the death penalty as societal self-defense. The fascinating question to put to Locke concerns his awareness of time and how lethal force in the face of an immediate threat to security is justifiable. For if one removes an offender from society and thus eliminates the immediacy of the threat to the security of individuals and the state itself, is there any justification for imposing a death sentence? Locke affirms the right of the state to defend itself from rebels and any who, as criminals, enter into a state of war with society. But if the threat is not immediate and has even been resisted and subsequently contained, does a state of war exist any longer? Locke seems to place weight on the time factor, justifying lethal force in self-defense when a threat to life is immediate. But what if the threat is removed and there are alternatives that might satisfy deterrence or reparation concerns?[23]

3. Although Locke implies that the death penalty should be imposed only where the law has observed the constraints of due process or "unbiased application," Amnesty International provides data to demonstrate that states actually do, as an empirical matter, abuse power and fail to observe these constraints. Locke's general position opposing state tyranny would naturally oppose the kind of abuse of power that would lead to the use of execution for political repression, yet he does not address the Amnesty International concern that states can unjustly use execution for this purpose. States can use execution as a means of terrorism, disregarding the respect that states must have for the inherent natural rights each citizen possesses to life and liberty; and this terrorism can be state sanctioned as legal activity when laws and governments are unjust. Nazi Germany, as is well known, relied on a legal but immoral policy of execution to

achieve repressive political ends, including the general, and sinister, policy of genocidal extermination. Amnesty International, however, in holding that the death penalty should be abolished without exception, claims that execution is an act so extreme and so violative of fundamental human rights—especially and particularly the right to life that all human beings possess—that the punishment itself is inherently unjust. Amnesty International points out abuses in the practice of the death penalty, citing in its various reports on state terrorism cases and instances where execution—even legal execution—is pressed into service to quash political dissent.

Amnesty International reminds us that history is replete with examples of states that have resorted to execution for purposes that extend far beyond punishment for the crime of murder. History—and even current events—reveal that in a politically unstable world, states can resort to violence to silence opposition, authorizing actions that involve human rights violations which can include the use of torture, unjust imprisonment, lengthy trial delays, and even execution itself. Citizens have been, and still are, punished by the state for political offenses, and that punishment may extend beyond imprisonment or exile to include execution. Through its endorsement of an absolutist abolition policy Amnesty International seeks to preserve the basic human right to life in the face of political power that can subordinate that right unjustly to various political ends.

4. This empirical and historical point allows us to draw a conclusion concerning the relative merits of the Lockean versus the Amnesty International perspective. It is my view that moral evaluation would find the Amnesty International perspective superior to the Lockean, but on practical rather than theoretical grounds.

Practically speaking, the Amnesty International perspective would necessarily prevent a state from resorting to execution as an instrument of political repression. Locke's perspective cannot prevent the abuse or misuse of execution power, or, to be more precise, it cannot prevent unjust executions between the time a political regime resorts to execution as an instrument of political repression and the time when people exercise their Lockean natural right to dissolve such a regime. Given that Locke's perspective cannot prevent at least some unjust killings through state-sponsored execution prior to dissolving a tyrannical and unjust government, and Amnesty International can, I would assert the Amnesty International position on the death penalty to be the superior interpretation of a human rights ethic. Locke's human rights–based theory of the state allows for the real possibility that prior to the people's exercise of a right to revolt against unjust and tyrannical employments of state power, corruptible governments can unjustly execute citizens. The Amnesty International perspective, not only theoretically but practically, eliminates such a prospect.

5. Amnesty International's stance against execution can be said to be a logical position in that it opposes an absolute penalty with an absolute opposition. The death penalty is absolute, but its claim to absoluteness is not that it is absolutely certain of guilt or even that the demands of justice have been met absolutely—only that the result of the penalty, death, is absolute. If justice demands that this absolute end be achieved through a process that is absolutely just and in accordance with a standard of absolute certitude, then the Amnesty International prohibition says that in a condition of human finitude and actual evidence of human rights abuse, such standards cannot be met. The fact that the absolute end achieved—the death—is the result of a finite and a flawed system feeds the illusion that our systems of justice are adequate to deliver the absolute certainty and absolute justice that this necessarily absolute end—the death by execution—logically requires. Amnesty International's absolute no is directed at the illusion that human justice can be delivered with certitude.

What is attractive about a natural rights perspective has been well articulated by Hugo Adam Bedau, a major legal and philosophical scholar of the death penalty. He writes that this perspective "purports to provide each of us with moral armor (our rights) that protects us against burdens and deprivations that might otherwise be imposed, on the ground that they are in the interest of the many or good for society in the long run."

Bedau adds, however, that

> Locke's theory requires any offender to forfeit the right to life whenever that is "deserved" by virtue of the nature of the offence. Surely the harm done in a crime is part of its nature. Hence, it can be argued that crimes other than murder (such as treason, espionage, arson, rape) also "deserve" the death penalty because no other punishment can provide comparable protection for society. One may well doubt whether a theory of natural rights not impervious to reasoning of this sort is worth defending.[24]

Bedau points out that nothing in Locke's view would prevent the state from imposing a death sentence on all manner of offences, not just murder. We know from history that this has happened. The expansion of the death penalty to cover a variety of crimes, a move made possible by pressing into service a utilitarian form of reasoning that justifies indiscriminate use of the death penalty to maintain the good order of society, led to a legal situation in England where, by 1800, English law acknowledged over two hundred capital offenses, some for petty thievery and pickpocketing more than a shilling.[25]

Out of the natural, universal, and inalienable right to life Amnesty International has constructed the rigid moral barrier Locke himself could not erect, grounding that right in a moral absolutism that cannot address or incorporate Locke's notion that the death penalty is to be justified on a theory of societal self-defense. I take Locke seriously and will address this issue in the pages ahead. What I wish to draw attention to at this moment is that Locke does not go in the direction of an Amnesty International ethical absolutism, but appeals, rather, to what we might term a utilitarian mode of thinking that defends state execution in the service of deterrence—the idea that capital punishment yields consequences that advance the good of the whole of society. This utilitarian appeal is deserving of more attention. This other moral option for thinking about the moral meaning of the death penalty—the utilitarian or "consequentialist" approach—will be examined in detail in the next chapter.

5

A Service to the
Greater Good

The argument can be made that the death penalty is morally justifiable because it advances the general welfare. Such an argument is grounded in a mode of philosophical thought and moral reasoning associated with utilitarianism. A utilitarian evaluation of the moral meaning of the death penalty discerns moral meaning by weighing the consequences of execution, not particularly to the victims of crime or to the executed offender, but to society as a whole.

A utilitarian analysis would consider the usefulness of the death penalty in light of the consequences that flow from its use. By employing a calculus on the "principle" that we ought to do whatever will promote the greatest happiness for the greatest number, the utilitarian would determine whether the beneficial consequences of capital punishment outweigh its harmful effects. If it can be demonstrated that using the death penalty will advance the good of the whole—the aggregate good—even if not everyone (i.e., the person executed) necessarily benefits, utilitarian analysis would conclude that execution is right action and that resorting to this punishment is morally justified. Locke, as we have seen, made use of such an argument.

In general, utilitarianism holds that human actions are to be morally assessed in terms of the value they produce. In its specific mode of operation, utilitarianism is *consequentialist* in that it makes the rightness of actions depend on the consequences of action; and it is *teleological* (from the Greek *telos*, meaning "end" or the thing aimed at) because it aims at the specific end of maximizing utility—meaning the greatest aggregate good or happiness—for the greatest number. Two distinctive forms of utilitarianism have formed over the years: act utilitarianism, which focuses on individual actions; and rule utilitarianism, which commends decision-making based on those rules which, if generally followed, would produce the most good for the most people. Although some argue for the distinctiveness of these two forms of utilitarianism,[1] others do not.[2] It is safe to say, however, that these two modes of utilitarian thinking can certainly lead to different decisions about how to act, since applying a rule against lying, for example, would in all likelihood prevent a rule utilitarian from telling the very lie that an act utilitarian might, in a specific situation, be able to justify.

There is no question that utilitarianism has a certain attractiveness, as even its critics admit,[3] for there is strong intuitive appeal in the idea that we should perform those actions that will produce more good than any other action. Furthermore, utilitarianism does take seriously the potential messiness of the moral life, assuming a posture of flexibility in response to that messiness unknown in the pre-Enlightenment era of religiously based moral absolutism. Utilitarianism takes seriously the need to ground decision-making in a mode of rationality that can have universal application, for what it promises is an orderly moral calculus, commended by reason and available to rational human persons for applying to difficult moral situations. The utilitarian philosophy accords with a modern scientific temperament and is a primary expression of the Enlightenment spirit, for the principle of utility—whether defined as happiness or pleasure or some other value—establishes for the moral life a rational foundation free of self-interest, caprice, and arbitrariness.[4]

Two figures tower over the development of what we call today classic utilitarianism: Jeremy Bentham (1748–1832) and John Stuart Mill (1806–1873). Both of these philosophers accepted reason as the true source of moral legislation; and both addressed punishment and the death penalty. But having employed the utilitarian calculus, they drew different conclusions. Bentham opposed the death penalty, Mill supported it.

Bentham presented his views on the death penalty in two essays, one in 1775, a second in 1831. Since those essays have been thoroughly explicated and interpreted by Hugo Adam Bedau,[5] a detailed examination of Bentham's views is not necessary here. I do think it important, however, to indicate for comparative purposes with John Stuart Mill, whose views on the death penalty I shall examine shortly in more detail, that Jeremy Bentham, the true originator of modern utilitarian thought, held that the reasons against using death penalty outweighed the reasons for it.[6]

Bentham was a hedonistic utilitarian who held that the end of life was, naturally, the pursuit of pleasure and the avoidance of pain. The aim of good and moral action was, for Bentham, to achieve the greatest sum of pleasure, and he devised a hedonistic calculus that considered how pleasure might be affected by intensity, duration, purity, and several other factors, which need not detain us. He applied this philosophy to a critique of society, and it is in this context that Bentham addressed crime and punishment. As his writings on these topics indicate, he was a severe critic of the British legal system and an advocate for various criminal justice reforms. He held that crimes should be classified according to the level of seriousness of offense, with "seriousness" to be appropriately determined by the misery a crime causes for its victims and for society. For Bentham punishment was to have as its purpose the canceling of whatever advantage a crime might have gained for the offender. Only an act that produced harmful consequences to others ought to be considered eligible for the status of crime.[7]

Bentham's view of the death penalty was grounded in the utilitarian view that punishment in general was an evil in that it caused pain and displeasure. Punishment could only be justified in the larger utilitarian consideration where the evil caused by punishment was outweighed by the benefits to the greater happiness of all. In this context, Bentham weighed the death penalty, doing so in the context of a utilitarian concern that alternatives to execution might more effectively achieve the end of increasing the general happiness. Bentham concluded that the death penalty was problematic on utilitarian grounds for various reasons. It induced positive harm by preventing any opportunity to correct an erroneous execution. It eliminated the possibility of compensating a person wrongly executed. But, more important, Bentham could not establish that the execution of an offender advanced the happiness of all, and it certainly was not preferable to alternatives such as imprisonment. When he considered the argument about deterrence, Bentham would become among the first to argue that in light of the harshness of prison life, the death penalty could actually be a less effective deterrent than imprisonment. Bentham even went further in his consideration of the effects of execution on the welfare of all. Noting that the death penalty was on the books but had fallen into disuse for certain crimes because society had come to believe death too harsh for, say, the crime of pickpocketing, Bentham suggested that having a death penalty "far from preventing offences tends to increase them by the hope of impunity."[8]

John Stuart Mill

As I mentioned earlier, Bentham's view was opposed by his most famous disciple, John Stuart Mill. Mill addressed the issue of the death penalty and even some of Bentham's arguments, not in any of his writing but in a speech delivered before the House of Commons opposing an amendment that would have abolished capital punishment:

> When there has been brought home to any one, by conclusive evidence, the greatest crime known to the law; and when the attendant circumstances suggest no palliation of the guilt, no hope that the culprit may even yet not be unworthy to live among mankind, nothing to make it probable that the crime was an exception to his general character rather than the consequence of it, then I

confess it appears to me that to deprive the criminal of the life of which he has proved himself to be unworthy—solemnly to blot him out from the fellowship of mankind and from the catalogue of the living—is the most appropriate, as it is certainly the most impressive, mode in which society can attach to so great a crime the penal consequence which for the security of life it is indispensable to annex to it. (p. 267)[9]

Mill defends the death penalty "as beyond comparison the least cruel mode in which it is possible adequately to deter from crime" (p. 267), having restricted the death penalty to the single specific "atrocious crime" of "aggravated murder" (p. 267). This remark from his only sustained philosophical discussion of the death penalty is the first of several references to "deterrence" Mill will offer in this speech.

Mill makes a direct utilitarian appeal by arguing that the death penalty is useful to society at large. Focusing on the specific benefit that accrues to society from deterrence, Mill argues that the deterrent effect yields to the greatest number a positive—"eminently beneficial" (p. 267), in Mill's words—consequence that, in the utilitarian calculation, outweighs the evil of extinguishing a life. Mill's utilitarian argument is that the deterrent effect protects the social order and helps preserve "security of life" for all. In promoting security and thus advancing the welfare of all, the death penalty constitutes a defensible action, a right action that is, in the utilitarian view, morally justifiable.

Mill addressed the deterrence issue because in the parliamentary debate over the amendment to abolish the death penalty, supporters of the amendment had argued that no such deterrent effect could be claimed. To support their case they drew on the recent experience in England of juries refusing to convict individuals who had been charged with certain capital crimes, like theft, where the punishment of death had seemed too harsh. The argument of amendment supporters was that just as the death penalty for theft had in previous years failed to deter thievery, so, too, would continuing the death penalty for murder fail to prevent murder. Mill clearly discerned that were this consequentialist argument to go unchallenged, the utilitarian defense he had offered would itself fail. Mill offered three different arguments concerning deterrence.

Deterrence as Grounded in Psychological Arousal

First, to his opponent's claim that hardened criminals are not affected by fear of the gallows, Mill responded by simply conceding the point. But Mill redirects the argument. The beneficial deterrent effect of capital punishment, Mill argued, was not appropriately directed to the hardened criminal but to the innocent person:

The efficacy of a punishment which acts principally through the imagination is chiefly to be measured by the impression it makes on those who are still innocent: by the horror with which it surrounds the first prompting of guilt: the restraining influence it exercises over the beginning of the thought which, if indulged, would become a temptation; the check which it exerts over the gradual declension toward the state—never suddenly attained—in which crime no longer revolts, and punishment no longer terrifies. (p. 269)

Mill is arguing that the expected experience of terror in the face of prospective execution will deter murderous action on the part of innocent persons, perhaps even blunting the formation of a murderous intent, which would be a necessary condition for the commission of the capital crime of aggravated murder.

But this claim is arguable. No necessary connection can be established between the experience of imagined terror and actually being innocent of aggravated murder. In fact, by arguing for such a connection, Mill opens himself to a logical drubbing. What separates the guilty from the innocent for Mill is that the guilty are insensitive to the terror aroused by the prospect of execution and thus are not deterred. The innocent, on the other hand, are sensitive to that terror and because they can be aroused they can be deterred. But what if it can be demonstrated that the innocent—those persons not guilty of aggravated murder—had also lost their sensitivity to terror at the thought of execution? The necessary connection Mill argues for—the connection between psychological horror and being deterred from the commission of a capital crime—would necessarily fail. Making a reasonable case that the innocent—all those in the class of persons not guilty of committing capital crime—are insensitive to the excitation of terror (as are the undeterred guilty criminal offenders) subverts the foundation of Mill's deterrence claim.

I think a reasonable case can be made that the death penalty, as it is currently carried out in the United States, does not produce the requisite psychological arousal on the innocent that Mill claims is necessary for deterrence.

Showing that the innocent are—or are not—affected by the terror of execution requires an empirical argument. I cannot make a strictly empirical argument, but Mill did not do so either. But in an empirical spirit and against Mill, I would say that it seems not far-fetched to appeal to certain facts of social experience that could lead reasonable people to conclude that such a psychological effect as Mill requires for deterrence is currently lacking in American society. To make this case I would argue that in American society, Americans cannot be affected behaviorally by Mill's "experience of terror" because in this society, the violent death visited upon persons by execution fails to stand out from a background of violence that is so much a part of our common social experience. Mill requires a social environment where execution death stands out by virtue of its ability to shock and horrify. But my question is, What if the society considering the death penalty is itself saturated with violence? What if violence is familiar in the culture and prominent in its social history? What if violence is a feature of everyday experience, so that even if individuals have not been its victim directly, they have been touched by violence, have had their lives and lifestyles affected by concern for violence, and even, in many cases, seek out exposure to violence for entertainment purposes?

Mill's argument for deterrence based on psychological arousal requires a society where the terrifying nature of execution can so stand out from the commonplace experience of everyday events that the prospect of an execution can truly shock and horrify. But this cannot occur in contemporary America. Execution cannot incite a deterrence-delivering horror when violent death is commonly presented in graphic detail in ordinary, everyday news reporting. It cannot arouse the imagination to provoke deterrence when media vendors compete for an audience by trying to outdo one another in the details of stories that concern human beings visiting cruelty, brutality, and savage death on one another; when newspaper tabloids publish autopsy photos of murdered children; when an entire industrial sector of the economy successfully places violent death at the center of entertainment, where much citizen leisure time and money is spent. This constant barrage of encounter with violence necessarily blunts—rather than heightens—the capacity of persons to experience shock and horror at the imagined thought of an execution.

Against such a background, it is all but impossible for execution to stand out by virtue of its singular horror and capacity to shock the imagination. Everyday experiences present too much stimulating competition for Mill's argument to claim efficacy today. But there is an even stranger complication. What if, against such a background, execution were removed from the arena where it could deliver its powerful deterrent effect? What if it were sanitized and rendered as close in the public perception to a nonviolent—even, ironically, a helpful, healing act—as could be imagined?

This too has occurred. Executions are not public; furthermore, the mode of execution has become increasingly associated with nonviolent images, which further begs the question, How is a lethal injection execution going to horrify and shock and thus deliver its positive deterrent effect?

For execution has become more palatable to more people as the method of execution has been intentionally robbed of horror by making it a seemly painless euthanizing medical procedure. Execution is no longer associated with the violent images of guillotine bloodshed, or the unseemly violence of choking, strangling, burning, and other forms of high-intensity pain infliction. Against the background of a social environment perceived to be violent, execution has taken on the appearance of putting an individual peacefully to sleep. This is hardly an obvious move in the direction of arousing shock for deterrence purposes. Foucault's presentation of the breaking on the wheel, an old medieval torture-style of execution—"The prisoner's arms and legs were propped up on a wheel-like platform and were broken in several places by the use of a heavy iron bar. The mangled remains were then turned rapidly, scattering gore about until the unfortunate victim was dead"[10]—might, were it to come back into fashion, more suitably generate the psychological arousal Mill's theory requires. The problem, of course, is that such cruelty would ill conform to modern tastes and standards of conduct, though it would no doubt come closer than lethal injection to inciting Mill's description of a deterrent effect. Receiving an IV is a commonplace experience; being drawn and quartered, disemboweled while still alive, or even guillotined is not. Why would a typical citizen, who has received an IV or knows someone who has, not conclude that lethal injection is a user-friendly mode of execution, finding it all the more acceptable because of its familiarity and nonthreatening nature? Shifting to this mode of death delivery does not, in my view, contribute to the sense that execution is a horrible prospect. On the contrary. This mode may in fact be perceived as "too easy," so that even as a poisoning injection delivers death to an individual through an act of violence, the perception is fostered that the killing is not horrific enough to generate the sense of retributive satisfaction due those who have been victimized by the capital criminal. How can an execution, held in secret and carried out in the guise of a peaceful medical procedure, incite the imagination to terror in a society where crime scene and autopsy photos of murdered children are published for an audience waiting in line to purchase groceries?

Mill's specific argument for deterrence fails in contemporary American society. Against Mill, I would argue that in the current American cultural situation, shock and horror at the thought of violent death are aroused, when they are aroused, by events other than state execution of convicted criminals. It seems reasonable to assert that the imaginations of the innocent are not sufficiently horrified by the prospect of execution to infer the presence, much less the efficacy, of the deterrent effect, upon which Mill rested his justification for capital punishment.

And the idea that citizens—those citizens innocent of capital crimes—can actually become anesthetized to the terror that an execution might hold has further complications for Mill's position. With so many killings, whether real or fictional, a part of daily life in America—the average child growing up in America will witness in the media sixteen thousand murders and over two hundred thousand acts of violence by the age of eighteen[11]—and with the blunting of sensitivities through constant, persistent, and increasingly graphic encounters with violent killings, something even more pernicious is occurring with respect to executions.

Psychic numbing to violence, along with the high percentage of support for the death penalty and the increasingly frequent use of nonthreatening modes of execution, suggests more than the fact that the death penalty cannot deter in Mill's sense. It suggests that execution may itself become a lure for the imaginations of those wanting an experience beyond the vicarious thrills and shocks produced by television news and Hollywood film. Execution is the real thing. It is a form of killing that really kills, and the reality of the killing can induce a new level of excitement and incite a desire for active, rather than merely imaginative, participation in the execution. That execution could so incite the imagination as to lead to an increase—rather than a decrease—in crime was a phenomenon suggested by Camus, who noted in "Reflections on the Guillotine" that of 250 persons hanged in England in the early nineteenth century, 170 had attended at least one execution: "And in 1886, out of 167 condemned men who had gone through Bristol prison, 164 had witnessed at least one execution."[12]

Although execution is secretively carried out today and is cloaked in nonviolent appearance, it may still possess power to engender a morbid fascination in certain minds. As a unique form of legalized and safe killing—safe to those who carry it out or witness it—execution is also real; and because it is real it possesses the capacity to excite the imaginations of some persons who are seeking—let us say for entertainment purposes—the experience of terror beyond what Hollywood film and local news broadcasts are able to provide. I am not saying that we have reached this point in our cultural life in any general sense, but I do see signs that in contemporary American society, the violence of execution has become its own attraction—to the innocent. We have witnessed efforts to broadcast executions over live television, and I have met people who have expressed the desire and even officially volunteered to witness executions. More than once in the wake of a capital conviction the media has carried interviews where the survivors of a victim of capital crime have expressed the desire to actually participate in the execution—personally to pull the switch or begin the poison flow. This is the ultimate expression of a desire to participate in an act of safe killing, and these expressions of desire are greeted in the public not with horror, but with sympathy, as if expressing such a desire constitutes an acceptable expression of the pain of loss. If it is acceptable, it is also a testament to the depth of insensitivity that a culture of violence fosters, nurtures, and finally, in the expression of sympathy to those who express such views, even condones.

Mill defended execution on the utilitarian ground that its deterrent effect, generated from a sense of shock and horror, would promote society's welfare. He does not consider that execution might actually become an incitement to violence, a lure for antisocial, violent impulses, rather than a means of preventing them. Mill would no doubt find in this development sufficient disutility to eliminate the execution practice. Were Mill to have discerned the possibility that execution could be so transformed that it served the interests of the thrill-seeking and easily jaded, even inciting in some the desire to act as the agent who intentionally visits violent death on another human being, he would, I believe, have deplored such a development. The death penalty opens the question about the effect of this kind of killing on the psychic state of certain individuals who may be psychologically fragile, or even aberrant. Although others with more expertise must pursue such questions, I would note that these ought to be live issues for the utilitarian, for the negative effects on society caused by those who are incited to violence rather than deterred from it are consequences that utilitarians must take into consideration.

Mill's case that deterrence, a utilitarian argument for the death penalty, consists in the capacity of innocent persons to be horrified at the thought of facing execution fails to the extent that the innocent—as well as the guilty—can become hardened to the horror of execution. Making this case necessarily robs deterrence of the only real grounding Mill gives it.

Who Knows Who Has Been Deterred?

Connecting the experience of horror to deterrence is Mill's strongest utilitarian defense of capital punishment, but not his only argument. To his parliamentary opponent's claim that because hardened criminals are indifferent to the gallows, the death penalty is a failure, Mill responded by saying, "Who is able to judge that? We partly know who those are whom it has not deterred; but who is there who knows whom it has deterred, or how many human beings it has saved who would have lived to be murderers if that awful association had not been thrown round the idea of murder from their earliest infancy?" (p. 269).

This second argument about deterrence has intuitive appeal and is, admittedly, hard to refute. But more significantly, it is also impossible to prove, since the argument is derived from a suppressed premise that is never established,[13] namely, that there are innocent persons whose innocence with respect to capital crime has been maintained because a single variable—the death penalty—has deterred them from crime. Relevant data to indicate a capital crime had not been committed because of the impact of deterrence is simply impossible to collect and reliably report. To the claim that one could make, "Prove that this doesn't happen," one could rejoin, "Prove that it does." It may be a research failing of this study, but I have not in my years of study of this topic come across examples of persons who have formed the intent to commit an aggravated murder but have then refrained from doing so because of one variable and one alone: fear of capital punishment. I have heard anecdotal reports of persons facing death who, when they thought about capital punishment at all, thought they would not be caught or in some other way would evade a death sentence; and of course there are persons who, in committing the crime that brought them to death row, did so unreflectively in a moment of extreme stress and thus did not think about the death penalty at all.

Mill's argument here is not without appeal, and he can always argue, as did Thomas Sowell and John J. DiIulio, that "we know that the death penalty definitely deters those who are executed. The fact that this is obvious does not make it any less important."[14] But Sowell and DiIulio, like Mill himself, point to no data, no instances, to support their assertion that any particular prospective murder was prevented because of the presence of a death penalty. They do not even offer as relevant testimony their own experience—that they have been so deterred personally. Nor is the case made that because the death penalty attaches to murder, a person forming a murderous intent necessarily surrounds the prospective act of murder with "awful associations." I would assume the opposite, namely, that by a self-deceptive logic an individual contemplating a prospective murder will act on that intent having become convinced that the act is really justifiable and good, even if others do not or will not understand.[15]

The Need for Consistent and Faithful Use—Fear of Disuse

Mill, as already mentioned, acknowledges that the deterrent effect of the death penalty for crimes other than murder cannot be demonstrated. He even says, "The failure of capital punishment in cases of theft is easily accounted for. The thief did not believe it would be inflicted" (p. 269). Pursuing this thought, Mill goes on in his third point about deterrence to concede that only by the diligent and faithful imposition of the death penalty for aggravated murder can the deterrent effect be obtained. Mill's conclusion is that a failure on the part of judges and juries to apply the death penalty where it is warranted robs the punishment of its deterrent effect and, thus, of its utilitarian justification. When the punishment is not used consistently, Mill avers, society is justified in deciding "to abrogate the penalty."

On this particular point, the argument can be made against Mill that in the United States, utilitarian grounds exist for abolishing the death penalty. The percentage of persons actually executed relative to the number of homicides committed is small—approximately 1 percent.[16] On the other hand, each of these homicides represents a loss of life, an irreparable loss. In the vast majority of cases, response to that loss does not come in the form of a demand from society that the life of the person who caused the death be forfeited as punishment, so the infrequency with which executions are carried out relative to number of homicides committed is evidence of a societal reluctance to use the death penalty in response to homicide. But Mill's case is not about homicide but a particular kind of homicide, aggravated murder.

At this point, what must be considered is that various factors can affect how killings will be categorized for legal purposes. What makes things difficult is that prosecutors may exercise discretion and refuse to pursue capital charges for reasons having nothing to do with the nature of the crime itself. The criminal charges brought against O. J. Simpson, for instance, reveal how, in a high-profile case, discretion to pursue a capital charge for a crime fitting the criteria of aggravated murder can be affected by factors other than the nature of the crime and evidence against the accused. Simpson was not charged with a capital crime even though initially the prosecution in the case believed the facts of the case clearly warranted pursuit of a death sentence. Readers may recall that the prosecution conducted some experiments in other jurisdictions to see if a jury would convict Simpson, and the result of their query was decisive: no jury would convict Simpson on a capital charge. This was sufficient evidence to convince the prosecution that they should drop pursuit of a death sentence. Mill worried that the death penalty could fall into disuse; disuse would necessarily have to include evidence of failure to pursue the death penalty in cases where it would be legally appropriate to do so. That reluctance may not be generally directed toward all aggravated murders but, as the Simpson case shows, is discernible at least in certain cases. But that still constitutes evidence for reluctance, and I find it difficult to believe that Mill would have sanctioned under utilitarianism the view that aggravated murder committed by a certain class of individuals—celebrities—is exempt from capital prosecution.

Mill held, rather, that in the utilitarian calculation every person is the equivalent of every other, and utilitarian justice is to be accorded by "be[ing] as strictly impartial as a disinterested and benevolent spectator." What Mill had to say about reluctance to use the death penalty in eligible cases is highly relevant to our discussion:

> When it is impossible to inflict a punishment, or when its infliction becomes a public scandal, the idle threat cannot too soon disappear from the statute book. And in the case of the host of offences which were formerly capital, I heartily rejoice that it did become impracticable to execute the law. If the same state of public feeling comes to exist in the case of murder; if the time comes when jurors refuse to find a murderer guilty; when Judges will not sentence him to death, or will recommend him to mercy; or when, if juries and Judges do not

flinch from their duty, Home Secretaries, under pressure of deputations and memorials, shrink from theirs, and the threat becomes, as it became in the other cases [e.g., capital theft], a mere *brutum fulmen* ["vain menace," from Pliny, *Natural History*]; then, indeed, it may become necessary to do in this case what has been done in those—to abrogate the penalty. That time may come—my honourable Friend thinks that it has nearly come. (p. 269)

Although certain states are carrying out death sentences with greater frequency—Texas, for instance, has executed a third of all those put to death in the United States since 1976—the utilitarian question relative to deterrence is whether the penalty itself is being used with sufficient regularity that persons forming murderous intent could conceivably be deterred from following through with a crime. If death sentences are handed down in approximately 1 percent of all homicides, and the actual number of executions carried out every year is an even smaller percentage than that, the argument could be put back to Mill that the system of execution as currently practiced is being used in such a way that the deterrent effect cannot be imputed to it. It thus ought to be abrogated. We can turn the statistics around to glean *positive disutility* for the common good by suggesting this: that a prospective murderer aware of the statistics, and calculating a 1 percent chance of actually facing execution, might decide to play those odds. Rather than being deterred, certain individuals might be *incited* to act on the murderous intent. The refusal of prosecutors to pursue the death penalty in the O. J. Simpson case is certainly not conclusive evidence that Americans are reluctant to impose the death penalty, but it is evidence that some persons can receive a kind of preferential immunity—can we call it, in Mill's terms, "mercy"?—not granted to all, and that this failure of impartiality affects the usefulness—the utility—of the death penalty to contribute to justice and the welfare or happiness "of all concerned." Failure to pursue and to administer executions for reasons having nothing to do with the legal process of determining guilt—something I think was evident in the highly publicized Simpson case—demonstrates that the death penalty system is corruptible and ought therefore, on Mill's terms, to be abrogated. In the O. J. Simpson case, the prospect of the death penalty became, for the prosecution, a "vain menace" as the prosecution recognized that no jury would do its duty in this particular case.

Effeminacy and the "Worst Punishment" Illusion

Mill's speech makes other points, and I shall briefly mention and comment on them. Mill laments the possible loss of the death penalty, because that loss will represent, "if they will forgive me for saying so, an enervation, an effeminacy, in the general mind of the country. For what else than effeminacy is it to be so much more shocked by taking a man's life than by depriving him of all that makes life desirable or valuable?" (pp. 269–70). Just so the point is not lost, resorting to a punishment that deprives a person of all that makes life valuable (freedom) is, in Mill's view, as harsh as execution, *if not harsher.* To prefer this deprivation over death because of being shocked at death is nothing but weakness and, as this profound advocate of women's rights characterizes it, "effeminacy."

We move in Mill's argument at this point from the substantive utilitarian argument about deterrence to the most interesting aspect of Mill's argument in favor of the death penalty. For in the wake of his statement about effeminacy, Mill, echoing Bentham, proceeds to explain his view that death is not the greatest of all ills, and because of that, execution is not the worst punishment that can befall a criminal offender:

> What comparison can there really be, in point of severity, between consigning a man to the short pang of a rapid death, and immuring him in a living tomb, there to linger out what may be a long life in the hardest and most monotonous toil, without any of its alleviations or rewards—debarred from all pleasant sights and sound, and cut off from all earthly hope, except a slight mitigation of bodily restraint, or a small improvement of diet. . . . There is not, I should think, any infliction which makes an impression on the imagination so entirely out of proportion to its real severity as the punishment of death. (p. 268)

What these words mean is that Mill's whole argument about deterrence, based on the fact that death is feared and thus yields a necessary shock, is actually based on an illusion. Death is not really so bad, he is saying, and it is clearly not the worst thing that could befall a criminal offender. Because Mill's utilitarian view was directed at happiness and the higher-order pleasures that contribute to happiness—the forming of friendships, intellectual pursuits, and the like— Mill very clearly saw that depriving persons of access to this happiness would be a fate worse than death, for at least death puts an end to the pain. It is on the basis of such a philosophical position that Mill argues that we ought not be so fastidious about execution—so "effeminate." Execution ought to be used as the punishment for terrible crime not because it is the harshest penalty, but only because it is perceived to be. In that perception lies the deterrence effect. So that when Mill says, "I defend this penalty, when confined to atrocious cases, on the very ground on which it is commonly attacked—on that of the humanity to the criminal; as beyond comparison the least cruel method in which it is possible adequately to deter from the crime" (p. 267), he is actually advocating the lesser punishment of death. He thus advocates a proportional response at the same moment he reneges on delivering it. Mill settles for the death penalty because he believes that the death penalty can arouse the shock and horror necessary to generate deterrence. The shock is based on an illusion, but for Mill the deterrent effect is real. In opting for death, society receives its benefit, and by resorting to execution, society is actually acting in the least cruel and most humane way toward the offender most deserving of the worst punishment.

The implications of this view are fascinating. Mill is arguing on utilitarian grounds that execution deters and thus yields a positive benefit. But he is also saying that it is an illusion that this punishment is in fact the worst punishment that could be fitted to the worst, most pernicious crime, namely, aggravated murder. The worst punishment appropriate to this crime on a simple proportionality argument would be not death but imprisonment. For imprisonment, not death, is the punishment whereby the life of happiness is denied the offender. Imprisonment imposes sustained unhappiness. Execution cuts off unhappiness in a short pang of death.

So why opt for death? Two reasons. First: It deters. And it deters because it is perceived to be the proportionately worst punishment fitting what is clearly the worst crime. Second, society should execute because by so doing an offender guilty of committing the worst crime can be dispatched via the most "humane" and "least cruel" punishment we can deliver. In making this second statement, it may appear that I have just offered a non sequitur. Mill endorses the idea that execution is defensible because it is perceived to be the worst punishment for the worst crime, yet by imposing it, society is actually acting in the most humane—and least cruel—fashion possible; and it is on those grounds—on its humanity—that Mill claims to be basing his defense of the death penalty. But the question that arises is why the society that executes in the belief that this is the worst punishment to deliver proportionate to the worst crimes would have any interest in actually delivering to the worst criminals a punishment less cruel and more humane than others available to it? Is this not denying proportionality once again? The non sequitur is Mill's, not mine.

As fascinating as I find this, Mill's position must be said to be contradictory. First of all, while I respect Mill for wanting to act humanely toward the offender, I consider his argument to be an expression of Mill's own fundamental decency and respect for humanity rather than a position consistent with utilitarian thought. For the fact is that if Mill is willing to execute as a way of acting humanely, Mill is operating from a concern for the happiness not of the whole but of the condemned person. How is the general happiness of society advanced by imposing on an offender a punishment that is in reality not proportionate to the crime? Mill is evidently of the mind that the general welfare of all is not served by the inevitable misery of imprisonment. But it could be argued that this kind of attention to the welfare of the offender—even though it results in the offender's death—borders on concern for the inherent dignity of the condemned as a person. Utilitarianism, however, does not require any action grounded in a principle of general respect for persons. It aims at maximizing happiness for the greatest number. Concern for the humanity of the offender is decent but extraneous to Mill's general mode of argumentation, especially if execution maximizes a benefit to the whole by delivering up deterrence. Mill's defense of capital punishment on the grounds that it is more humane and less cruel than imprisonment is misplaced as a utilitarian argument unless it can be shown that this nonproportional response to the worst crime actually delivers more deterrence, thus more happiness, to more people and thus advances the security of society. Mill does not show this, and his defense of capital punishment does not aim at this. It aims at the welfare of the prisoner who is, in Mill's terms, delivered "the least cruel mode" of punishment consistent with yielding a deterrent effect. But if imposing a harsher, more proportionate punishment would increase the deterrent effect, why would a utilitarian like Mill not advocate such a punishment? Why all this concern for the humanity of the criminal? I am not denying that this could be a sound argument. I am only denying that it expresses a consistent utilitarian argument.

Another question that can be put to Mill involves the illusory idea that death is the worst punishment. Mill's idea that society can endorse execution because it yields a deterrent effect, even though that effect is itself based on an illusion that death is worse than imprisonment, begs the interesting question: If illusion can be relied upon to effect deterrence, why could we not use illusion in other ways if by so doing we still generated the deterrent effect? Because of Mill's blithe acceptance of the efficacy of illusory beliefs, we should be able to ask why we could not elicit the deterrent effect by pretending to execute. Executions are already held in secret. With even more secrecy imposed, reports about execution could be issued that indicate that they are quite cruel events so as to ensure the excitation of horror and thus heighten the deterrent effect. And because we know that imprisonment is actually the punishment more proportionate to the worst crimes, we could actually impose that punishment in the interests of justice until such time as the effeminate majority of the population were to recognize, as Mill himself did, that the worst punishment for the worst crime was actually not execution.[17]

This scenario would satisfy all of Mill's requirements for generating a deterrent effect, while actually delivering what Mill would concede as the harsher punishment—imprisonment. And for those who might object that this would be lying, I can only respond that Mill has already shown himself to be willing to act on a societal perception that he believes to be false, and on that false perception human beings are actually put to death. If we are going to compare lies, my scenario would at least conform to the idea that the worst crime should receive the worst punishment; and it would more likely generate deterrence by increasing the likelihood of shock and horror without having actually to kill human beings.

Utilitarian argument against utilitarian argument, I think my case for faking executions wins hands down.

Mill and the "Acceptable Losses" Theory

I have been engaging Mill's arguments in a critical spirit and cannot conclude this foray without attending to one other point Mill raises—the execution of the innocent.

> The very fact that death punishment is more shocking than any other to the imagination, necessarily renders the Courts of Justice more scrupulous in requiring the fullest evidence of guilt. Even that which is the greatest objection to capital punishment, the impossibility of correcting an error once committed, must make, and does make, juries and judges more careful in forming their opinion, and more jealous in their scrutiny of evidence. If the substitution of penal servitude for death in cases of murder should cause any relaxation in this conscientious scrupulosity, there would be a great evil to set against the real, and I hope rare, advantage of being able to make reparation to a condemned person who was afterwards discovered to be innocent. (pp. 271–72)

Mill then goes on to comment that the possibility of correction must be kept open "wherever the chance of this sad contingency is more than infinitesimal . . . where there remains anything unexplained and mysterious in the case, raising a desire for more light, or making it likely that further information may at some future time be obtained" (p. 272).

This concern on Mill's part springs from his own decency and sense of fairness. The only reason I say this is that in my understanding of utilitarianism, there is no necessary connection between justifying capital punishment and requiring that the accused actually be guilty of the crime. The utilitarian argument for capital punishment attaches like a leech to deterrence, and the deterrent effect is generated from the shock and horror aroused by the thought of death. It is deterrence that justifies execution. If that effect can be produced from the execution itself, I see no clear utilitarian reason to require that guilt be established. An innocent person will do quite as well. Of course the argument could be made that were it to become known that innocent persons are actually executed, such knowledge would lead to general unhappiness, which is no doubt true. But that unhappiness would have to be weighed against the added terror and increased fearfulness such knowledge would produce in society, conceivably providing a stronger basis for deterrence. Utilitarians have to consider such things in their calculations, for even though such potential consequences may seem far-fetched they must be weighted and weighed in rendering moral meaning. If the point of execution is to arouse horror and thus deter murder, execution of the innocent—even if known—could contribute to the increased likelihood of generating the beneficial deterrent effect. Mill is concerned about executing the innocent, but, I am saying, that concern is not itself a necessary expression of a utilitarian viewpoint. Mill would have to show why more harm than benefit would come from such executions, and this he does not do.

Second, Mill makes the argument that executing the innocent is not likely. The argument, still made and widely accepted today, is that the likelihood of judicial error in capital cases decreases because a life is at stake, and that increases the scrupulousness of the criminal justice system. This may be true as a generalization. But even increased scrupulousness on the part of judges, juries, prosecutors, and defense attorneys does not eliminate the possibility of wrongful execution. In a fallible criminal justice system, mistakes continue to be made, and lack of scrupulousness in handling capital cases is unfortunately to be found. A reasonable person could conclude from the examination of the Willie Darden case (chapter 2) that sufficient evidence exists in that case to meet Mill's test that executions should not proceed if the chance of innocence is "more than infinitesimal." I conclude that Mill would have opposed Willie Darden's execution or any other execution where exculpatory evidence was denied a hearing.

A final point about Mill's view of executing the innocent pertains to the implications of his comment that "there would be a great evil to set against the real, but I hope rare, advantage of being able to make reparation to a condemned person who was afterwards discovered to be innocent." In this statement, Mill, I think, concedes that in point of fact, persons accused and convicted of capital crime may be executed by mistake. I have already commented that Mill discerns a great evil in executing the innocent, although I would claim against Mill that this great evil is not a necessary consequence of utilitarian thinking. But there is another point to make in relation to this comment. For Mill in the remark to which I have just referred acknowledges that despite the greater scrupulousness exercised by judges and juries in capital cases, mistakes not only can be, but actually are made, with no reparation possible to the person wrongly condemned and executed. But Mill argues that the execution practice ought not to stop because of occasional mistakes. That reparation cannot be made to those innocent persons who were wrongly executed says, first of all, that mistakes are inevitable; second, that it is terrible that mistakes occur; and third, that they occur is not sufficient to stop the practice of execution. Despite the potential for this great evil occurring, the amount of evil generated from a mistaken execution does not outweigh the benefits of continuing the practice, not so long as the deterrent effect yields a greater positive benefit to a greater number. By refusing to oppose executions knowing that errors will be made, Mill is calculating that it is worth preserving the death penalty even if execution is occasionally, even rarely, visited upon the innocent. I do not mention this to point to internal inconsistency but to articulate that Mill seems to hold an "acceptable losses" view of capital punishment: a certain number of wrongful executions are an inevitable and high but still acceptable price to pay for continuing the practice of execution. In other words, as much as society should work to prevent wrongful executions, wrongful executions are an insufficient reason to stop executions.

I applaud Mill's honesty on this point but find his view unacceptable. For if we justify the possibility that an innocent person may be executed, we justify executing any innocent person. We would necessarily be committed to sanctioning the wrongful execution of that rare individual not saved by judicial scrupulousness who would, as an innocent person, come from the class of innocent persons, any of whom would be eligible for this death. I do not need to work my moral imagination strenuously to perceive that if one person from the class of innocent persons is eligible for such a killing, I, inasmuch as I am a person innocent of aggravated murder, am eligible. My wife and children are eligible. I trust my reader is eligible. We are all eligible, yet our deaths would be, on the "acceptable losses" utilitarian calculation, justifiable. Mill is concerned with the problem of wrongful execution, but not to the point of ensuring that it would not occur at all. If I accede to Mill's argument, making the utilitarian move of suppressing my own interests in the face of impartial justice and equal consideration for the good of all, I consent to any particular member of the class of innocents being that rare case of the person who, out of the class of all innocent persons, is mistakenly put to death as an acceptable price for maintaining execution. I am not willing to condemn myself or my loved ones or my reader to such a fate.

For his part, Mill honestly acknowledges that wrongful executions are impossible to prevent. But against Mill I would argue that the benefits of execution, even if I were to concede that they yield the benefits Mill claims, do not justify killing the innocent. In order to be consistent in holding that the societal benefit from capital punishment justifies the rare but inevitable death of any particular individual from the class of all persons innocent of the crime of aggravated murder, I would have to consent to my own wrongful execution and that of my loved ones. This I cannot—and will not—do.

Problems with the Utilitarian View

Utilitarians have to weigh costs and benefits. They have to predict consequences, discerning what will—and what will not—contribute to a maximizing of goodness. Utilitarianism as a philosophy has been subject to many criticisms over the years, but there is one criticism that goes to the basic problem with this way of looking at the issue of moral meaning. And that is the fact that the utilitarian must be smart. Arriving at moral meaning was not for Mill a matter of intuition or fellow feeling but of intellectual assessment and evaluation. What was required for achieving happiness was not a good heart but a superior intellect invested with power to predict future states of affairs confidently and with certainty. Predicting the outcomes of a decision and the consequences of a possible action is so difficult a matter for most mortals, since such predictions are so fraught with unknowns, that most of us would shrink from constructing moral meaning solely on such a calculating and speculative method. Those who try are those who equate reason with intelligence.

But if the moral life is properly the arena of persons whose moral commitments are not dependent on superior intelligence—and I hold that this is the case—then utilitarianism, inasmuch as it requires people to be smart in order to be moral, necessarily fails, at least if one wishes to hold that the moral life can be lived well by reasonable people, whatever their level of intellectual ability.

Utilitarianism's position on capital punishment is also unsatisfactory. Bentham used utilitarian arguments to oppose execution. On the other hand, if my analysis of Mill above is fair, Mill used utilitarianism to justify—unhappily, I admit—the execution of innocent persons. I find that a terrifying admission. It is morally wrong to execute innocent persons—any innocent person; and if the only way to guarantee that innocent persons are not executed is to stop executions altogether, does moral reason itself not commend that executions cease?

Mill's position is fraught with problems. If we wish to use his version of deterrence in our contemporary culture, we could justify executions only if they generate to a broad spectrum of society shock and horror. What that would require in our society is almost beyond my imagining—perhaps some return to the old practice of hanging, drawing and quartering, and scooping out the entrails of the condemned before the condemned's own, still living, eyes. But such cruelty, gratefully, ill accords with modern sensibilities. We have gone in the opposite direction, making execution more sterile and more akin to a friendly, nonthreatening medical procedure, perhaps from the idea that we can punish in society without violence. But execution is violent—it directly visits destruction on human beings, members of our moral community.

If executions fail to shock and horrify, which, in my view, they do fail to do, then Mill's grounding for deterrence is undone. And if deterrence is undermined, so is his general justification for capital punishment.

Those who even today advance utilitarian deterrence arguments and appeal to a proportionality argument to defend capital punishment would do well to study the logic of Mill's position. As an advocate of proportionality, Mill held that the worst crimes should be met with the worst punishment. Mill identifies the worst crime. He also identifies the worst punishment. They do not correspond. They do not meet Mill's own requirement of proportionality. In advocating death as the appropriately proportionate response for the crime of aggravated murder, Mill can only do so by holding up the illusion that has bewitched his contemporaries into believing that death is the worst evil.[18] For Mill logically denies that a forfeiture of life in response to aggravated murder is the truly appropriate and proportionate response. As Mill says, execution is not so severe a punishment as it seems: "Is it, indeed, so dreadful a thing to die?" (p. 270), while imprisonment, in that it deprives a person of all that makes life desirable or valuable, is worse than it appears.[19] So it is imprisonment that is the more severe punishment. It inflicts the inhumane torture of deprivation and denies the opportunity for happiness, which, for Mill, was the only intrinsic good. Depriving persons of the opportunity to acquire the pleasure or good of intellectual inquiry, creative accomplishment, experiences of beauty, and friendship was, for Mill, to suffer such "disutility" that death would be preferable and a more humane alternative. Mill thought sensitivities about death were much too pronounced in his era and that what was required was a cultivation of moral sentiments such that death ought to have "no more than the degree of relative importance which belongs to it among other incidents of our humanity" (p. 270). Mill thus implicitly acknowledges that imprisonment is a proportionate and therefore just response to the worst crime.

Mill is thus committed to the view that there is an alternative to execution—imprisonment—that conforms the worst punishment to the worst crime while also assuring security for the commonwealth and yielding a positive deterrent effect. If a punishment that was truly "worst" and thus fitting to the worst crime could generate positive consequences and do so only requiring that illusory and "effeminate" notions of death be denied, then it seems to me that Mill and any other utilitarian ought logically to support that alternative, which is imprisonment rather than execution.

6

A Just Retribution
for Murder

On the basis of a theory of moral meaning that held good consequences to be the fundamental justification for action, John Stuart Mill defended the death penalty as morally sanctioned because it yielded through deterrence an overriding societal benefit. Like Locke's human rights ethic before it, Mill's utilitarian philosophy expressed an Enlightenment-era confidence in reason as the arbiter of moral meaning; and reason, in both cases, commended the death penalty.

In this chapter another major ethical theorist from the Enlightenment period will be examined. Like Locke and Mill, Immanuel Kant will support the death penalty. Like Locke and Mill, Kant will invoke reasons for defending capital punishment that surface even today in debates over the moral meaning of the death penalty. Kant holds that capital punishment is just retribution for a specific crime, murder; and we can gain access to the retributive justice position by examining Kant's argument defending the principle that those who kill ought themselves to be put to death.

Immanuel Kant

In the writings of the Immanuel Kant (1724-1804) we find one of the most influential ethical philosophies the world has known. Kant held that duties, rather than consequences, were fundamental to determining right actions, a perspective more formally known as deontological ethics (Greek *deon,* "necessity" or "obligation"). A "duty-based" deontologist is one who holds that the rightness of actions is independent of consequences and that right actions are those required by a list of duties to others, such as: Be fair, inflict no harm on others, keep promises, show respect to others, express gratitude; and duties to one's own self: Refrain from killing oneself, develop one's talents, seek to improve one's character. What makes a duty recognizable to reason as a duty is that a duty satisfies three essential conditions: it expresses an unqualified command for autonomous agents; it is universalizable, or expressible as a universal principle that applies to all; and it commands respect for persons. A brief look at each will clarify this formalistic ethical philosophy.

First, in saying that a duty expresses an unqualified command for autonomous agents, Kant meant that duties prescribe actions categorically, that is, without qualification or condition. Although in our daily life we might act in response to many nonmoral or *hypothetical* imperatives that attach to some condition, such as, "If you want to slim down, stop eating so much, " or "If you want to protect your belongings, buy insurance," moral duties are categorical. That is, they allow no conditions. They are duties because reason recognizes that they must be done whether or not one wants or is inclined to do them. Categorical imperatives are moral: "Don't lie." "Keep your promises." They are the laws of morality. One obeys these imperatives simply because reason bids us to obey them and we ought to—it is our duty as moral persons. It is our duty to obey them whether or not doing so makes us happy. The categorical imperative bids human persons act from what Kant believed was our autonomous commitment to morality itself, not because of any ulterior motive.[1]

Second, categorical imperatives are binding on us only if they are binding on everyone. Thinking out of the Enlightenment appreciation of universal laws of nature, Kant sought to give morality a foundation as objective as any in nature, so that the laws or commands—the maxims, rules, or duties that reason prescribes we obey—are to be followed only if they are principles we are willing everyone else should have to follow as well. We should be able to imagine everyone obeying them, so that in this sense they are *universalizable*. The Golden Rule passes this test; even the imperative "Keep your promises" does. But a rule that cannot be universalized and apply to all as if it were a law of nature (objective) should not command our assent or action. If one were to consider breaking a promise, Kant would require that this proposed action be universalized in a maxim or rule that would apply to all: "Keep only those promises that you feel like keeping." The power of the universalizability test is immediately apparent, for acting on this command would at the same time authorize everyone else to break whatever promises they made. If promises were universally eligible for breaking, we simply would not make promises, for the very idea of a promise is thereby emptied of meaning. Making a promise that everyone understood would be broken actually creates a contradiction, for, as Kant says, "The promise itself would become impossible, since no one would consider that anything was promised to him, but would ridicule all such statements as vain pretences."[2]

Third is the principle of respect for persons. Unlike Mill, who said the only intrinsic good was happiness, Kant attached value to the good will, by which he meant the intention to do one's duty. Like other deontologists, Kant held that the value of actions lies in their duty-related motives and intentions rather than the consequences that might happen to flow from them. Recognizing that the human person is more than a creature of desire and appetite, Kant held that persons possess a unique capacity to exercise the will in rational control of desire for the purpose of right action. It is this capacity for right and dutiful action that gives persons their moral worth and dignity. Unlike the accidental possession of intelligence, or strength, or talents of one sort or another, which can command our admiration, possessing moral worth commands reverence and respect. Persons are to be treated, Kant says, as ends in themselves. They are never to be treated disrespectfully as means to some end, for there is no end beyond the person of good will. We show respect as persons to persons by seeking to fulfill the duties we owe them, and, similarly, we demonstrate self-respect by acting in such a way that we fulfill those duties we owe to ourselves.

This brief summary of Kant's fundamental moral philosophy provides background for Kant's theory of punishment, and for his particular views on capital punishment. Kant's position on crime and punishment is grounded in external, legal, or what Kant calls "juridical" rights and duties. Juridical rights entail a recognition that every person is potentially a violator of another's freedom, and every person is also potentially the subject of violation by others. Coercion by the state in restraint of such violation can be deemed just, when, in the realm of external action and in the face of an unlawful interference with another's freedom, the state acts through lawful coercion to protect persons from those who would unlawfully violate their rights of freedom. In the realm of external law, such infringement on the rights of others constitutes those violations we identify as crime. Kant defines crime as the transgression of the public law "that makes him who commits it unfit to be a citizen" (p. 99).

Kant held that coercion could be used legitimately to promote freedom by restraining those who would unjustly violate the right each person possesses not to be hindered in the just exercise of freedom. From this theoretical commitment, Kant proceeds to define punishment as the right a magistrate has to "inflict pain in consequence of having committed a crime" (p. 99). Punishment for crime is, in Kant's view, a form of justifiable coercion, and it is justified on grounds of retribution:

> Juridical punishment can never be used as a means to promote some other good for the criminal himself or for civil society, but instead it must in all cases be imposed on him only on the ground that he has committed a crime; for a human being can never be manipulated merely as a means to the purposes of some-

one else and can never be confused with the objects of the Law of things. His innate personality [that is, his right as a person] protects him against such treatment, even though he may indeed be condemned to lose his civil personality. He must first be found to be deserving of punishment before any consideration is given to the utility of this punishment for himself or for his fellow citizens. The law concerning punishment is a categorical imperative, and woe to him who rummages around in the winding paths of a theory of happiness looking for some advantage to be gained by releasing the criminal from punishment or by reducing the amount of it. . . . If legal justice perishes, then it is no longer worth while for men to remain alive on this earth. (p. 100)

In this passage Kant explicitly rejects as a justification for punishment any appeal to notions concerning deterrence or societal benefit, including security or protection. No reason other than the violation of law itself ought to be used to justify the punishment. Persons, being of intrinsic worth, are not to be manipulated or used as a means to an end, even the end of advancing human happiness or the security of society. The dignity of the offender's "innate personality" suffices to ensure protection from such manipulation, and Kant affirms a universalizable prescription that recognizes the inherent worth and dignity of persons who possess as persons the right to be free of violation and who merit punishment insofar as they perpetrate such violations on others.

Kant accepts that just punishment should be in some manner "proportional" to the crime (p. 101), but he finds his standard of justice not in any utilitarian consideration but in the principle of returning "like for like"(p. 102) and thus compensating for the offense. This identifies Kant's principle of retributivist equality, or what we might call just retribution. Kant's "principle of equality . . . [is] the principle of not treating one side more favorably than the other" (p. 101). In the next sentence we see universalizability at play: "Accordingly, any undeserved evil that you inflict on someone else among the people is one that you do to yourself. If you vilify him, you vilify yourself; if you steal from him, you steal from yourself; if you kill him, you kill yourself. Only the Law of retribution (*jus talionis*) can determine exactly the kind and degree of punishment" (p. 101).

Kant couples the view that all persons possess inherent moral worth, which yields a view of the "pure and strict equality of persons even before the law" (p. 101), with the universalizability principle, which renders any action that a person performs with respect to another reciprocally applicable to one's own self—so that if I steal from another, I consent to another's stealing from me. In such wise, we reach Kant's view of the death penalty as a punishment justifiable on the grounds that by taking the life of another, murderers create an inequality between taking a life and continuing to possess life themselves. The just retribution demand that equal compensation for an offense be paid by the criminal offender necessitates, in Kant's view, death.

Kant held that "anyone who is a murderer—that is, has committed a murder, commanded one, or taken part in one—must suffer death" (p. 104), and for the following reason:

> In this case, there is no substitute that will satisfy the requirements of legal justice. There is no sameness of kind between death and remaining alive even under the most miserable conditions, and consequently there is no equality between the crime and the retribution unless the criminal is judicially condemned and put to death. But the death of the criminal must be kept entirely free of any maltreatment that would make it an abomination of the humanity residing in the person suffering it. Even if a civil society were to dissolve itself by common agreement of all its members (for example, if the people inhabiting an island decided to separate and disperse themselves around the world), the last murderer remaining in prison must first be executed, so that everyone will duly receive what his actions are worth and so that the bloodguilt thereof will not be fixed on the people because they failed to insist on carrying out the punishment; for if they fail to do so, they may be regarded as accomplices in this public violation of legal justice. (p. 102)

Kant's position on the death penalty thus seems to incorporate features that correspond with the key provisos of his general moral theory. How Kant presents a defense of the death penalty through that moral theory, referencing the categorical imperative, universalizability, and respect for persons, is summarized in the following sections.

1. *Categorical imperative.* From his starting point that punishment for the violation of the rights of others constitutes an inescapable and unconditional demand of justice, Kant proceeds to say of the wrongdoer who has committed murder that "he must die." Though Kant argues in general that for many crimes room for discretion exists and a range of possible sanctions may be considered, there is nothing conditional in fitting the punishment of death to the particular crime of murder. Murder demands forfeiture of the murderer's life. The law of retribution commands that when a murderer faces punishment, nothing more—such as adding torture prior to execution—and nothing less than the death penalty will do. (Because he held that magistrates may only grant pardon for those crimes where they have personally been the victims of injury themselves [pp. 107–8], Kant excludes the possibility of pardon for murder.) The death penalty for murder constitutes a juridical duty that obliges death to be the necessary and unconditional punishment for the crime of murder in all particular cases, without exception.

2. *Universalizability.* Kant's assertion of a principle of equality in punishment invokes the idea of universalizability. Kant wrote in the *Metaphysics of Morals* that as a member of society who is potentially both a perpetrator and a subject of violation of rights of freedom, every person who enters society consents to be limited by law. Breaking a civic law to which individuals have consented violates unjustly the rights of the victim to be free of such violation, and justice requires that any who violate the fixed distribution of rights and duties[3] to which all have given consent be punished. The degree of punishment is determined by considering the kind of violation involved and the cost that the crime has exacted of the victim, but punishment itself springs from the demand of justice that those who break the law be punished for their violation. This retributive view of punishment applies in general to all lawbreakers, with particular punishments being made to fit particular crimes so that a loss incurred by the victim of crime might in some manner be equalized by the loss incurred by the punishment. But in the case of murder, the loss of life cannot be equalized short of demanding that the perpetrator be judicially put to death. Moreover, the state is expected to conform to the requirement of justice and mete out punishments to criminal offenders evenhandedly, in conformity with the principle of equality. In this delegation of authority to the state to punish, all have consented, so that punishment for those who violate rights held to be inviolable is required in every instance of violation.

Kant exempts no one from this rule of law and punishment. As punishment is universally applicable, so too the death penalty is applicable to any person guilty of killing another person. Kant obviously conceived of the death penalty as a universally applicable punishment for the crime of murder, the necessary and just mode of demanding that murderers accept responsibility for their crime and thus conform to the requirements of justice. By willing justice for all, including one's own self, the citizen in civic society accepts rational, fitting, and just punishment—the kind and degree to be determined by courts of justice rather than private judgment (p. 101)—and accepts a law of retribution on the theory that if one robs from another "he makes the ownership of everyone else insecure" (p. 102). In the idea of not treating one side more favorably than the other and of universalizing one's violations of law so that "if you vilify him, you vilify yourself; if you steal from him, you steal from yourself; if you kill him, you kill yourself," Kant conforms juridical punishment to the moral requirement of universalizability.

3. *Respect for persons.* Kant clearly maintains that the status of the violator as a human being is not to be disregarded in setting punishment—there is to be no "manipulation" of the offender, no "maltreatment that would make an abomination of the humanity residing in the person suffering it" (p.102). The offender's

"innate personality protects him against such treatment" (p. 100) even though the offender loses "civic personality" through punishment. There is no doubt that Kant continues to accept that offenders are members of the moral community and that as persons are to be held responsible for any violations of law. Kant's view is that a just state will, through just criminal justice institutions, hold the criminal directly responsible for the loss of life incurred by the murder and let no other considerations affect the disposition of justice. Not only does Kant show in this discussion of punishment and the death penalty an abiding commitment to the idea of respect for persons, but to a view of punishment as a means whereby individuals are treated with respect in light of their criminal offenses.

In the case of the death penalty, Kant asserts that anything less than the death penalty would offend against justice and the principle of retributive justice. Anything less than the infliction of death would be to treat a murderer disrespectfully. In light of the offense of murder, the only way to continue to show respect to those who commit this most grievous of crimes is to recognize that by their act they have made their own lives forfeit. Only punishment of death will satisfy the demands of justice and the principle of equality.

In sum, then, Kant views the death penalty as an unconditionally binding punishment for the crime of murder, thus referencing the notion of the categorical imperative. Second, Kant invokes a principle of equality that has moral force because it is extended to all and is thus universalizable. Third, the defense of this punishment is promulgated in such a way that it shows not only respect for the victim of capital crime, whose sacred rights have been violated, but for the humanity of the criminals who have violated those rights and thus brought the death penalty upon themselves. Murderers have not relinquished their membership in moral community by their crime. The moral community, rather, holds murderers responsible and in that way treats the murderer with continued respect. Even in the face of egregious crime, the murderer continues to be shown respect so long as justice is administered in conformity with the requirements of impartial justice; and in demanding that justice be served in delivering punishment to a murderer, the moral community, through the state and its coercive power, continues to attach responsibility, demand retributive accounting, and demonstrate respect for the person who cannot be shown respect unless justice is served. That the just punishment for murder is, in Kant's view, necessarily death diminishes not at all the formal respect that is shown not only to juridical law and to the victim whose rights have been unjustly violated, but by demanding just punishment—by demanding the death penalty—even to murderers themselves.

One last point is worth making in regard to Kant's duty-based defense of the death penalty for the crime of murder. Kant addresses himself to an argument

Cesare Beccaria had advanced in his influential 1764 work, *On Crimes and Punishments.*[4] Beccaria had held that capital punishment, to be legitimate, would have required in the original contract with society that citizens consent to forfeiting their own lives if they commit murder. This they cannot do, Beccaria objected, for citizens cannot dispose of their own lives. Kant, believing Beccaria to be opposed to capital punishment because of having been moved "by sympathetic sentimentality and an affectation of humanitarianism" (p. 105), replied to this argument by saying, "No one suffers punishment because he has willed the punishment, but because he has willed a punishable action. If what happens to someone is also willed by him, it cannot be a punishment. Accordingly it is impossible to will to be punished" (p. 105).

Yet Beccaria's argument gives Kant reason to explain how individuals in society and under the rule of law rationally submit to punishment, including their own. It is not that individuals will their own punishment, but that they submit to the penal law they co-legislate. Were individuals required to will their own punishment, they would be required to assess their own liability for wrongdoing and thus become their own judges. This reason will not permit. In the case of the death penalty, it is a court that dictates this punishment, so the criminal's own judgment that he must forfeit his life in punishment for murder—and Kant attributes this judgment to "his reason"—is not to be confused "with a resolution of the Will to take his own life" (p. 106). With this confusion eliminated, Kant reasserts that by submitting themselves to penal law persons in society rationally subscribe to the possibility of their own execution. They submit—without willing their own destruction—to a punishment that could not be a punishment were it also willed. Punishment falls on the wrongdoer not because punishment is willed, but because wrongdoers have willed punishable acts.

Critique of Kant

Kant's perspective on the death penalty has several features that recommend it, although critical questions can be raised at almost every juncture. Among Kant's strengths is his formidable ability to addresses the death penalty both informally, in the context of his general moral theory, and formally, in the context of a theory of the state and its right—and duty—to punish. In his formal argument justifying the death penalty, Kant moves from a social contract theory of the state founded on a principle of general consent to consideration of the just state. And it is within this discussion that Kant articulates the view that the just state not only promotes but also dispenses justice through its institutions. Accordingly, the just society conforms to the requirements of justice by acknowledging its duty to punish those citizens who become criminals when they violate the penal law and offend against the rights of others. Justice requires punishment for crime, but punishment must itself be just, that is, it must observe a principle of equality and be applied in a manner consistent with fairness and proportionality. Just punishment observes the law of fair retribution.[5]

In holding that punishment is a necessary response to violation of law, Kant directed this categorical imperative at actual offenders who were to be punished not only in accordance with the law, but fairly and impartially in a moral sense. Since I have defended the view that exempting the innocent from execution is an impossibility where fallible justice is concerned, Kant's view on this matter is clearly important, for he could make no utilitarian appeal to the idea that some good, some benefit to society, might come even from such a unjust death. As Kant held that punishment must attend the guilty, he would likewise have held that the only execution for murder that was justifiable was of a murderer indisputably guilty of the crime. The possibility of executing the innocent would have received his contempt. I say "would have" because Kant pays this issue no attention. Executing the innocent would, in Kant's view, constitute a grave injustice exempt from the possibility of justification, so profoundly would such a death violate a person's right and dignity. The evil of such an undeserved death is obvious and beyond argument: executing the innocent violates not only Kant's principle of respect for persons but also the categorical imperative, which attaches punishment necessarily to actual offenders. Such a death, were it to occur, could not be universalized, for justifying the execution of the innocent would justify the execution not of an occasional innocent person, but any innocent person at any time.

Kant would clearly not accede to the "acceptable losses" position I imputed to John Stuart Mill, yet how he could justify the death penalty in light of the fact that justice administration is fallible and makes mistakes, even to the point of occasionally executing an innocent person, is mysterious. Kant, just to be clear on this point, upheld a categorical principle that murderers must suffer execution as the only just punishment for the crime of murder. What is to be challenged is the assumption that justice will always be administered fairly, never making the mistake of executing an innocent person. Clearly, an innocent person wrongfully executed would lose life unjustly, and Kant could be expected to find such a deed contemptible. Executing the innocent, an inevitable prospect given the fallibility of the justice system, would be to act in such a way that one would have to universalize the execution of the innocent in order to put into practice the principle that the murderer must die. The principle that the murderer must die, for Kant a just principle, shipwrecks on the empirical reality that the innocent are occasionally executed, which is unjust. Kant certainly would not have advocated the execution of the innocent or advocated any principle that would have justified, through universalization, such executions.

Admittedly, Kant addresses the question of justifying state execution by limiting use of the penalty to murder. But history shows—and Kant would have known this from his own experience as a citizen in eighteenth-century Europe—that the death penalty could be abused, not only attached to crimes less grave than murder but employed for terrorist purposes by states or political entities of one sort or another. That Kant would have opposed such use of the death penalty is clear, at least implicitly, but given how execution has been used as an instrument of state oppression and repression, or used by revolutionaries in rebellion against tyranny—Kant regarded the executions of the king and queen of France during the Reign of Terror "with horror"[6]—it seems odd that Kant would not have insisted that those accused of capital crime be protected from the possibility of unjust execution.

Kant addresses the issue of capital punishment assuming that no mistakes are made in determining actual guilt, for actual guilt is a necessary condition for imposing the necessary and categorically commanded death sentence. But if that assumption is itself highly questionable, and perhaps even more so in his day than our own, a theory of execution that ignores this problem is clearly incomplete or inadequate. The bumper sticker on Kant's carriage, "Every execution a justified execution," necessitates that every execution must, if it is to satisfy the requirements of just retribution, fit the crime deserving of death—murder—and be applied to the person actually guilty of murder.

But not every person sentenced to death is actually guilty of murder. Kant, in other words, advances his principle that the murderer must die assuming in the system of justice a perfection that does not exist. Any execution that takes the life of an innocent person fails the "Every execution a justified execution" test, and it is impossible that only the truly guilty—actual murderers—are executed (or, conversely, that no guilty party evades punishment). So by maintaining the view that murderers are to die for their crime and that their guilt must be actual and not simply imputed as the result of legal proceedings, Kant is led logically to the point that he must either continue to assume perfection in the system of justice, or he must justify execution as a mode of justice that sometimes—even if only rarely—violates the very rights that Kant held to be inviolable. Execution of the innocent cannot be universalized or justified, and the system of perfection needed to assure that only actual murderers are executed is beyond the power of humans to create. If Kant admits that a fallible justice system could allow an innocent person to be executed—even one—he can maintain support for use of execution only by resorting to a form of analysis that would justify that killing by some kind of utilitarian appeal to "acceptable losses." That may be how one would typically justify executions in a system that occasionally makes mistakes, but it is not a Kantian way.

Kant's justification of the death penalty, in my view, applies only to an ideal state. With that qualification, Kant's position maintains its strength and philosophical consistency. But the reality is that systems of justice make mistakes. In the United States, for example, it is estimated that over four hundred innocent persons have been convicted of capital crimes in this century, twenty-three of whom were actually put to death. In addition, fifty-nine innocent persons sentenced to death since 1970 found relief in judicial review and release from death row. From these statistics it is clear that criminal justice, at least as practiced in this country, fails to meet the standard of perfection. My view is that Kant can consistently hold the principle that a murderer must die. But I also hold that that principle requires a system of justice administration that does not make errors, or else one would have to universalize the killing of persons who are not murderers, which is contradictory to the principle. Kant's principle cannot coherently be put into practice in the real—imperfect—world.

I find this criticism the most damaging to Kant's position. This argument I have presented against Kant so positions Kant that he must either admit that justice can be delivered with such perfection that only those executed are actual murderers, which I find preposterous to assume; or he must universalize the execution of the innocent, since it is certain that at least one innocent person will be executed and even one such wrongful death undermines the claim that state-sponsored execution is a universally just and justifiable form of killing. Students of Kant ought not to wince when I say that this second alternative—this idea of Kant universalizing such a killing—is even more preposterous than the first.

Kant, of course, makes other points about the death penalty worthy of consideration and critical assessment. His commitment to a principle of equality, for instance, seems to me commendable. There is a harshness to this principle of equality, however, for the command that death be imposed for murder without condition or qualification lacks concern for details of situation and circumstance—Kant does not identify capital crime as the "aggravated murder" Mill was careful to specify. Qualifications and various distinctions categorizing types of homicide are integral to our present system of justice; and although this is an observation rather than an argument, I doubt that in contemporary America, even in light of widespread citizen frustration with crime, Kant's "mandatory" death sentence would meet with approval, either morally or legally—certainly not legally.

Kant's position does, in a practical way, eliminate arbitrariness and caprice in imposing death sentences, an important point since history has shown that arbitrariness and caprice are no strangers to state-sponsored execution. When the

U.S. Supreme Court imposed its moratorium on executions in 1972, it did so on the grounds that death sentences were being imposed in an arbitrary and capricious manner; and one state, North Carolina, responded by passing a law that eliminated any possibility of arbitrariness by making the death penalty mandatory for first-degree murder. In *Woodson v. North Carolina*, the Court held that such a law was unconstitutional because it did not provide "objective standards to guide, regularize, and make rationally reviewable the process for imposing a sentence of death." The Court upheld the non-Kantian notion of "particularized" consideration of cases, thereby refusing to grant mandatory death sentences standing in the law.[7] Moreover, the Court found evidence of inequality and arbitrariness in the practice of deciding who does and who doesn't receive a death sentence, and in the 1972 *Furman* decision, eliminated execution for rape, taking note that execution for rape was clearly discriminatory in that it was imposed only in certain jurisdictions and overwhelmingly against black males.

While Kant's mandatory sentencing policy has not been received into America's legal system, the Kantian concern for eliminating arbitrariness or caprice in sentencing is apparent in these decisions and attempts at legal reforms. A Kantian-like perspective is also apparent in the actions states took to rewrite capital punishment statutes in conformity to the Supreme Court's call for creating objective standards and criteria when imposing the death penalty. That objectivity standard was satisfied when states rewrote death penalty laws incorporating guidelines—those specific aggravating and mitigating circumstances—that juries are to consider in determining whether the death penalty is appropriate for a specific crime. This is a more liberal view than Kant held, more attentive to circumstance and situation, but it is not inconsistent with the Kantian equality principle that appeals to moral objectivity while abhorring arbitrariness.

Kant established through his equality principle that no side should be treated more favorably than another, and I assume from this that evidence of unfavorable treatment of any group before the law should be examined and evaluated. If that be the case, it is my view that the equality principle continues to be violated in practice, for there is still cause for holding that race and gender affect the disposition of justice in sentencing. It is beyond dispute that the death penalty falls more consistently on blacks than on whites, especially when one considers that black males, who make up approximately 6 percent of the population, make up 41 percent of the death row census. And although there were forty-eight women on death row at the end of 1995, only one woman had been executed. The U.S. Supreme Court does not acknowledge such statistics as evidence of any pattern of actual discrimination, but Kant's equality principle, I think, would suggest the need for examination and assessment of these figures. Evidence that a punishment is being meted out unfairly or arbitrarily runs afoul of Kant's equality principle. The issue is, What counts as evidence? Would Kant himself acknowledge racially imbalanced "trends" as evidence sufficient to impute inequality in imposing the death penalty? I would hope Kant might ask, If capital punishment is a sanction reflecting social policy, why should broad evidence relevant to the operations of a social policy, including the use of statistics to indicate possible trends, not be at least considered? That is my question, not Kant's, but it is asked in a Kantian spirit.

Kant lights at times on the idea that persons ought not to be punished more severely for a crime than the nature of the crime warrants, but in the end he advocates through the categorical imperative that individuals must receive punishment proportionate to the crime. Kant offers no argument for his view that the death penalty must be inflicted on the murderer except that retribution requires it. The question could be asked why death is required for just retribution. Kant allows that rapists ought not to be punished by being raped themselves—he claims this punishment is "impossible"—but castrated.[8] Kant allows, then, that punishment other than like-for-like retribution is appropriate for certain crimes. Why not for murder? Kant's principle that a murderer must die is itself simply an unexamined assumption on Kant's part. It is an assumption not proven but asserted; and it is asserted in light of remarks Kant makes, previously quoted, concerning the *jus talionis* in relation to the prospect of "blood guilt" falling on the people who fail in their duty to execute murderers. The idea of blood guilt is quite foreign to modern constructions of justice and I would assert, contra Kant, that this idea holds—and should hold—no weight in any contemporary conception of retributive punishment that claims to be grounded in reason. That religiously conceived appeal fails to provide adequate rational grounds for justifying the death penalty as a form of killing sanctioned by morality.

If that argument of Kant's is weak, another is stronger. Kant's moral justification for the death penalty seems to hang on the idea of universalizability—the idea that by killing another, killers kill themselves. Kant provides more detail on this point, saying later in the *Metaphysics of Morals* that the murderer by the murderous act universalizes that killing and "draws back onto himself [as a punishment]" the act itself, thus rendering himself eligible for suffering "that which according to the spirit of the penal law—even if not to the letter thereof—is the same as what he has inflicted on others" (p. 133). This is a coherent appeal to retributive justice and a philosophically strong view that makes appeal to universalizability in language resembling the Golden Rule—that as I have actually done to others, I should expect others to do to me.

But making such an argument does not provide necessary, or even compelling, grounds for saying that a murder necessitates the death of the murderer, not if the aim of punishment is just retribution and alternative retributive punishments exist that would satisfy the demand of justice. Universalizability seeks to guide action by making an appeal to rationality. Kant, however, does not address the thorny issue of how this universalization can be applied when a murder is committed by individuals whose rationality is seriously impaired, yet who form intent and kill unjustly. Kant claims that the demand for a murderer's death is itself a rational response, but the question is whether all those who murder can be considered rational persons such that we can apply the principle of universalizability and claim that by their acts of murder they necessarily—rationally—draw the punishment of death back on themselves. Does the application of a rational principle of universalizability appropriately apply when the capital crime has been committed by children, mentally ill persons, or murderers who act in the heat of passion with rational constraints broken?[9]

This provokes a question to Kant about freedom and whether the free exercise of the will is a necessary condition for action that would merit the death penalty. If the murder does not arise from a free and rational exercise of the will, Kant could only execute such offenders—children, the mentally ill, or the temporarily insane—on one of two assumptions. Such incapacitated murderers could be said to be subject to the rule of rationality by virtue of species membership—and there is evidence in Kant to support such a statement; or because of a belief that condition and circumstance have no effect on the applicability of a rational rule of law. It is conceivable that persons who murder yet lack sufficient rational capability to grasp the meaning of such an evil act are, in Kant's view, not persons. Since they are not persons, they do not deserve respect and thus can be disposed of through execution. But in Kant's theory nonpersons, those creatures lacking not only rationality but the freedom necessary for moral action, *are not fit subjects for punishment.* Punishment must fall on persons who by their misuse of freedom violate the rights of others and thereby—rationally—draw back on themselves as punishment the very violation they directed at another. Kant does not attend adequately to the "diminished capacity" problem of those wrongdoers who are to be considered persons yet whose rationality is qualified by age, maturity, or mental ability.

Another problem with Kant's perspective on punishment has been noted by John Kemp: "For Kant, excessive punishment is, of course an injustice, but it seems to be no worse an injustice than insufficient punishment or no punishment at all."[10] Were we to grant that excessive punishment is clearly worse than some form of underpunishment, we would do so by appealing to a hierarchy of evil—some wrongs are clearly worse than other wrongs. Kant clearly abides by some such hierarchy, but he does not invoke it when considering punishment. This is perhaps because Kant configures punishment as rational response to evil so that punishment is formally exempt from being considered itself an evil.

Again, this is an arguable point philosophically. Empirically, it is indefensible. Kant could only hold such a view by defining punishment against the background of an ideal, uncorrupted and incorruptible system of justice administration that would never pervert the rational nature of punishment to harm persons beyond what reason requires. This conception of punishment represents yet again an empirical failure on Kant's part.

And because motive is so critically important to determining right action in the Kantian moral view, it is important to note that Kant the retributivist holds the motive for execution to be justice grounded in reason, not passionally seated revenge. Kant does not countenance vengeance as a legitimate motive for the death penalty or for any punishment; the word "vengeance" never enters his discussion of punishment. It is forced off the page by a retributivist appeal that rests on a principle of equal justice. Vengeance, Kant wrote elsewhere, is "to insist on one's right beyond what is necessary for its defense," so that when it appears it is "vicious," forcing us to "think only of the damage and pain which we wish to the man who has harmed us, even though we do not thereby instill in him greater respect for our rights."[11]

For Kant, the motive for just punishment must be located in rational retribution, not vengeance. But Kant curtails other concerns relevant to punishment that it seems most reasonable to include. For instance, Kant, a social contract theorist, avoids any reference to the Lockean idea that society has a right to defend itself and that punishment can serve the end of self-defense. There is nothing patently irrational about such a notion, and reason, I suggest, finds such an appeal attractive. Kant also refuses, as one would expect, to reference in any way the utilitarian idea that society can in some way benefit from using the death penalty. His refusal to go the route of consequentialist thinking has the virtue of relieving moral judgment of the intellectual difficulties that attend utilitarian approaches, where all kinds of consequences would have to be weighted and weighed to determine morally right action. Kant's appeal to principle avoids these problems but invites others, including the problem that his theory concerns itself with no impulse to act from a generous or sympathetic motive in reckoning punishment. Kant thus shows no overt sympathy for the idea of tempering justice with mercy: justice itself—retributively conceived—suffices.

Kant's general moral theory has been criticized, even lampooned, for its abstractness and its absoluteness. In seeking to avoid consequentialist thinking, Kant fails to bid us act in some way that advances human well-being. In his stress on doing one's duty and obeying the law—moral and penal, he shows no concern for the need to improve the welfare of all by acting as we would want others to act.[12] Kant's general theory of a motive for action is confined and nonexpansive—and I would say incomplete, even inadequate when applied specifically to punishment. Using force against lawbreakers as a means of societal self-defense is a rational Lockean notion worth maintaining against Kantian abstraction; and attending to the well-being of persons in society and society as a whole is worth including in a theory of just punishment, even if Kant excludes them.[13]

Kant's theory of retributive punishment returns to the offender the very harm the offender has visited on another. This is justice. This is *jus talionis,* or the law of retribution that redresses the imbalance created by a criminal offense. But we must push the issue further. The criminal offender has done more than harm another and create an imbalance—the criminal has abused freedom itself. Should not punishment be directed at the freedom of the criminal? If crime is finally an abuse of freedom, the rational, proportionate, and appropriate response to that abuse is to take the criminal's freedom away. The death penalty does not respond in kind or proportionately to the abuse of freedom represented by the criminal act, but launches, rather, a deadly attack on the body. On a strict accounting of retributive proportionality, the alternative principle would suffice as well as Kant's demand that the murderer be put to death. The alternative principle would be that the abuse of freedom involved in the crime of murder demands that the murderer forfeit freedom.

Kant mentions that crime may condemn the criminal to "los[ing] his civil personality," and such a loss is clearly a terrible punishment for crime. But just retribution can effect this end by means other than killing the criminal offender. Execution clearly forces a loss of the civil personality, but it does something more than that as well—it destroys the body. The body is not evil; it is not the center of the moral personality. It is not the seat of rationality or of freedom itself. The body is itself a subject of nature, not free, but determined: it serves the will and does not debate, object to, or override decisions for action that are legislated by the will. How is justice served by destroying the body? Another punishment— incarceration—directs the punishment to the source of the abuse of freedom, located in the will. Consistency ought to demand that the will be the focus of the punishment, not the body.

Execution destroys the will, true enough, but more than the person is punished by destroying the person's body. Personhood, for Kant, attaches to the rational will, not the body. A sly problem arises in that execution can so focus on the destruction of the body—on all that is entailed in the act of rationally killing a criminal—that the body becomes, practically and empirically, the true object of punishment. Destroying the body can become an end in itself so that persons condemned to punishment by death become the means by which the end of destroying the body occurs. In making this claim I do not refer to the public perception of criminals on death row whose acts have merited death. This perception could continue to conform to Kant's view that the condemned person is to be subjected to death out of respect for the person who by misusing freedom freely draws this punishment to him- or herself. Again, that is an ideal construction. The death row experience and the execution process are, as empirical matters, not so clearly focused on the person and the abuse of freedom. Rather, death row and execution, in constantly attending to the end of successfully destroying the body, subject the condemned to a process where the person becomes a means that serves this end of bodily destruction. This may sound abstract, but it is simply a Kantian way of describing what has often been described as the experience of dehumanization that comes with occupancy of a cell on death row: "Condemned prisoners tend to see the death row regime as a calculated and gratuitous assault on their humanity. For them, the physical setting is punitively spartan; rules and regulations are means to inflict pain. The intrusive procedures associated with visits do much to fuel the prisoners' angry perception that their keepers meant them harm."[14] The death row experience is one of powerlessness and hopelessness, with psychiatrist Seymour Halleck testifying in the case of *Groseclose v. Dutton* in 1985 that a normal reaction to such an experience is "depression and lethargy." Death row prisoners have even described the experience as "living death."[15] One prisoner described by author Robert Johnson said, "You need love and it just ain't there. It leaves you empty inside. Really, you just stop caring."[16]

What brings this "living death" about is the dehumanization process of the death row experience—the isolation, the treating of the person condemned to death as if the person were not a person but a body: "Death row guards are enjoined solely to preserve the corpus of the condemned—to feed them in their cells or in common areas, to conduct them to out-of-cell activities, to watch them at all times."[17] The point of raising this issue about the body as the end to which the person is sacrificed is that by such action, Kant's principle of respect for persons is violated. A prisoner condemned to death is objectified, reduced to body and then treated as body to be killed. This is the empirical reality of the death row experience, not the high ideal of Kant's punishment principle. It is this attention to the body as the true object of punishment that I believe underlies the experience of dehumanization on death row. This experience of dehumanization may be necessary for those who tend the condemned: it is—and ought to be— hard to kill a person. It is not so hard to kill a thing, a body, an animal, a nonperson. Dehumanizing the condemned masks the violence of execution and the execution process, which sometimes comes to public light in stories of guards pleasuring themselves by forcing inmates to take a trial sit-down and strap-in on the execution apparatus, or stories of botched executions.[18] And when execution commences, the moral personality cannot help but be subordinated to the task of killing the body, so that the person—the moral personality—is inevitably treated not as an end in itself but as a means to the end of execution, that end being—plainly—the destruction of the body.[19] This is another way to construe the failure of the death penalty to punish the person, since what is required to enact the punishment necessarily renders the body, not the person, the primary focus of the punishment.

At the commencement of one well-publicized execution in Florida, a condemned man who had insisted on his innocence and thus refused a plea bargain that would have spared his life went unwillingly to his death. He resisted as guards attempted to stuff cotton up his rectum to ease the clean-up job after the execution, and a struggle ensued. Reports that John Spenkelink was savagely beaten on his way to Florida's electric chair led to an investigation that, not surprisingly, exonerated all prison officials of any wrongdoing. An exhumation of his body two years after the execution attributed broken bones to the violence of the execution itself. While it seems that the claim that Spenkelink was actually dead before the execution was not true, the claim that he had been beaten is less easily denied. Florida today requires an impartial party to be in attendance during the condemned's last hour to assure no mishandling or maltreatment of the prisoner.[20]

I mention this because Spenkelink's protest of injustice—evidence that his moral personality had not been eradicated—had to be quashed and silenced so that the body could be attacked and destroyed. The executioners did not treat Spenkelink as a person, but having dehumanized him, brutalized him on the theory that what was about to be destroyed was not a moral personality or a member of the moral community, but a dehumanized nonperson, an animal. If this is how Spenkelink was treated in actual practice, and if dehumanization is an experience imposed on persons condemned to death, Kant would object to such treatment on the grounds that only persons can be punished and persons—even those facing the death penalty—must suffer no maltreatment but be treated with respect, and never as a means to an end. In the practice of execution today, persons are subordinated to the end of destroying dehumanized individuals who are presented to the execution process as bodies to be destroyed. Such a description clearly violates Kant's strict injunction that such dehumanization not occur.

I have not challenged what Kant says in justification of the death penalty because I believe that his few words on this subject reveal a principle-centered approach obviously flawed by internal inconsistency or poor logic. My aim, rather, was to test his principles against the reality of practice, that is, to test the applicability of the theory in the world of empirical experience. In that test, I have found the death penalty as practiced at odds with Kant's conception of it, which suggests in my view that Kant, by consistently maintaining his principles, would refuse to support the death penalty as we practice it today. Kant's theory is itself not without problems. He clearly makes certain assumptions that ought not to be granted, including the glaring assumption that retribution rather than restitution or restoration ought to guide a principled theory of just punishment. My point in challenging Kant's assumptions on the empirical level, however, is that by such means we expose the disparity between Kant's principles of just punishment and the practice of the death penalty. Kant's easy conclusion about the moral validity of state-sponsored execution is thereby thrown into doubt, serious doubt, not in light of an alternative theory, but, in a very real sense, on Kant's own terms.

7

A Theory of Just Execution

No inquiry into the moral meaning of the death penalty ought to ignore the issue of human rights and whether human persons, in the exercise of their fundamental human right to life, have a right not to be executed. Likewise, no such inquiry should avoid confronting the deterrence issue, or the oft-heard position that capital punishment is retribution that justly visits on murderers the same fate—violent death—that they have unjustly visited on others.

We have thus far considered each of these perspectives as they have been argued by strong and influential proponents of capital punishment. Each perspective has been subjected to critical analysis, with the result that none of the positions provides a clear moral justification for capital punishment. In fact, when examined in light of the real circumstances involved with the American practice of execution, these theories oppose capital punishment rather than support it.

But perhaps these arguments in favor of capital punishment, even though they are commonly employed and often heard in public debates, especially when a particularly notorious or well-publicized capital case is under public scrutiny, are not the strongest arguments. Is there a different and better way to formulate a moral theory more likely to justify capital punishment?

There is an alternative to the viewpoints we have examined. Given the moral absolutism involved in two of the approaches we have examined thus far—Amnesty International's categorical opposition to execution and Kant's categorical support for executing on principle all who murder, I want to consider a "morally moderate" perspective. Not only does such moderation reflect the American penchant for avoiding extremes and absolutes in moral thinking, but the American legal system has, in my view, sought to conform execution policy to a nonabsolutist moral perspective. The moderate alternative to the extremes of death penalty abolition and principled mandatory execution of all who commit murder is what I shall call the theory of just execution. The model of moral reasoning that structures a theory of just execution is one with which I am personally sympathetic and have actually advocated for use on other issues, particularly the abortion issue.

In what follows I shall construct an alternative theory to the human rights ethic, the utilitarian deterrence position, and a justification of the death penalty based on principled retribution. The alternative theory of just execution will draw on the strengths of the other perspectives already examined and provide a structure for nonabsolutist thinking on the question of the moral meaning of capital punishment. Our attention is now directed to the task of articulating the theory of just execution, then connecting it to legal practice.

The Meaning of Moral Presumptions

The moral theory that supports a theory of just execution is associated with a natural law tradition. While this is a complex tradition that can be associated broadly with a diverse crew of philosophers in the West,[1] natural law, broadly conceived, holds that ethics is founded on reason and reason's natural recognition of basic human goods. A natural law ethic holds that goods are more fundamental than rights,[2] that they are irreducibly and self-evidently good. What this means is that we as persons are naturally endowed with the capacity to recognize the goods of life as good, and it is on this basis that duty and virtue become integral to moral life and thought. For our natural capacity to know good and the goods of life imposes the obligation on us to pursue and promote these goods to the end of human flourishing. Moreover, because moral excellence demands that we act consistently with what we know ought to be done, we inculcate habits of conduct consistent with our vision and understanding of goodness, so that we undertake to cultivate the virtues that are then expressed in our actions, our patterns of action, and in how we intend to act.

Duty and virtue both complement natural law ethics, but the core of the perspective rests in the goods of life that reason recognizes as intrinsically valuable. Specifically, the goods of life upon which this "natural law" moral theory is based include life itself, procreation and family life, physical integrity, self-consciousness, aesthetic enjoyment, the capacity to work and play, friendship, and, among other qualities, practical reasonableness itself.[3] The goods of life are perhaps more practically defined as those things parents would want for their children—the things one would wish for them and want them to enjoy and help them acquire through good parenting. In that light, the goods of life are vital and close to us in our everyday lives, and we value them as essential to any life that would be meaningful and purposeful.

Although I hold that the good of life itself is a preeminent good in that the other goods of life necessarily depend upon it, the goods of life—all of them—are intrinsically good and ought not to be directly violated, dishonored, or destroyed. The goods of life naturally direct our action and express the heart of our common moral vision, but they are not absolute values even though honoring these goods ought always to be our intention. The goods of life provide moral grounding—and theoretical foundations—in a world that is imperfect and complex, a world where there is wrongdoing and evil, where values, even the goods of life themselves, can become the focus of conflict and give rise to difficult moral dilemmas. The goods of life ought always to ground our moral visions, but they ought not in my view find expression in principles that express moral absolutes. This sometimes happens, as when in the abortion debate we hear it said that life is an absolute value so that honoring this value ought to brook no exceptions and therefore justify no abortion killings. Such absolutism is, in my view, inconsistent with the natural law view and its practical understanding of the finite world in which we live. For in that finite world, the moral life must be developed in a way that pursues that vision of goodness in light of the realities of the finite world and our limited capacities to know, to understand, to appreciate fully, or to act purely. Our pursuit of the goods of life conforms us to a moral vision of goodness and hopefully renders us increasingly sensitive to moral complexity. Moral absolutism turns in an opposite direction and by its constraint on action denies complexity.

The goods of life are not absolute values, and certainly not relative values. They are, rather, relational realities that present themselves to moral reason and the human heart in the complexity of life. Relational realities engender a kind of moral thinking that in its sensitivity to human finitude avoids formulating action guides in the language of moral absolutes. Given the imperfection of the world and the finitude of the human condition, the action guides that in a perfect world could be absolute principles allowing no exceptions or qualifications are transformed into what I have called "moral presumptions."[4] Moral presumptions embody a vision of the good, right, and fitting. They define the springs of action that constitute moral selfhood. They express the action guides that regulate our common life in community and manifest themselves in operational norms of everyday action and decision-making. Moral presumptions define widely accepted standards of action that we use and rely on for life in moral community: they embody in action our deep-seated and shared moral beliefs and value commitments, and they manifest the core values and the vision of the good life we use to construct our moral communities.

The Moral Presumption against Capital Punishment

Because we in moral community recognize and affirm life itself as a good—even a preeminent good—of life, we understand and accept a moral obligation to pursue, protect, and promote this good. Conversely, we understand that killing deprives persons of this basic good. The moral community thus regards killing as a transgression or moral violation of the most serious kind and does not sanction or justify killing except for specific and morally compelling reasons, such as self-defense.

Capital punishment is a killing. It has been subject to intense moral scrutiny because it inflicts a directly willed and intended killing, the very kind of killing that is most suspect from a moral point of view. It is a form of killing that springs not from the heat of irrational passion, but from reason and an invocation of justice, yet, ironically, for all its appeal to rationality, it makes no obvious appeal to the most rational reason for justifying a killing one could offer—self-defense. And the lack of grounds for appeal to a rational self-defense argument is practical as well as theoretical, since the person facing execution, by virtue of being confined and removed from society, has been rendered impotent and incapable of harming others.

This is not the only point relevant to the chore of assigning presumptive moral meaning to capital punishment.

One of the reasons used to justify the killing of animals—and even human fetuses up to certain points in pregnancy—is that these forms of life are not considered members of the moral community and thus do not enjoy the protections afforded by membership, including the right to life. That controversy can surround the issue of membership in the moral community is all too obvious, as the abortion debate, and even the animal rights debate, has dramatically demonstrated. But no such issue of conflict surrounds the capital punishment debate. Killing a condemned person cannot be justified on the grounds that the condemned's membership in the moral community—and his or her fundamental status as a person—has been denied or disavowed or is even in serious dispute. The protections that attach to membership in the moral community, including the protection afforded by an inherent "right to life," are granted by those who support the death penalty so that justifying the execution of a condemned person never rests on a claim that the condemned is, in fact, not a person, or is only potentially a person, or was once a person but is no longer. On the contrary, capital punishment cannot be justified without recognizing the full personhood and humanity of the condemned person, for without such recognition, the one facing capital punishment cannot be held fully responsible as a person for his or her acts. Capital punishment, as it has developed, requires for its justifiable infliction a person who is capable of understanding both the gravity of the capital offense and the justice that is rendered by imposing death as a response to that offense.

Justifying an act that deprives individuals of life is no easy task from a moral point of view; and capital punishment is handicapped morally from the outset because the ordinary appeals for moral justification recognized in the moral community are not available. An argument for self-defense would be strained theoretically and impossible to make practically, at least so long as society takes those who do pose a threat of harm to others and effectively eliminates that threat by removing the person from free society.

So what this analysis shows is that capital punishment inflicts a willful and intended killing on a human person, and it does so for reasons that do not reside in such graspable and rational arguments as self-defense or the subject's nonpersonhood. In light of the moral community's presumption that killing is wrong, that it violates a good of life—the preeminent good of life itself—by willfully seeking to destroy it, it is reasonable to conclude that the moral presumption at issue in capital punishment is a presumption *against* using the death penalty. Capital punishment, being a killing, is itself not a good of life. It does not advance the moral life or build up the moral community. It is not a means by which we seek to pursue the goods of life and does not consist in the kind of activity we should ordinarily, because of its inherent goodness, want to promote. Its basic moral meaning resides in the fact that it destroys a good of life and does so without appealing to the most reasonable and obvious moral justifications. The presumption of the moral community, therefore, would most reasonably reduce to the view that capital punishment is, as a killing, an act contrary to promoting the good of life. It is therefore to be avoided, which is to say that supporting the possibility of just execution entails the moral understanding that this punishment ought not be ordinarily resorted to as a usual means of punishment for crime. The idea that it could be a just punishment for many crimes or widely used is, on such a theory, inconceivable.

Although supporters of capital punishment might object to this characterization, the moral presumption against capital punishment is, I believe, widely affirmed in practice and would be affirmed as reasonable among even outspoken supporters. For this presumption, because it is a presumption and not an absolute prohibition, identifies the widely shared moral understanding that capital punishment is a form of killing that will require justification; and this way of articulating the presumption establishes the weight of the presumption against capital punishment, which is considerable. The presumption against capital punishment explains why the use of capital punishment has evolved in the direction of greater and greater restriction over the years rather than in the direction of increasingly wide application. Furthermore, that presumption against use of the death penalty explains the fact that capital punishment is, as a punishment, rarely used to punish persons for crimes, and more than that, it is rare as a cause of death in our society.[5] These facts provide empirical confirmation that we, not only as a moral community but as a society—a society that overwhelmingly supports the death penalty—observe the moral presumption against capital punishment. It is vital to establishing a theory of just execution that we acknowledge our reluctance to inflict this cause of death on members of the moral community, for in that reluctance we find evidence to support the claim that the moral presumption at issue in the death penalty debate is actually a presumption against its use. And this, I would hold, is true even if particular individuals also happen to believe that we possess as a society the right to inflict this form of punishment and that there are criminal acts of such a nature that persons committing them bring this punishment upon themselves justly.

Morally speaking, capital punishment is governed by a moral presumption against execution. Members of the moral community would see in capital punishment a form of killing that does not honor the good of life in an obvious way, that deprives the person subject to capital punishment of this good by violence, and that prevents in an absolute way further pursuit of any other of the goods of life. From a moral point of view the act of inflicting capital punishment destroys the good of life—and all other goods that depend upon life itself as a condition of their pursuit—rather than protecting it. In formulating the presumption against capital punishment this way, I do not mean to say at the outset that capital punishment is thereby exempt from any possible justification in certain circumstances. We are constructing a theory of just execution, and the foundation of that theory consists of a moral presumption *against* capital punishment.[6] In the moral community of which we are a part, capital punishment is not a good of life but a destruction of the good of life; as such, members of the moral community hold that the punishment of death, which is an extreme and problematic punishment, ought not ordinarily to be inflicted on persons for their criminal offenses, even when that offense is so serious that another person, the victim of the offense, loses his or her life.

But there is more to the story. Capital punishment is not a killing of one person by another. It is the killing of one person by all. It is, as a punishment for crime, a societal sanction enforced by law and through the power of the state. This lends it a special status and invites a reconsideration of the moral presumption at issue, for the question could be raised, Does the moral presumption against capital punishment hold if the state has been granted authority from the people to impose this punishment, so that its legitimation can be located in the law and in the collective will of society?

The moral response to this question would consist in pointing out that the will of the majority, even if it lends authorization to a penal sanction like execution, does not thereby confer moral legitimacy upon the act. Invoking a "might makes right" ethic, as I have said before, points us in the direction of moral relativism. If capital punishment is morally permissible, it is not because the majority wills its use or the government claims power to inflict it. Alexis de Tocqueville warned Americans long ago of the potential harm to be caused by "the tyranny of the majority," and locating justification for capital punishment in power and the will to use power—whether of the majority or of an individual tyrant like Hitler, who provided a sanction of legal legitimation for all the death inflicted on innocent persons in pursuit of Nazi policies—simply begs the moral question. The moral presumption against killing does not suddenly, because of state involvement, become a moral presumption for killing. We can assume that when the state kills a citizen, that killing falls under the same moral presumption as any other killing, so that we could amend our moral presumption against capital punishment to say the following: The moral presumption against capital punishment is itself entailed by the presumption that the state ought not to kill its own citizens.

That the state ought not to kill its own citizens is not, upon reflection, a controversial moral claim, but a widely held expectation that persons in moral community hold. The state, it could be said, serves to protect and advance the good of life and ought not ordinarily to be about the business of killing its citizens. This is a most rational claim that ought to be even more important to political conservatives than to liberals, since political conservatives have traditionally expressed a deep and natural suspicion of the state and its exercise of power. No power is more to be distrusted than the claim of the state to exercise extreme or absolute power, and it is extreme, even absolute, power that is used when the state executes a citizen. I would hold that this conservative view is—and ought to be— normative, and that the state ought not to be entrusted with the exercise of such power. The fact that in contemporary American society, political conservatives are more likely than liberals to support the exercise of state power to deprive a citizen of the preeminent good of life itself demonstrates how confused we are in the foundational philosophy of citizenship in relation to state power, how contradictory conservative support of the death penalty is, and how irrelevant the labels conservative and liberal have become when it comes to drawing moral conclusions about policy issues from basic political orientations.

The moral presumption at issue in capital punishment is against use of the death penalty. Furthermore, this view attaches to the view—a classically conservative view distrusting the exercise of power—that the state ought not ordinarily be entrusted with the power to execute its own citizens, even in seeking to dispense a proportionally extreme penalty for an extreme offense. This is a political exercise of power fraught with danger in two ways. It is practically dangerous in that an exercise of absolute power may be difficult to contain or restrict, as history has demonstrated too many times to warrant further remark. It is metaphysically dangerous, since the exercise of absolute power—and I confine this remark to matters of justice dispensation—ought reasonably to be undertaken by an agent possessed of the ability to dispense justice on the basis of absolute epistemological certainty and thus be incapable of error. That is what we attribute to God in God's absoluteness. It is not how I have characterized our criminal justice system.

So, keeping these potentially important qualifications in mind, let me assert once again that as a theory, just execution will affirm at its heart a moral presumption against capital punishment and against the moral permissibility of the state executing its own citizens. But not holding these presumptions to be absolute, the theory moves to its next step, which is to ask: Can this presumption against capital punishment ever be lifted? This opens us to the second stage of the theory, which is to consider the criteria that would have to be satisfied if the moral presumption were to be justifiably lifted so that a morally permissible execution could commence.

The Requirements of Justice

A theory of just execution would establish that in light of a moral presumption against capital punishment, an execution could not proceed unless that presumption were lifted. That presumption could only be lifted—and an execution justified—if the requirements of justice were met and the safeguards that ensure justice were preserved. The following criteria serve to indicate what would be required to justify lifting the moral presumption against capital punishment, and, as in other "presumption/exception" theories, such as "just war" or "just abortion," all of the criteria have to be met. Failure to satisfy all the criteria would block the effort to lift the presumption, so that moral permissibility would necessarily fail to attach to capital punishment or, more precisely, to particular instances of it.

Legitimate Authority

In order for an execution to be deemed just, it must be imposed by legitimate authority. Execution must be authorized and sanctioned as a tool in a state's justice system. This requirement prohibits vigilantism or any extralegal execution by mob violence or terrorism. The extralegal practice of lynching so common in the United States, which did not have a lynching-free year until 1953, is rendered morally impermissible.[7] The point of this criterion is to assure that no criminal act that has deprived a person of life be punished by a private citizen or citizens. In the political commonwealth governed by a rule of law, it is the law, not the individual victims of crime or their families or clans, that determines how response shall be made to a criminal offender, the theory being that the harm committed in political society is not only to the immediate victim of crime but to the state itself. Capital punishment, to be morally just, must therefore be imposed under the rule of law and in the name of the collective will of the sovereign power. It is the sovereign power that justly authorizes capital punishment though a legal system of justice administration, and this is the case even though appeals for moral justification are sometimes referred out of the authority of the legal system to a religious source of sanction and legitimation. But even when appeal is made to a source of religious legitimation for the death penalty, it is clear that the particulars of any given case where it is believed the religious sanction would apply are determined by some kind of legal system that exercises, on behalf of the religious sanction, sovereign power—or else God (or whatever transcendent or ultimate religious source is in question) could simply effect the execution directly without any delegating of the divine will to human agents.

Just Cause

A just cause for imposing the death penalty must be claimed in order to justify using it. Just cause can be established by considering the nature of the crime itself and applying a principle of proportionality so that extreme crimes would be met with extreme punishments. The death penalty is an extreme penalty. Resorting to the death penalty would be justified under this criterion as an extreme but proportionate response to an extreme offense. This criterion takes account of an "evolving standard of decency," as the phrase has found its way into American law,[8] so that the tendency would be to restrict the extreme penalty to truly extreme crimes, such as aggravated murder. Executing a person for stealing a calf—the first crime in America that brought about a death sentence and an execution—or for any of the larcenies that legally called for the death penalty in the societies of Locke, Kant, and John Stuart Mill no longer meets this test. Such crimes lack sufficient gravity to establish just cause. Practically speaking, only a very restricted class of crimes—murder and perhaps treason—are thus considered justly eligible for the death penalty, and then only the gravest instances of offense within that class.

But focus on the nature of the crime itself does not exhaust the just cause criterion. And it ought not to, since what does—and what does not—constitute a "gravest of the grave" crime will always be subject to a relativistic interpretation. Although it is beyond dispute that we who are members of the moral community today consider Daniell Frank's execution in 1622 for the crime of stealing a calf unjust and disproportionate, it clearly was not beyond dispute in the moral community of 1622 Colonial America. Stealing a calf was just cause for hanging. If just cause were to be determined only by appealing to what a society held at any given moment to be a crime sufficiently grave to establish just cause, we would have to conclude that justice was served by the execution of Daniell Frank in 1622, even though that execution offends our modern standards of decency. And these standards would then be subject to such contextualization themselves, for we could situate the American penchant for execution within the wider context of the family of nations.

Although countries that have poor records of respecting human rights still employ the death penalty—Saudi Arabia, Iran, Iraq, and China come to mind— the fact is that most nations that Americans would identify as affirming values that correspond to our own have abolished the death penalty, which means this: that on the basis of an "evolving standard of decency," the death penalty *even for murder—even aggravated murder—has been abolished as failing to satisfy just cause.* Were we to determine just cause by such a relativistic mode of evaluation, the American continuation of the death penalty could be viewed within the wider moral community of which we are a part as being out of sync with the evolving standard. Even the American who supports the death penalty has evolved morally beyond the view that found the execution of Daniell Frank for stealing a calf acceptable, or the Hebrew Scriptures view that cursing a parent merited death, or the Muslim view, found in the Qu'ran, that imposes for the crime of armed robbery death by sword or crucifixion or a cutting off of foot and opposite hand.[9]

China considers opposition to the government just cause for execution. As Americans have leveled human rights abuse charges at China and debated the propriety of extending to China most-favored-nation trading partner status, it is clear that Americans in general find this assertion of just cause for legalized execution inadequate, reflecting a morally deficient barbarism. But if just cause is to be determined relativistically and not morally, China's use of the death penalty is morally wrong only in light of American standards. By the same token, America's use of the death penalty is deficient in light of the move in the wider moral community to abolish the death penalty. Viewed in the context of democratic societies around the world, our retention of the death penalty is as aberrant as the execution of Daniell Frank in Colonial America appears to us today.

One could reply that just cause is established by only one crime, murder, thus making the move Kant made. But this is to mandate capital punishment in the face of the moral presumption against capital punishment that I have taken pains to articulate. By opting for a theory of just execution, we are necessarily excluding—by definition—any absolutist move, including the Kantian move that would support on principle a mandatory use of the death penalty for certain crimes whenever they are committed. If I am right in claiming that we have put just execution into practice in contemporary American society—a point I shall address below—that would mean that many crimes that could fit the description of that crime for which Kant required the death penalty do not, in fact, receive the death penalty, because a morally moderate position will exclude a mandatory death penalty. (I have already pointed out that even the Supreme Court, which has upheld the death penalty, refuses to endorse mandatory death sentences.)

If we deny that just cause consists in requiring a mandatory sentence of death for the crime of taking another's life, just execution theory requires that we determine which murders are deserving of death, how the ones we single out for execution are distinctive and thus merit death in ways others do not, then go about the business of using discretion in imposing the death penalty. To mandate a death sentence for a particular crime would be to deny all that we mean by a morally moderate just execution ethic, for just execution would then mean nothing other than resolving to impose death for, say, every murder; and we do not do and will not do that. The moral presumption against the death penalty is too strong and withstands such a challenge.

But the Kantian position has the merit of simplifying just cause by attaching just cause to a particular crime. In holding that this is insufficient and even contradictory to the just execution ethic, I wish to locate just cause in something other than the offense, which may or may not—as it is considered and deliberated on—give rise to a demand for the death penalty. The foundation of just cause that seems most reasonable to me for calling for the death penalty is one Locke advanced and Mill seemed to address, however obliquely: self-defense.

In the idea of self-defense, we have a justification for execution that natural reason can recognize as sufficient for establishing just cause. When self-defense is the foundation of just cause, we would hold that a criminal offender not only harms innocent persons but poses a continuing threat of harm to persons. Against that threat, society, acting on behalf of the welfare of all, has a right to protect itself. In opting for the death penalty, the society is acting to protect persons from the actual and potential harm a criminal offender embodies for society, and the execution is an act of self-defense that ends a threat that can in no other way be ended with certainty. If the criminal justice system fails to impose sentences consistently and severely, and there is no guarantee that an individual criminal offender guilty of terrible crimes will not later be free to subject innocent persons to harm, then execution is justified—and meets the criterion of just cause—on grounds of self-defense. Capital punishment becomes the means not only of punishing such a criminal, but of assuring that the threat posed to society is definitively removed.

The strongest case for establishing just cause consists not in arguing that murder is the only crime worthy of the death penalty. That is certainly a case to be made and it has merit, but it is not without problems, especially for a theory of just execution that will honor the moral presumption against capital punishment and refuse to insist that capital punishment be imposed for the crime of murder. The strongest case for just cause rests in a self-defense claim. In cases where the threat to the common good is enormous because of the nature of the offender's crime, and there is no way short of execution to ensure that the threat posed by the offender is eradicated, the just execution theorist can appeal to self-defense. When this claim is made and justified, the execution of a criminal offender for reasons of society's self-defense would satisfy the criterion of just cause.

Justice, Not Vengeance, as Motivation

A just execution theory will require that the motivation for an execution be justice and not vengeance. That is not to say that those who survive in the wake of a capital criminal's offense should be expected not to want revenge. The loss of a loved one to murder is a moral horror that only the deepest passion can fathom and for which a desire for retribution is natural. But in the commonwealth of society, as Locke reminded us, "men being partial to themselves, Passion and Revenge is very apt to carry them too far, and with too much heat in their own Cases."[10]

This criterion serves to remind us that the natural desire to harm those who have wronged us must be checked. While retribution seems to be one legitimate motive for punishment, the agent of retribution must never become an individual acting out of a desire for revenge but the collective of society itself, acting through its legal system to dispense justice in accordance with a rule of equal protection and "due process of law." Private vengeance, which would issue from an unchecked desire for revenge, threatens the well-being of all, for we are not, as Locke said, likely to be good or fair judges where our own feelings and interests are concerned, especially when we have been greatly aggrieved. Were the motive of revenge sufficient to justify a killing, that motive would have to be recognized as justifying any and all killings springing from the same motive. This would surely undo any hope of dispensing justice dispassionately or even fairly, since passion might, in the heat of the moment, jump to conclusions and exact vengeance on the wrong party. Kant considered even the desire for vengeance "vicious," but we can acknowledge that desire here as an understandable response by victims of terrible crime or their survivors.

But vengeance is not justice. If what vengeance is seeking is to put right the balance of justice when a capital crime has been committed, we must recognize that vengeance is blind to the irreplaceable nature of the loss suffered. The fact is that the wrongful injury of death is so severe that it cannot be put right. Vengeance can seek justice, but justice is not to be had. Vengeance only serves the illusion that the loss resulting from death can be put right by the death of another. Such a view is folly, sad folly. An irreplaceable loss cannot be replaced; an irretrievable loss cannot be retrieved. And ideally, it is the replacing of the irreplaceable and the retrieving of the irretrievable that justice would require.

We cannot have perfect justice, just execution theory would say—and we ought not have an illusory justice based on vengeance. The best that can be hoped for is dispassionate justice and fair legal adjudication. Dispassionate justice, rather than serving vengeance, might well impose a retributive punishment, but in doing so it would be motivated by justice and not revenge. Such justice, even if clearly retributive, would seek to protect persons from the immoral acts that can spring from vengeance.

Fair Imposition

According to this criterion, imposing a death sentence ought not to be based on considerations of race, religion, class, sex, or other accidental features not relevant to establishing that a particular crime is "gravest of the grave" and thus eligible for death penalty consideration. Fairness in just execution theory is not reducible to a Kantian equality principle where the nature of the crime mandates a death sentence. Fairness requires making a determination that capital punishment is a just response to a certain kind of crime, and establishing fairness is accomplished by assessing the crime in light of all kinds of relevant factors. The fairness question is whether imposing the death sentence is fair and just in one case and not another, that determination being affected by mitigating and aggravating circumstances. The law allows consideration of such factors in the penalty phases of capital trials, so that a conviction does not lead inevitably to execution but to an assessment of those factors that have a mitigating effect on punishment, or, conversely, those factors that so aggravate the severity of the crime that the crime is pushed into the category of "gravest of the grave" where death sentences are imposed as proportionate punishment. The law can mitigate punishment and even prohibit consideration of the death penalty for reasons of age and mental ability. Children under sixteen are currently exempt from execution, although this has not always been the case, and mental status is relevant: Arkansas, for instance, prohibits the execution of defendants with IQs below 65.[11] Such persons are held to be not fully responsible for their crimes. It is worth noting that a de facto mitigation of the death penalty occurs in the application of the death penalty relative to class and gender, though pointing out how this occurs provokes fairness questions rather than satisfying the criterion.

The point of the criterion, however, is to require fairness in the imposition of the death penalty because justice demands it. The standard of fairness is brought to bear to determine the appropriateness of the death penalty in particular cases on the assumption that how such determinations are made can be and ought to be affected by factors that have bearing on the attribution of full responsibility for committing a capital crime. Conviction even in a death penalty–eligible case does not necessitate imposing the death penalty. Even upon conviction in a capital case, a defendant has the opportunity to demonstrate how mitigating factors in his or her particular case ought to prevent the moral presumption against capital punishment from being lifted. Consideration of such factors squares with an ideal of fairness in the imposition of the death penalty.

For all the discrimination that goes on in assessing whether a particular defendant merits mitigation of the death sentence, any discrimination that would affect an impartial distribution of justice would, under this criterion, be disallowed. Disallowed discrimination under this criterion would include considerations of race, religion, class, gender, or any factor incidental to evaluating a case that would regard one person as in some sense more or less valuable than another. This criterion of impartial justice requires that the person who confronts a death sentence do so as a person, a fully endowed member of the moral community, who is neither more nor less deserving of a death sentence than anyone else in a similar situation.

And as a last point, the standard of fairness avowed by this criterion of just execution requires procedural impartiality in the system of justice administration. This aspect of the criterion is potentially troublesome in that fairness that conforms with the moral requirements of justice will require something more than formal observance of a general rule, such as "All persons accused of a capital crime ought to have competent legal representation." The fair imposition criterion is violated if wealth and class can affect the dispensation of justice such that the more resources one has the better chance one has to secure legal representation that will in turn increase the likelihood of evading a death sentence. This is a gray area where disputes will inevitably arise, but just execution demands a moral assessment of those particulars beyond formal observance of a legal rule.

Prohibition on Cruelty

This criterion holds that the humanity of persons condemned to death must be respected so that the punishment of death, being extreme, cannot demand more than death. Torture of a condemned person is thus disallowed. Furthermore, the method of execution must be such that it delivers the person to death with dispatch. The force of this criterion is such that it leads to the development of increasingly humane methods of execution. Once-common methods of execution such as boiling in oil, drawing and quartering, garroting, and crucifixion all fail to meet the humaneness standard imposed by this criterion, for these methods involve torture and abuse of the condemned. A botched execution is, in my view, inherently cruel, and although a botched execution is no legal impediment to continuing with the execution, I would argue that morally speaking, an executioner's failure to dispatch an individual in such a way as to eliminate torture renders execution impermissible for this individual, whose sentence of death must then be commuted.

That executions should be humane is certainly not controversial, but the implication of holding firm to this criterion is serious indeed, particularly for those who want to argue that the true foundation of just cause for capital punishment is deterrence. By making execution methods more humane, and then carrying them out in secret, we practically eliminate any justification for the death penalty based on deterrence, at least if deterrence is grounded in Mill's idea that psychological arousal ought to provoke shock and horror at the prospect of execution so that others are deterred from committing capital crimes. Just execution theory would not, to be sure, rest its case on deterrence, and this criterion, if accepted as a legitimate aspect of a just execution theory, in a practical sense, eliminates that possibility.

Last Resort

The willful destruction of human life is presumptively wrong, and capital punishment ought not to be a live option unless the decision to use the punishment comes at the end of a long reasoning process that concludes there is no alternative other than demanding forfeiture of life that will satisfy the demands of justice. The presumption against capital punishment is strong and abiding, and it is not to be waived except after thorough deliberation and exhaustive consideration of alternative punishments. Those alternatives must be found wanting. Deciding on capital punishment must in this sense be a last resort, with all other alternatives to execution having been found deficient in delivering proportional justice to the defendant.

Preserving Values

This criterion is clearly consequentialist in its focus, and the consequence it points to is this: capital punishment ought not to contribute to a subverting of the value of the good of life in the moral community. This criterion insists that capital punishment be justified by attending to the positive contribution capital punishment makes to advancing and enhancing the value of life. If using this punishment does not make such a contribution but can be shown to subvert the moral community's valuing of the good of life, capital punishment would be deemed morally impermissible.

This is a troubling criterion because it posits a contradiction. The contradiction is obvious enough: capital punishment ought to enhance and advance the value of life, yet inflicting the death penalty constitutes a killing and is therefore a direct and willful societal assault on the value of life. The contradiction can dissolve if it can be successfully argued that in the name of justice capital punishment assaults the value of a particular life, not the value of life in general; and that by acting to effect the forfeiture of this particular life, society—the moral community—acts to enhance rather than diminish or subvert the value of life. A just execution theory cannot be justified except by such a rationale, and the staunchest and most consistent defenders of capital punishment will make this case. One such defender of capital punishment, Senator Orrin Hatch of Utah, has recognized the importance of this criterion of just execution by stating, "Capital punishment is our society's recognition of the sanctity of human life." Although just execution theory would deny that life is to be valued in accordance with a "sanctity of life" claim, for that would attach absolute value to the value of life and thus deny the foundational premises of just execution as nonabsolute,[12] Hatch's statement does attach capital punishment to the preservation and advancement of the value of life in the moral community. Defending capital punishment on the argument that capital punishment enhances the value of the good of life is, in my view, a necessary move in any just execution theory effort to lift the moral presumption against capital punishment.

This criterion ought to direct our attention back to our moral presumption against killing and the particular destruction of the good of life at issue in capital punishment. For this criterion requires that the integrity of the moral presumption against capital punishment be preserved, even if the criteria of just execution theory have been satisfied and the presumption is justifiably lifted. The effect of an execution ought to be to enhance the good of life and not subvert it. The consequence of capital punishment ought to be that by such action we promote the value of life and thus restore the moral presumption against killing persons—even by the state—to its status as a functioning norm to be honored and observed in the moral community. In other words, an execution performed consistently with a just execution theory ought to reinstate the binding power of the moral presumption against capital punishment, and in no way contribute to a slackening of the force of that presumption. Moral presumptions may be lifted, but it is a condition of lifting them justly that the lifting itself contribute to preserving the values at stake in the presumption. Lifting the presumption in certain circumstances must in no way undermine the value of the good of life or subvert it.

The End of Restoring a Just Equilibrium

Another consequentialist-related criterion of capital punishment is related to the hope that the death penalty will restore equilibrium to the upset balance of justice and thus bring peace to the social order and even to the surviving victims of capital crime. Capital crimes, especially aggravated murder, leave many victims in their wake. The direct victim of the crime is of course the subject of greatest loss; and that loss is absolute and irretrievable. But loss is experienced by those who loved the victim. They too lose in an absolute way a friend, a family member, a person whose value in the interconnectedness of a relational world is beyond measure. The pain of such loss can be excruciating. In the demand society makes for just punishment in the face of absolute loss, the intent of punishment must be directed at bringing the upset scales of justice back into balance to the extent possible. When criminal wrongdoers are punished, a positive benefit accrues to society in that society sees itself acting consistently with its own professed commitment to protecting the innocent, ensuring freedom, promoting the value of life and liberty, and pursuing justice. Acting vigorously to prosecute crime and deliver justice through the legal and penal system is what society does to address the disruption in the social equilibrium created by acts of criminal wrongdoing. Social harmony cannot exist in the presence of crime or in the ineffective pursuit of justice in response to crime. The vision of a just society is a shared societal vision: where justice is pursued, a society's common values and its bonds of unity are strengthened; so too when injustice is confronted and unjust acts are punished. Capital punishment ought reasonably to effect the end of enhancing and advancing the cause of justice. By so doing, it promotes social harmony, strengthens the society's bonds of unity, and aims at the end of societal peace.

For the victims of crime, a benefit will hopefully issue from witnessing the society as a whole acting through its system of justice administration to address, correct, and punish individual acts of injustice. For the victims of crime to feel that the offense directed at them has been directed at everyone else as well, and that the power of the collective will be directed toward responding consistently with its professed commitment to justice, reinforces the bonds of social inter-connectedness, allowing them to experience the hope that in society's pursuit of justice, peace may be restored in their own lives as individual victims. This is of course a hope. For those who are affected by the irreparable harm of murder, this hope is not easily realized. But delivering justice is always a move in the direction of peace toward the end of peace. And no punishment—including capital pun-ishment—that does not aim at such a restoration of peace should be considered a just punishment.

Capital punishment, in other words, must aim at restoring peace to the sur-viving victims of capital crime and do so in a way no other punishment can ac-complish. That is the message and the requirement of this criterion, and this wor-thy end—peace—is a necessary feature of any theory of just execution.

Proportionality

This is perhaps the most important criterion in a theory of just execution, but it arises in at least three different ways. First, proportionality requires that the pun-ishment fit the crime. This criterion thus invokes a hierarchy of moral evil and restricts capital punishment to only the gravest crimes, aggravated murder being the most obvious candidate for the death penalty in the serious crime category of homicide.

In accordance with proportionality, capital punishment must, second, not yield an effect disproportionate to the end being sought, whether that end be de-livering a just punishment or restoring equilibrium and peace to society and to surviving victims of capital crime.

And third, proportionality requires that capital punishment not violate a person's inherent dignity, whatever that person may have done, however heinous his or her crimes may be. Denying an individual's humanity and refusing to ac-cord the respect he or she is owed by virtue of membership in the moral com-munity constitutes action disproportionate to the crime. As Kant said—and on this point he was clearly right—only persons can be punished. Only fully en-dowed members of the moral community are capable of assuming responsibility for their actions. Only persons can be held morally accountable by the moral community for acts of wrongdoing. Adding torture or treating a capital criminal in a way that does not accord basic respect to his or her fundamental humanity violates the proportionality criterion and in turn would deny capital punishment justification.

These nine criteria establish the conditions that would have to be met if the presumption against capital punishment is to be justifiably lifted. A theory of just execution would require that all of these criteria be satisfied, and failure to meet them—any one of them—leaves the moral presumption against capital punishment securely in place, functioning as an operative action guide that prevents the granting of moral justification to a proposed execution.

Moral Background for Legal Developments

The law governing capital punishment in the United States has, I contend, made implicit appeal to a theory of just execution. Appeal to such a framework of justice—a moral theory—is made by defenders as well as opponents of capital punishment, for the theory can be shown to be in play affecting, even if only inferentially, the course of legal debate over execution policy. Even a cursory examination of the legal evolution that has occurred over the past twenty-five years will substantiate this claim, for those developments can be shown to accord with what a theory of just execution requires.

Consider, for instance, that developments in American law can be understood in light of a moral presumption against capital punishment. That is, capital punishment is recognized as a grave punishment that must not be commonly and indiscriminately used but reserved for only the gravest crimes. The U.S. Supreme Court, which has refused to abolish the death penalty and has thereby tried to strike a moderate, nonabsolutist position, has addressed legal issues relevant to the death penalty by consistently, if not overtly, affirming a moral presumption against capital punishment. I do not offer this as a provocative or controversial statement. A moral presumption against capital punishment is what remains when the penal law refuses to endorse an absolutist stance on capital punishment, and absolutism can go in either of two directions. Legal abolition of the death penalty—categorically—would represent one form of absolutism; the state's exercise of a power to mandate death sentences for particular offenses deemed by the state to be capital crimes would represent absolutism in the other direction. If these options are disavowed, what remains is a moral presumption against capital punishment, and this I believe the U.S. Supreme Court, the final arbiter of legal authorization for execution as a specific tool of penal law, has endorsed. It has endorsed the presumption by, on the one hand, refusing to abolish the death penalty. The Court has not found capital punishment to be an instrument of penal law that is inherently cruel, thus abolishing it. This would represent an absolutist stance, practically speaking. On the other hand, the Court has insisted that use of the death penalty be highly restricted. The Supreme Court has further required that imposing the death penalty can be accomplished justly (and morally) only if defendants' rights are protected, only if the irrevocable nature of the penalty assures that great latitude is given to a defendant in seeking to avoid the penalty, and only if a variety of necessary conditions safeguarding the defendant and burdening the prosecution are met. Because of this avoidance of the absolutist options, and because the restrictive use of the death penalty authorized by the Supreme Court demonstrates adherence to a presumption against, rather than for, state killing, I think it clear that the moral presumption against capital punishment can be inferred in the basic orientation of the legal system toward capital punishment and the use of state power to kill citizens.

But just execution theory deals with more than the presumption against capital punishment. As a "moderate" or nonabsolutist perspective, it also allows that capital punishment may be justified if certain conditions are met. I have specified nine conditions I think necessary for a theory of just execution. If we consider how current execution policy in the United States has developed, I believe we can discern a correspondence between those moral criteria and the legal requirements that are designed to ensure that the death penalty serves justice. These developments are the result of the American judicial review of capital punishment.

Authority

The question of authority has been addressed, and legal authorization by both state and federal governments has been affirmed. The Constitution nowhere mandates or even mentions capital punishment but it clearly implies its legal validity in the Fifth Amendment, which states that no person "shall be deprived of life, liberty, or property, without due process of law." The implication, of course, is that a citizen may be deprived of life if due process is observed, and that could presumably be effected by means of capital punishment. The Constitution establishes that Congress shall "provide for the punishment" of counterfeiting and "declare the punishment of Treason," so that the power to punish criminal offenders is clearly established and duly authorized by the constituting political and governmental agreement of American society. Capital punishment is not mandated or required, but left for legislative determination and judicial review. On both fronts, its legal authorization has been unquestionably affirmed. Legal authority for capital punishment, therefore, can be said to rest in those legislative acts that specify capital punishment as an allowable penalty under the power granted the state to legislate punishments of various sorts. Capital punishment, so long as it passes the tests of constitutionality, can be said to be legally authorized.

Just Cause

The law has specified just cause by restricting death penalty eligibility to certain crimes that are thought to be the gravest of the grave. The crime of aggravated murder seems at present to be the center of just cause, but growing frustration with crime in American society has been an impetus to legal expansion of the number of crimes for which death can be imposed. On this criterion I would say that to the extent that this expansion represents a clarification of the meaning of aggravated murder—that an aggravated murder would be murder committed in commission of a crime, or the killing of a police officer, or the killing of a rape or kidnap victim—then this expansion could be viewed as consistent with the restricting of just cause for execution to aggravated murder.

Justice, Not Vengeance, as Motivation

Legal motivation for seeking to impose a death sentence could reasonably be said to be justice rather than vengeance. This can be inferred from the lengthy review process that has developed to ensure that justice in the form of equal protection and due process is afforded the capital defendant. It is also apparent in the demand that death sentences be imposed in accordance with a jury's consideration of the "objective" sentencing guidelines. Those guidelines set down what is to be considered in imposing sentence upon a person who has been found guilty of death penalty–eligible crime, with attention being given to those circumstances or factors that would persuade jurors to withhold the most severe penalty due to mitigating circumstances. This move to objective sentencing standards conforms to a principle of equal justice dispassionately distributed. The sentence of death is then subjected to a substantial and mandatory "due process" review to ensure that no unfairness has infected the proceedings that led to the conviction or sentencing. In all of these safeguards, one sees a concern for justice and the protections of justice at work, so that one could reasonably infer that in a capital trial where a death sentence is handed down, justice, not vengeance, has been the primary motive.

Fair Imposition

Death penalty statutes have blinded the law to any individual factors that would legally position a person to receive—or not receive—the death penalty if the crime warranted. Restrictions on eligibility for the death penalty have been legally put into place with regard to minimum age and mental ability, and in general the whole process of death penalty imposition has been objectivized to avoid the unfairness of arbitrary or capricious death sentences. Death penalty statutes that are vague or unclear in setting out the objective requirements for what is to guide a jury in sentencing have been disallowed. Objectivizing the death sentence imposition process has been legally demanded by the courts to ensure that persons are not denied either due process of law or equal protection before the law.

Fair imposition has been a major thrust of legal reform of the death penalty. This criterion, incidentally, is an action criterion distinct from the motivation of justice criterion above, since just execution wants to conform observance of the letter of the law (acting justly with respect to imposition) with its spirit (motivated by justice). With a life at stake, nothing less would be appropriate.

Prohibition on Cruelty

State courts, as well as the U.S. Supreme Court, hear challenges on this issue, especially in the wake of a botched execution. The focus of attention with regard to this criterion has been on methods of execution, with certain methods being adjudged indecent and impermissible. The prohibition in this criterion pertains to the system of death delivery—and some states even give prisoners a choice of method—rather than on the inherent cruelty of the punishment itself. Again, a judgment that capital punishment is inherently cruel would constitute in a theory of just execution an absolutist move at odds with the foundation of the theory.

Last Resort

That the legal review process is as extensive as it is contributes to the understanding that when an execution is actually carried out, it constitutes a last resort. Not only is a jury presented with the option of the death penalty, which it can refuse to impose in consideration of mitigating circumstances, but the numerous opportunities that have been made available for a defendant to challenge a death sentence and its appropriateness in an individual case mean, on a just execution theory, that reasonable alternatives to execution have been exhausted. The execution represents a last resort with respect to just punishment.

Preserving Values

Although this criterion is somewhat difficult to encapsulate as a focus of legal attention, this much seems clear: The thrust of legal decisions on capital punishment has satisfied this criterion in the sense that the legal system has failed to find capital punishment an action or punishment policy that subverts the value of life. Those who support capital punishment and support the legal right of states and the federal government to impose it do so because they hold that by killing a murderer, the state is demonstrating in a dramatic and powerful way that life is a cherished value not to be taken away from any citizen unjustly; and that society so affirms the high value placed on life itself that those who take life unjustifiably commit an intolerable offense which justly merits demanding that the offender forfeit his or her own life. That forfeiture is demanded because the offense committed against the value of life is so terrible. By exacting the forfeiture, the value of life is enhanced and society's commitment to protecting life is demonstrated for the good of all. The quote I offered above from Senator Orrin Hatch expresses how those who work to support and apply the death penalty, who write laws and evaluate candidates for court positions, understand the death penalty to be a primary and visible legal means of demonstrating how society can take action in regard to preserving the value of life against those who offend against it.

The End of Restoring Equilibrium

The survivors of victims of capital crime have become more and more important to lawmakers. Some states, like Texas, will allow the families of victims to witness executions on the theory that by so doing some closure on the trauma of losing a loved one will commence. In the background of state support and judicial sanctioning of the death penalty is a recognition that justice is accomplished by inflicting this punishment, and when justice is accomplished, the equilibrium of justice put out of balance by a criminal act is restored. Healing may even be effected in those individual survivors of victims, whose suffering may be eased by knowing that their loved one's murderer has been put to death and can do no more harm.

Proportionality

Execution has been sanctioned upon judicial review as a just and proportionate response to the crime of aggravated murder. Attention is given to the details of cases so that factors that might mitigate punishment even in such a case can be considered and a nonproportionate penalty avoided. The move toward lethal injection demonstrates legal concern that methods of execution not impose any undue or excessive punishment beyond the execution demand that the life be taken; any nonproportionate behavior that would impose excessive punishment through torture is disallowed and appealable.

That the American judiciary has attended—however unconsciously or even unwittingly—to a theory of just execution, as laid out above, can be demonstrated by examining the particulars of various post–*Furman v. Georgia* Supreme Court decisions. It can be seen in the *Gregg v. Georgia* decision, which imposed a requirement of objective standards for juries to use in sentencing and required automatic state appellate review of cases; in *Woodson v. North Carolina*, which required particularized attention to cases and thus denied mandatory death sentences as inconsistent with "evolving standards of decency"; in *Coker v. Georgia*, wherein it was held that Georgia's death penalty for rape was a punishment disproportionate to the offense, thus affirming the death sentence for crimes in which a victim lost his or her life; in *Lockett v. Ohio*, which recognized the unique nature of capital cases and the inevitable consequence of the death penalty's irreversibility, so that full consideration of mitigating circumstances in imposing a death sentence was required. Just execution is also the moral theory informing the *Godfrey v. Georgia* decision, which required recognition of a defendant's right to be judged in light of clear and unambiguous sentencing guidelines. Other decisions over the years have addressed a variety of related issues: death penalty eligibility for accomplices in murder; the need to weigh and separate substantive from frivolous appeals; issues of fair and consistent application; the prohibition on executing a person who during death row confinement went insane and could no longer understand why he was being put to death; and racial discrimination.

A theory of just execution provides Americans with a distinctive moral model that can be used to explain how the law has evolved as it has. For it has evolved in the direction of restrictive use between the extreme options of mandating death on the one hand or abolishing it on the other. The just execution theory that endorses such a moderate, nonabsolutist stance can clearly be discerned in the history of legal interpretation over the past twenty-five years. For the law has authorized capital punishment, but clearly in light of a presumption against it, authorizing it only in restrictive cases and only on condition that the demands of justice—and the criteria that justify lifting the presumption against capital punishment—have been satisfied.

8

Just Execution: Testing Practice against Theory

The theory of just execution is a strong theory. And it is so practical a mode of moral thinking and evaluation that I believe we in the moral community commonly appeal to it when we stake out positions on the moral meaning of the death penalty. We frame our moral debates in light of specific criteria that we deem must be satisfied if capital punishment is to be morally justified, and we can agree on the criteria whether we wind up supporting the death penalty or opposing it.

The criteria emerge from deep and common agreements over what is appropriate to the determination of moral meaning, even if, in consideration of specific cases, disagreement ensues, so we can say that just execution provides a theoretical structure for framing a reasoned debate over moral meaning. Not itself a position on capital punishment, the just execution theory provides a common and reasonable framework for arguing whether the moral presumption against capital punishment can be justifiably lifted. Even the legal system reflects this structure, for the thrust of American law on the question of the death penalty has been that capital punishment ought ordinarily not be used as a state-sanctioned punishment for crime but may be used if certain stringent criteria for just and fair imposition of the death penalty are observed.

Court decisions and continued legal refinement of issues related to fair imposition of the death penalty reflect a legal system working in the direction of ensuring that capital punishment be rendered a just punishment. The general move of the law has been in conformity with the requirements of a just execution moral theory. If it can reasonably be said that legal developments related to the death penalty over the past three decades appeal to a particular moral view, I would offer just execution as the strongest candidate for such a moral appeal.

But despite the ability of this theory to synthesize important aspects of human rights ethics, consequentialist ethics, and even universalizability features from Kant's deontological perspective, this theory—the best theory—does not, in my view, finally deliver to us a convincing moral justification for capital punishment. The criteria of just execution set a standard of justice that from an empirical point of view cannot be met. Let me offer the following points in support of this claim.

On the Authority Criterion

If what one means by authorization for the death penalty is legal authorization, then the authority criterion is satisfied whenever and wherever capital punishment is carried out in conformity with the requirements and protections of law. The true function of this criterion of just execution is to prohibit any extralegal executions, such as lynchings, vigilante killing, and blood-vengeance retribution. On this criterion, such killings, even if motivated by a desire for justice, would fail the test of moral justification.

We must keep in mind that the criterion of proper authority is insufficient to establish moral meaning, and that the authority criterion considered legally points to an exercise of political power and to nothing beyond that. The vast majority of Americans support the legal sanctioning of the death penalty for specific crimes, and the legality of the penalty sometimes permits the inference that the moral meaning of execution is thereby itself assured. But this is not so. Such a conclusion is the relativist's conclusion, which conforms morality to power rather than subjecting even power to a vision of the good.

While necessary for a theory of just execution, the legality of the penalty is simply question-begging from the point of view of morality. A necessary ambivalence attaches to the authority criterion when we consider that Hitler, for instance, because his will had the force of law and he willed execution in pursuit of genocidal policies, killed no one illegally. Unless we move from legal authorization to moral authorization, we shall be left with the relativist's "might makes right" ethic, where morality is determined not by a vision of the good but by power, whether the power of a democratic majority or the power of a tyrant to force submission to a despotic will. This first criterion of just execution theory, then, addresses the question of law, but does not specify a *moral authority* for capital punishment. But clearly an appeal to moral authority is in order on the question of just execution, so that this criterion can be invoked for the purpose of considering *moral authorization* for the death penalty beyond the *legal sanctions* this criterion requires.

Because a moral presumption against capital punishment exists, moral authorization for the death penalty ought reasonably to be located in practical reason itself. Practical reason would have to establish that punishing a person by killing that person has positive moral worth and that the execution constituted an act promoting the goods of life. Were practical reason to establish such positive moral worth, the value of execution would be obvious and incite no strenuous moral opposition, for the goods of life and acts that flow from them in promotion of those goods do not hide goodness but manifest it to practical reason. The goodness is there to see. My contention, however, is that the death penalty is not luminous with regard to the good. By resorting to execution the state acts to deprive a condemned person not only of particular goods of life—aesthetic enjoyment, self-consciousness, physical integrity, friendships, and so on—but of the good of life itself.

Moral authority for capital punishment ought so to express itself through reason that the positive moral meaning of the execution act is clear. And what ought to be clear, taking this first criterion to be a requirement for moral authorization, is that by the act of execution the goods of life can be advanced and promoted.

But that seems not at all obvious. Reason can see that it is just to punish a person who commits moral offenses against other persons and even against the society of persons. Reason can see that by requiring punishment, justice is promoted and goodness pursued, for justice is done to the victim of crime (ideally) while punishment serves to reintroduce and conform the offender to the moral values that by criminal acts the offender has subverted.

But this appeal to justice and goodness seems outside the range of what the death penalty visits on the offender. The light of goodness does not illumine the execution act, for execution is shadowy and sinister; and it is recognized as such within the moral community by being hidden away and kept from the public witness. That can only be because its goodness is not luminous and not apparent. Destruction of the goods of life is the obvious moral meaning of capital punishment. The moral presumption against capital punishment is based on that simple fact.

Thus the authority criterion does not establish moral authority, and in the legal authorization it does demand, it only prohibits execution practices that are outside the law. Given that the law itself can fail in spectacular ways to meet the moral demands of justice, this is not to say much.

On Just Cause

In the theory of just execution, the moral presumption against capital punishment cannot be lifted without just cause for doing so. In American law, just cause for seeking the death penalty has been identified with the specific crime of aggravated murder. Two critical points deserve to be made about this.

The first point is that restricting the use of the death penalty to such a specific crime—and even then discretion is permitted in sentencing because death sentences are not mandatory—is a rather recent development in American law. Pointing this out reminds us that legal execution has typically been used for many crimes besides aggravated murder, including property crimes, political crimes, and racially charged crimes (rape). The death penalty has been used in all kinds of wildly outrageous acts of oppression of undesirables as a tool of state power and governmental policy, as well as an instrument of law; and it has been susceptible to misuse and abuse. Amnesty International, incidentally, reminds us that this continues to be the case today. In reflecting on just cause for execution, we must remember that the death penalty has been justified over the span of human history for lots of different reasons, and those justifications have been asserted with the power of moral force. We are therefore urged by such a reflection to consider that even restricting the death penalty to the specific crime of aggravated murder is susceptible to misuse and should be greeted with suspicion. For in arguing that aggravated murder suffices to establish just cause for a use of the death penalty, we thereby concede that all those executions carried out in the course of human history for some reason other than aggravated murder lacked just cause, and thus could not claim moral justification. In recognizing that capital punishment has historically failed to satisfy the demand of just cause because use of the punishment has not been restricted to aggravated murder, we must note that capital punishment bears, then, a history of moral taint.

Socrates was not executed for aggravated murder; neither was Jesus. Neither was Steve Biko or Dietrich Bonhoeffer or any of the student protesters in Tiananmen Square whom the Chinese authorities sentenced to death. Historically, political communities have not only resorted to using the death penalty for the crime of political opposition or nonconformity, but they have done so believing they have good and compelling justifications for doing so. Making this point does not in itself undermine the claim that aggravated murder is a just cause for using the death penalty, but it reminds us that the power to execute is a power that can be wrongly used and that justifications for wrongful use can be the products of self-deception. If we assume that those who endorsed and carried out executions when aggravated murder was not the cause justified their actions even when their actions were immoral, then they did so having deceived themselves that they had satisfied just cause when in fact—according to our lights—they had not. If the history of justifying the death penalty is itself affected and marred by self-deception, that fact, too, is worth keeping in mind as we seek to assure ourselves today that we have finally established just cause and so defined it that abuse is unlikely.

But we can push the issue beyond a history of immoral practice and self-deceptive justification. The idea that capital punishment ought to be restricted to the specific crime of aggravated murder in order to establish the moral warrant of just cause is inherently problematic. The fact that American law has moved in this direction has not been accompanied by a compelling justification for executing those who commit such crimes. No obligation to execute the aggravated murderer has been established in law. In fact, just the opposite has occurred. Decisions to impose a mandatory death sentence for murder have been reversed on appeal, so whether one receives a death sentence will depend upon all kinds of factors and how they are weighed and weighted. Murder is universally wrong, and justice requires that murderers be punished. But justice does not require that murderers be executed as punishment for their crime. No moral obligation to punish by death those persons who satisfy America's determination of just cause can be identified, for many of those eligible under just cause are not subjected to death. Furthermore, such an obligation is not recognized in the wider moral community. The fact that American law recognizes a just cause for execution in aggravated murder does not morally compel Switzerland or England to do the same. The fact of relativity in the human moral community robs this criterion of any universal appeal or obligatory force.

Aggravated murder has not been established by moral argument to be a compelling just cause for justifying the execution of persons. In fact, the only reason that reason itself would recognize as compelling for a state-sponsored use of lethal force against members of the moral community would involve self-defense—the state acting to defend itself or those who are being threatened with unjust harm. Killing in self-defense or in defense of the innocent can be justified, but whether capital punishment can be reasonably construed to be an act of self-defense is highly questionable. For those individuals who have so threatened to harm others that by their threat they merit a response that would include deadly force *do not merit that response once they have been subdued and no longer pose a threat.* The threat to others must, from a moral point of view, be immediate. Once the threat is eliminated, punishment is in order, but not a continued justification for using deadly force.

Criminal offenders who have been captured, incarcerated, and deprived of the means whereby they can threaten harm to others lose the condition that logically invokes self-defense, so that arguing for the death penalty on grounds of self-defense misses its target empirically. If the response to this is that particular offenders ought to be executed because they continue to pose a threat to society, especially if they receive a parole that returns them to the streets where they will kill again, I say that is a problem with our criminal justice system, not a moral justification for execution killing. For the justice administration system can adopt policies that fail to deliver justice and fail to provide citizens with continued protection. Focusing on capital punishment as a way to correct failures in the administration of justice is a conceptual confusion that plays on a widespread public concern for safety. When this version of a "self-defense" argument is made, the suppressed—and sometimes not so suppressed—reason for capital punishment is not that we have now discerned in a period of moral enlightenment a duty or obligation to impose the death penalty but that we discern in the death penalty one sure means whereby the person subjected to it will be prevented from ever again inflicting harm on innocent persons.

The reason that capital punishment enjoys such high levels of support in the United States can be traced to the collision of the widespread fear of crime with an equally widespread suspicion that our criminal justice system is ineffective in controlling, reducing, and even punishing crime. Citizens have a natural right to expect their governing authorities to protect them from harm. They have a right to expect the governing authorities to enact laws and penal sanctions that punish criminal offenders while enhancing the public safety. Executing a criminal certainly eliminates any threat that a particular offender may pose as a potential repeat offender, and the prospect of such absolute action may generate a greater public sense of security and safety even though it is clearly established that murder is the least repeated felony offense. But the argument from self-defense and public safety can be satisfied short of execution if a defendant is in custody and deprived of the power to assault society or any individual within it. Incarceration adequately defends society from a threat of harm. There is no need for killing on top of that protection if justice is done in sentencing murderers to prison terms.

If the response comes back that the criminal justice system cannot be trusted to keep murderers in prison—the average murderer is released within six years[1]—then I want to point out that the ability of the law to keep convicted murderers in prison is not a moral issue about the moral warrants for capital punishment but a public policy citizens concerned with safety ought to take up with legislators. The criminal justice system is in need of reform—that is the hidden message to legislators and politicians when high marks appear in support of the death penalty. If the system needs greater consistency and continuity across the various jurisdictions, then reforming and improving the system so that it delivers and administers justice in greater conformity to the demands of justice is what is in order—not an exercise of state power to authorize the killing of people we fear will "beat the system" and go unpunished for their crimes.

A criminal justice system that was working effectively and consistently, and that was able to assure society that potential repeat offenders would not escape punishment, would satisfy the reasonable expectation—and the right—citizens have for protection and security from harm. Public discussion ought to be focusing on public policy issues, addressing the failures in our system of criminal justice administration and examining the complex causes of crime, rather than allowing capital punishment to serve as political code for concern about crime.

Capital punishment distracts us from debating public policy and addressing failures in our system of criminal justice administration. A society's failure to respond to crime in such a way that its citizens feel secure is an issue conceptually distinct from the debate over the moral meaning of capital punishment. The capital punishment debate is about the justifiability of a specific kind of killing burdened with a powerful moral presumption against such killing. That we should as a society justify the killing of members of the moral community—even those members guilty of heinous crimes—because we are skeptical that our justice system can deliver justice is a terrible indictment of our criminal justice system. But it is not a moral argument and certainly not a moral justification. The strongest just cause argument for capital punishment is self-defense—and it fails. Society can defend itself adequately—and even with retributive harshness—by demanding that offenders forfeit the very freedom they have abused in perpetrating crime.

On Justice, Not Vengeance, as Motivation

Just execution requires that punishment be motivated by a concern for justice because a wrong has been done. This is a motive distinct from vengeance, which does not require the presence of a wrong but can be incited for an injury, a perceived injury, even a slight.

Emotions, being interconnected with rationality and even a function of rationality itself,[2] can so grip an individual as to shape and define the person through the emotion: love can be like this, as well as jealousy and greed and hatred. Vengeance and the desire for revenge can clearly follow a logic of unchecked passion where no limits apply. This is quite the opposite of a retributive justice that seeks to redress wrong by connecting offenders with correct values, doing so through proportionate punishment imposed by authorities who have no personal ties to the victim of the wrongdoing.[3] Given that revenge can be a defining and holistic passion that flows from personal injury and lacks internal restraint, the desire for it can, where the death penalty is concerned, overpower the concern for justice. Where life and death are in the balance, the desire for vengeance can so affect one's judgment that, as Kant said, "we become implacable and think only of the damage and pain which we wish to the man who has harmed us, even though we do not thereby instil in him greater respect for our rights."[4]

The motivational criterion specified here is aimed at questioning whether the process that leads to a death sentence in individual cases can observe the requirement that impersonal justice be delivered without appealing to vengeful passion. Rendering the sentencing phase of a capital trial "objective" would clearly speak to the desire to remove undue emotional influence from sentencing deliberations, and in American law, the effort to avoid arbitrariness in imposing death sentences has led to the development of guidelines that a jury must use to evaluate a case and test the propriety of the death penalty. This is a process of "guided discretion," as *Gregg v. Georgia* described it, and what is at issue is not fact-finding, but moral evaluation. The aim is objectivity and even a formal dissociation from any kind of vengeance motivation. But the moral evaluation of the criminal's act is offered by persons who have been selected for the capital jury because they have passed a "death test" of jury eligibility, with the result that their objectivity is compromised by being disposed emotionally toward imposing the death penalty.

Impersonal justice free of passion is the objective of the law and sentencing guidelines, but sentencing practices can be shaped—even exploited—by all kinds of affective appeals. The desire for vengeance can be allowed to enter into sentencing deliberations, and the process, despite its guise of objectivity, can be manipulated so that affective factors will influence, perhaps even determine, sentencing decisions that are supposed to be free of the taint of vengeance.

A study of capital case jurors showed convincingly that inclusion of death penalty questions in jury selection introduced "systematic biases"[5] in those who witnessed other prospective jurors being asked questions about the death penalty. Subjects who witnessed such questioning were more likely to convict, more likely to hold that the judge and prosecutor were supportive of capital punishment, more likely to think that the law disapproved of people opposed to capital punishment. Since jurors exposed to seeing other jurors questioned about capital punishment were three times as likely to impose the death penalty as the control group not so questioned, this particular study yielded results that led the California Supreme Court to require that prospective jurors be questioned individually and apart from other jurors.

This criterion pertaining to motivation reminds us that the process of determining who should get the death penalty seeks to be free of subjective factors even though it is clear that it cannot be. The process of imposing the death penalty is highly subjective, highly manipulable, and highly susceptible to being influenced by authority figures who are perceived to support the death penalty.[6] Once a jury has completed fact-finding and convicted in a capital case, the sentencing process gets under way, with jurors being asked to consider any aggravating circumstances that might overrule any mitigating circumstances and thereby legitimate the imposition of death. Court instructions do not specify how much weight to give factors and how to compare them once weighted. The weighing process is, despite its appearance of objectivity, quite subjective. In many capital cases, weight is assigned to certain aggravating factors on the basis of passional excitation, which those seeking the death penalty deliberately seek to arouse.

Recall that prosecutors referred to Willie Darden as an animal. They asserted Darden's lack of humanity and the horror of his crime. The impact of that prosecutorial summary was not to argue deterrence but to inflame the jury to vengeance. What occurred in Darden's case is not uncommon. I have read appeals from attorneys protesting the inclusion of crime scene photos in the penalty phase of trials. Including such photos in the penalty phase of a trial inevitably generates appeals, for the deliberate reflection required to devise a just sentence is compromised as the horror of a crime scene is introduced to affect psychological and emotional arousal. The aim is to affect rational deliberation by arousing a passion for vengeance, as if the horror of a crime scene makes the fact that a member of the moral community has been unjustly deprived of the good of life—the central moral horror—worse. Practical reason's demand for justice in sentencing is thrown open to whichever side in the adversarial process is most adept in swaying by means of emotional appeal. Those defendants able to acquire representation adept at playing the "emotion card" have a better chance of deflecting a death sentence than those who, like Willie Darden, face a courtroom of bias with no skilled help available. Justice demands that no defendant be subjected to the dehumanizing disrespect Darden received in his trial. All the arguments in a sentencing phase are directed toward creating in the jury an affective state that will direct deliberations and evaluation. As has been noted from a study of prosecutors, "the overall pattern of their arguments in the penalty phase suggested that they perceived the emotional dimensions of the decision to be paramount."[7] An appeal to emotion in this way is an appeal to vengeance, and the appeal to vengeance, directed as it is toward jurors selected for their support of the death penalty, works against the ideal of impartially and dispassionately rendering a decision where a life is at stake.

If fairness based on practical reason is the ideal, just execution would demand that justice be attended to, with no victim's life more important than another's, with no defendant's humanity being allowed to be assaulted. Extrapolating from Kant, inflicting punishment from a desire only to cause harm to the defendant for what the defendant has done, without thereby instilling in that defendant greater respect for the rights the defendant is accused of violating, is to fall into a consuming passion directed toward vengeance. And the negative and destructive power of vengeance cancels the positive and creative call for justice. Any decision to execute a human person arising from a desire to exact vengeance rather than impose a just punishment aimed at connecting the condemned to correct values necessarily fails to satisfy the criterion of a just execution. Wherever decisions about imposing death sentences are affected by emotional manipulations at the expense of impartial and dispassionate evaluation, this criterion cannot often or even usually be satisfied.

On Fair Imposition

It is a continuing debate whether the death penalty is fairly imposed. A just execution theory would require that the process involved in capital punishment not be affected by bias or unfairness. Claims that racial, sexual, or class discrimination affects the process of imposing the death penalty would subvert the argument that capital punishment serves the end of justice.

Patrick Langan, a statistician with the Bureau of Justice Statistics, looked into the problem of racial bias in the criminal justice system and concluded that racism no longer constitutes a significant variable in how individuals are arrested, prosecuted, adjudicated, and sentenced.[8] Langan acknowledges a history of racism in the justice system, yet argues that prosecutors do not prosecute black offenders at higher rates than whites and judges do not dispense longer sentences to blacks than whites. The average sentence received by blacks convicted of a felony is five and a half years, one month longer than whites receive. Although blacks convicted of a felony receive a prison sentence in 51 percent of cases compared to 38 percent of white defendants, Langan concludes that those blacks had been convicted of more violent crimes than whites. Accordingly, they were likely to receive stiffer sentences, and more blacks than whites are repeat offenders. Langan claims that an "aggravating effect" can be discerned in sentencing that has skewed statistical perception of racial bias because jurisdictions differ in how they sentence: black defendants are more likely to be sentenced in jurisdictions where sentences are in general tougher for both blacks and whites. Given that one in three convicted blacks but only one in five convicted whites were in these harsher sentencing jurisdictions, Langan concludes that racial disparity in sentencing is only appearance, and that it can be explained by the fact that blacks are convicted of more serious offenses, have longer criminal records, and are sentenced in areas where harsher sentences are imposed on all defendants.

Langan does not investigate discrimination and the death penalty, but it is clearly reasonable to infer that the appearance of a statistical racial disparity has *something* to do with race, although, admittedly, we may have to discern racial bias in some way other than simply comparing the number of whites in prison or on death row versus the number of blacks.

A theory of just execution requires that the death penalty be imposed fairly. Yet, if it is reasonable to conclude that discrimination still infects the capital punishment process, it also follows that this particular criterion of just execution is not satisfied and that particular death penalty sentences affected by discrimination cannot be justified. And if there is evidence that the death penalty is, as an instrument of societal policy, inherently discriminatory, then capital punishment as a form of killing would be morally disallowed. In three areas persuasive evidence of discrimination in imposing the death sentence is apparent. Let me briefly indicate some "discrimination factors" in the areas of race, gender, and class.

Race

Whites make up 48 percent of the death row population, blacks 41 percent, so those who claim more whites than blacks are sentenced to death row are right. But blacks make up 12 percent of the population, so the death penalty falls disproportionately on blacks given general population figures. The argument could be made that blacks commit a disproportionate number of capital crimes. What must be factored into this charge is the fact that in some southern states where capital punishment is often imposed, African Americans make up 60 percent of homicide victims. Yet over 80 percent of the cases in which the death penalty has been carried out involved white victims.[9]

It might be true that a disproportionate number of blacks receive death sentences because a disproportionate number of blacks commit capital crimes. That argument would dispense with the charge of racism. But it is the system of imposing the death sentence that is under scrutiny with regard to the fair imposition criterion, so that we must look elsewhere for evidence of racism—beyond the apparent disproportion of numbers of blacks on death row. And where we find evidence to justify the inference of racism infecting the capital punishment system is in the examination of the "race of victim" factor.

A 1990 study by David Baldus of the University of Iowa revealed that even after thirty-nine nonracial factors were taken into account in 2500 Georgia murder cases between 1973 and 1979, defendants charged with killing white victims were more likely to receive a death sentence than defendants charged with killing a black victim.[10] The capital sentencing rate for all white victim cases was 11 times greater than the rate for black victim cases: blacks who killed whites were sentenced to death nearly 22 times the rate of blacks who killed blacks, and more than 7 times the rate of whites who killed blacks. Prosecutors, according to the study, sought the death penalty for 70 percent of black defendants with white victims but for only 15 percent of black defendants with black victims.

As of April 1991, in 144 executions carried out in the United States after the 1976 reinstatement of the death penalty, not one white person was executed for killing a black. In that population of the actually executed, 92 percent of the victims were white.[11] Of the over sixteen thousand—other sources say close to eighteen thousand—legal executions in the course of American history, only thirty cases involved a white sentenced for killing a black,[12] and some of those executions were not for murder since they occurred in the time of slavery and the executions were undertaken as punishment for destroying property. The U.S. Supreme Court accepted the validity of evidence that in Georgia those who murder whites were 11 times more likely to receive the death sentence than those who kill blacks—and it was the "Georgia way," the Court noted—and that blacks who kill whites were 3 times more likely to face execution.

The strongest evidence of racial bias appears in the race of the victim, and one anecdotal example shows how this can function on a local level. Since 1976, the district attorney in Columbus, Georgia, has sought the death penalty in 38 percent of murders in which the victim was white and the defendant was black. But in cases in which the defendant was white and the victim was black, not one death penalty prosecution has occurred. The death penalty was sought in 48 percent of cases in which a white woman was murdered but in only 9 percent of cases in which a black woman was the victim. In Georgia in general, 87 percent of all cases where the death penalty is sought involve white victims, though only 40 percent of homicides involve white victims. In Florida, blacks who kill whites receive the death penalty 22 percent of the time compared to whites who kill whites, where death is imposed in only 4.6 percent of cases.[13] In Maryland, killers of whites are eight times more likely to get the death sentence than killers of blacks; in Arkansas, six times more likely, and in Texas five times more likely.[14]

It is no wonder that a 1990 report of the General Accounting Office found that there exists "'a pattern of evidence indicating racial disparities in the charging, sentencing, and imposition of the death penalty. . . . In 82 percent of the studies, race of victim was found to influence the likelihood of being charged with capital murder or receiving the death penalty.'"[15]

What Langan has to say about felony convictions and racial bias may be true for felony crime in general, but death penalty cases reveal a persistent "race of victim" effect that shows up in all manner of controlled studies, so that the evidence is clear on this point: killing a white person is much more likely to result in a death sentence than killing a black person.[16]

Racial disparity in death row statistics can reasonably be attributed, therefore, to racial factors, which the "fair imposition" criterion of just execution theory would disallow.

One last point. The United States was, with South Africa, the only industrialized Western nation to have the death penalty. South Africa abolished it in February of 1990. Prior to abolition, South Africa boasted one of the world's highest rates of execution frequency, with over twelve hundred persons put to death between 1980 and 1989. South African use of the death penalty demonstrated a "race of victim" effect similar to that in the United States. In 1988, 47 percent of black defendants accused of murdering whites were sentenced to death, with 2.5 percent of blacks convicted of murdering other blacks so sentenced. Not one white convicted of killing a black person was given the death penalty in that nine-year period.[17]

Gender

Race is not the only form of discrimination. Of the over three thousand inmates on death row in 1996, forty-nine (or 1.5 percent) were women. Mothers kill their children in the United States an average of 600 times per year, or 12,600 times since 1976, but since 1976 only four women convicted of that crime have been put on death row. None has been executed. Most women on death row are there for killing a husband or lover. In 1990, documented evidence of battering was available in each case of a woman sent to death row for having committed such a murder, but no jury was presented with a self-defense argument or was allowed to hear testimony about battered woman syndrome.[18] Only three women have been executed since 1976, and only thirty women since 1930.

It is clear that a gender bias is working in favor of women with respect to actual numbers of persons executed for capital crimes. There is prima facie evidence from these numbers to indicate sexual discrimination in the imposition of the death penalty. I do not know of a well-thought-out feminist critique of this kind of discrimination, but cultural reluctance to execute women, while it may be rooted in chivalry, probably points to a deep sexism that expresses a paternalism or imposed infantilism that refuses to value women as fully responsible moral agents. It is bizarre to consider, but the presence of this discrimination yields the conclusion that reluctance to kill women through legal execution is also evidence of American society's devaluing of women.

My focus here is on the death penalty and not other justice issues that arise in consideration of women and criminality. I recognize that few women convicted of killing their abusive partners are acquitted and that up to 80 percent are convicted or plea-bargain, often receiving unduly harsh and long sentences. In fact, the evidence is clear that women who commit "counter-type, 'manly' offenses are as likely as men to serve lengthy sentences."[19] This harshness, however, does not extend to imposition of the death penalty. The failure of a woman's claim to self-defense when a killing occurs as a response to battering is clearly a justice issue that demands attention, but so is the fact that a large body of research evidence suggests that in general men, especially black men, are more likely to be incarcerated than are women.[20]

A sex bias is discernible in the criminal justice system, but my point is that the bias against executing women is pronounced. Though it favors women, it is discrimination nonetheless—sexual discrimination—especially if we know over twelve thousand instances of mothers killing their children have occurred and no mother has been executed for that crime. If we consider this sex bias in light of the racial discrimination noted above, we can reasonably conclude that the death penalty is falling most heavily as a percentage of population on black males. The moral point at issue is this: A system of execution that fails to confront cultural biases and impose penal sentences fairly, evenhandedly, and without discrimination is, according to this criterion of just execution, morally impermissible.

Class

The Death Penalty Information Center established that in 1991 more than 90 percent of those on death row were financially unable to hire an attorney to represent them at trial.[21] If the likelihood of receiving the death penalty increases in the face of an inability to hire attorneys able to invest time and resources in presenting an adequate defense, then we must note a discrimination factor relative to poverty. This points to a financial or class bias—that the death penalty falls disproportionately on the indigent. And on the uneducated, since 60 percent of those on death row never completed high school.[22] Of the three thousand individuals on death row I am unaware of any who would be considered wealthy.

Just execution demands nondiscrimination, yet evidence of discrimination in imposing the death penalty exists in three categories: race, gender, and class. In its various decisions on capital punishment the Supreme Court has demanded revision of the procedures that lead to the imposing of a death sentence, but it seems that little has changed since 1976. Those awaiting execution today are no different from those who faced it prior to the "legal evolution" that commenced with *Furman v. Georgia:* they are still the poor, the uneducated, minorities, males, and persons suffering mental impairment.

American law addresses discrimination, and through constitutional provisions seeks to protect persons from unfairness before the law. The sad fact about American law, however, is that the process of establishing discrimination has been made difficult in capital cases, so much so, in fact, that proving discrimination under current law is easier to do to save a person's job than to save a person's life. The whole system of capital punishment is fraught with discriminatory practices that have been ruled legally tolerable and permissible. But they are not morally tolerable or morally permissible.

Furthermore, there is a hidden discrimination in the death penalty process— prosecutorial discretion. Los Angeles prosecutors, recall, decided not to seek the death penalty in the O. J. Simpson case—not for reasons concerning the fair imposition of justice but because prosecutors accepted that fairness was not possible. It is prosecutorial discretion that allows two homicides of similar type to be disposed of in quite different ways in different jurisdictions. The exercise of this discretion allows a disproportionate number of minorities and poor persons to face death sentences. In the view of Representative Henry Gonzales, inconsistencies in the legal system have made capital punishment a "grotesque lottery."

Sufficient evidence of bias and discrimination is available to draw the reasonable conclusion that capital punishment does not satisfy the fair imposition criterion required for the state to act consistently with a theory of just execution.

On the Prohibition against Cruelty

A death sentence under law authorizes the state to execute persons, not to torture them. The Kantian standard of so acting toward the condemned that their fundamental humanity is not demeaned is essential to just execution, and even methods of execution must conform to this standard.

Many methods of execution are disallowed on this criterion, not only morally but legally. Cruelty is prohibited. The U.S. Supreme Court decided in *In re Kemmler* that "punishments are cruel when they involve torture or a lingering death; but the punishment of death is not cruel. . . . [Cruelty] implies there is something inhuman and barbarous, something more than the mere extinguishing of life."[23]

Modern methods of execution have attempted to meet this requirement that death be delivered without unnecessary pain or cruelty. Electrocution, the gas chamber, and lethal injection were all introduced as methods that would satisfy this demand for quick, painless, and decent execution.

But cruelty has not been eliminated. Electric chairs are notorious for malfunctioning. In 1946, a seventeen-year-old male facing execution in the Louisiana electric chair petitioned the U.S. Supreme Court to prevent his being subjected to a second execution attempt. The first one had failed due to technical problems. Willie Francis had been prepared for execution, placed in the chair, and rocked with two jolts of electricity. He was not killed and complained of the terrible physical discomfort of the experience. As Sheriff Harold Resweber described it, "Then the electrocutioner turned on the switch and when he did Willie Francis's lips puffed out and he groaned and jumped so that the chair came off the floor. . . . The condemned man yelled, 'Take it off. Let me breathe.'"[24] In a 5-4 decision the U.S. Supreme Court conceded that this first execution attempt did cause "mental anguish and physical pain," but because these effects were not deliberate but "an unforeseeable accident," the Court held that the Constitution was not offended in its prohibition on cruel and unusual punishment. Willie Francis was told he would be subjected to execution a second time. And he was. The second attempt succeeded.

While lethal injection may conform to American society's current standard of decency as legally defined, the indignities and terrors that attend all the methods currently in use to kill by direct, deliberate, and violent action a member of the moral community gravitate against allowing the "prohibition on cruelty" standard to go unchallenged. And, as we know from many botched lethal injections, no method of execution is foolproof with regard to assuring quick and painless dispatch. Which executions will be botched—possibly even by a malevolent executioner—cannot be anticipated, so that any execution is potentially cruel. This fact would seem to lend weight to the moral presumption against execution rather than serve to help lift that presumption in the interests of a just execution.

But more is at stake in the cruelty issue than execution method. In 1973 Amnesty International offered this definition of torture: "Torture is the systematic and deliberate infliction of acute pain *in any form* by one person on another, or on a third person, in order to accomplish the purpose of the former against the will of the latter."[25] The United Nations Declaration Against Torture adopted in 1975 furthered this notion by saying torture "means any act by which severe pain or suffering, whether physical or mental, is intentionally inflicted by or at the instigation of a public official on a person for such purposes as obtaining from him or a third person information or confession, punishing him for an act he has committed, or intimidating him or other persons."[26]

On these definitions, a strong case can be made that torture attends death row confinement and isolation, which become as much a part—even more—of the punishment as the execution itself. The death row experience, which can be drawn out over many years, subjects the inmate to conditions that enforce a sense of powerlessness. Inmates can be harassed by prison officials, suffer from extreme isolation in the face of an uncertain fate, and experience psychic debilitation and physical exhaustion. Basic needs can be ignored, including the need for medical services. Physical complaints are sometimes dismissed by prison officials, who feel under no obligation to acknowledge a death row prisoner's complaint. In late 1996 in Tennessee, a death row inmate, Terry Barber, complained of acute pains in his back, and had difficulty receiving medical attention. Not only did he have to pay $3.00 to make a trip to the infirmary, but he was mistakenly diagnosed as suffering a pinched nerve and given nothing more than Motrin. Prison officials can ignore complaints from prisoners on the grounds that the prisoner is simply seeking drugs—an "institutional attitude" toward the prisoner that denies the prisoner basic respect and assumes prisoner dishonesty. Barber's pain became excruciating. Rev. Joseph Ingle, a minister with over twenty years' experience on death row and one of Barber's regular visitors, demanded that Barber be taken from the prison for X rays. The medical examination revealed that Barber had metastatic lung cancer. His pain was caused by the cancer eviscerating his spine, so immobilizing him that prior to intervention he had been forced to lie in his own feces and urine. Barber died not long after diagnosis.[27] Death row confinement justifies ignoring such complaints only if the powerlessness of the inmate is accepted and a process of dehumanization is at work.

Death row confinement is a kind of torture: "The goal of this confinement regime, and indeed of all forms of torture, whether explicit or not, is to 'destroy the victim's personality, to break him down.' To 'break' a person means, quite simply, to 'destroy his humanity'—that is, to literally dehumanize him, often completely. . . . Under no lawful punishment can offenders be treated in this way."[28]

The law, as we have noted, can authorize what morality cannot. The process of dehumanization violates, from a moral point of view, the "respect for person" principle that a just execution theory requires, for morality can justify no act of torture that would add to the infliction of pain and assault on a person's dignity as a person, even when the person in question is a death row inmate. Since 1973, forty-four inmates on death row found a way to commit suicide; others, desiring death, volunteer for execution and drop their appeals. The effect of death row confinement can be discerned in how news of a commutation is received. Since 1973, 1,519 inmates have had their convictions reversed, and 74 received commutations.[29] One person who received a last-minute commutation, Isidore Zimmerman, responded to the news this way:

> I didn't believe it. What was more I didn't care. For nine long months I'd been rehearsing my death, dying a little every day, dying a little more every night, while just up the hall from my cell they were killing men, thirteen of them. I knew my role as victim too well, knew it by heart, couldn't back down now. "I don't want clemency," I heard myself saying.[30]

This infliction of pain by lengthy confinement on death row constitutes cruelty, presenting the terrible paradox of capital punishment we have previously noted. On the one hand, the pre-execution confinement, because it is so lengthy, subjects prisoners to dehumanizing isolation. On the other hand, preventing the moral horror of wrongful execution requires extensive legal review. Appeals are time-consuming, occasioning many delays. But shortening the appeals process to make death row confinement less protracted and consequently more humane would come at the expense of concern for justice. Just execution begins to fade as a real possibility on the horns of this dilemma.

On Last Resort

Of all the conditions required for just execution, last resort seems the most difficult to satisfy. For if we consider one description of capital punishment, what is going on this: A person in a condition of confinement and powerlessness posing no immediate threat to others is deliberately killed. There is no moral obligation to do so. If a criminal offender who has harmed persons and threatened the security and welfare of society has been captured, then subjected to incarceration so that no actual threat can attach, the idea of executing this person as a last resort is counterintuitive if not altogether preposterous.

As already argued, the failure of a criminal justice system to deliver justice and provide for the public safety in no way constitutes a positive moral argument for justifying capital punishment. All this kind of argument does is establish the need to improve and reform the system of justice administration so that citizens can reasonably expect that justice will be done and the threat posed by criminal offenders will be effectively neutralized. That a society lacks confidence in its criminal justice system is not an argument for capital punishment, and to make it one is a conceptual confusion.

I would go even further. I would go so far as to say that in the face of this argument, capital punishment is not only not justified, but ironically, the very appeal to it in such a circumstance represents one more failure of the system. Any system of justice administration that advocates capital punishment as the corrective to its own ineffectiveness continues to express its ineffectiveness by appealing to capital punishment as the corrective needed to make the system work. Capital punishment, because it is restricted to aggravated murder and is rarely inflicted relative to the number of crimes committed each year, even relative to the number of homicides, will not and cannot possibly transform an ineffective justice system. Arguing last resort in the face of justice administration failure distracts us from attributing responsibility to the elected officials whose job it is to attend to those failures and correct them. Capital punishment is offered as a quick shorthand acknowledgment of the failures of justice administration while also being a means by which accountability for those failures can be directed away from those responsible for correcting them.

The last resort argument based on a societal admission that its justice administration system is ineffective is more sad than it is absurd. Capital punishment is never a last resort. The demands of justice can be satisfied in even the most extreme cases without resorting to a state-sponsored killing, as all those countries that have abolished capital punishment have recognized. There are always alternatives to capital punishment, alternatives that will satisfy the demands of even a harsh retributive justice.

On Preserving Values

Although defenders of the death penalty will—and should, because of this criterion—make the case that the death penalty aims at protecting and enhancing the preeminent value of life and in no way subverts it, this is not an argument grounded in empirical reality. An opposing argument, at least as rational but also nonempirical, would claim that responding to the act of killing by killing the killer adds to the killing and logically perpetuates a cycle of violence. The argument could be made that such killing contributes to anesthetizing the society to the killing that occurs in capital punishment, the result being that no moral horror—or even a sense of tragedy at the loss of life—attaches to the legalized killing of capital punishment. Were that to be the result, the argument that capital punishment contributes to a subversion of the value of life could be advanced with some confidence.

I think there is reason for holding to such a position. My citizen's perception is that the loss of life that occurs in capital punishment is not greeted with a sense of tragic loss, for even defenders of the death penalty should want to express that an execution is tragic. And it is tragic because a life has been lost. Even those who support capital punishment and deem it a just action should still—out of respect for this criterion of just punishment—logically acknowledge that it is a terrible thing to exact a life by execution.

But I detect no such reaction to capital punishment. I detect indifference, even satisfaction; and sometimes, as in the vile scenes of persons making merry outside the prisons where the executions are performed, actual celebration—celebration of a killing. Such reactions demonstrate that in those who experience either indifference or joy that a killing has occurred, the value of life is being subverted. This constitutes limited empirical evidence for subversion even if it is also anecdotal, and the fact is that we do not have a serious gauge of how deeply some of these attitudes go.[31] But to the extent they are present, a reasonable case can be made that capital punishment contributes to the subversion of the value of life. Furthermore, practical reason finds this conclusion much easier to draw than the paradoxical and contrary position articulated by Orrin Hatch that society shows its respect for the value for life by killing those who kill. Such a view provokes the charge of inconsistency, even hypocrisy; for at least the appearance of hypocrisy attaches to the claim that society can justifiably inflict as a means of promoting respect for the value of life the very act of direct and deliberate killing that it claims to deplore.

As much truth as there might be in this position, no expression of this way of thinking can evade evoking paradox and even actual contradiction. The opposite viewpoint—that *refraining from killing* is logically consistent with seeking to promote the value of life—is not paradoxical; neither does it require mental gymnastics to understand. In the absence of empirical data that would convincingly substantiate one side of this argument over the other, there is at least good logical support for the noncontradictory and consistent view that the killing that occurs in capital punishment subverts rather than supports respect for the value of life.

On the End of Peace and Social Harmony

The case is often made that capital punishment has a salutary effect on society and on the surviving victims of capital crimes. Just execution theory would include this consequentialist effect as a necessary criterion, since the good to be gained by restoring peace to society and to the individuals devastated by the loss of loved ones who have been victims of capital crimes is a positive good that would strengthen the effort to lift the presumption against capital punishment. The case needs to be made, however, that capital punishment promotes the welfare and peace of society and relieves surviving victims of the pain associated with the terrible loss they have experienced. Just execution would require that the utilitarian aim of attaining societal peace be effected, and that those affected by loss through capital crimes receive emotional and psychic comfort from knowing that the capital criminal has been punished in the extreme and is dead.

This argument is not empirically based, and neither will my argument against it be. But the claim that society is rendered peaceful by capital punishment policy seems counterintuitive, since capital punishment continues the cycle of violence begun by the capital criminal's violent acts. This could actually reinforce the sense that violence is an acceptable solution for violence. Recognizing that peace is in part sustained by the association of just punishment with a restraint of power and reliance on nonviolent means of punishment, we can infer that capital punishment undermines this association and harks back to schemes of justice where society has inflicted violence on its designated criminals, attacking their bodily integrity and assaulting their human dignity. Systems of justice administration that have sanctioned corporal punishment or literal "eye for an eye" cruelty have been repudiated in the humanitarian advance of civilization and in the evolution of law; so that the presence of such a use of violence hints at atavistic barbarism and undermines reliance on the nonviolence that is logically consistent with the end of peace. This is a logical rather than an empirical point, but it is not unreasonable to conclude that the end of peace is not advanced by a society willing to resort to violent force to solve problems when there is no logical or moral requirement that it do so.

And the idea that individual survivors of a capital crime—those who have lost a loved one to murder—can receive psychic peace as the result of knowing that the killer has been killed strikes me as a psychologically confused notion. Survivors of capital crime will undoubtedly fantasize about "killing the killer." They may focus on the offender in the aftermath of tragedy as a way to redirect or postpone grief or channel the tragedy of their loss. But the loss of a loved one to murder is so emotionally devastating and psychologically crushing an event that no action short of restoring life to the loved one can realistically mitigate the pain of that loss, not even "killing the killer." Responding to a killing by yearning for more killing hardly seems a realistic means for effecting a restoration of psychic peace.

The easy psychology that claims that killing killers effects peace for the surviving victims does no justice to the depth of grief experienced by those who lose loved ones to murder. That is a grief that no execution should have power to assuage. That is a grief so severe that it has actually occasioned suicide among victim survivors. A recently published article reported: "Almost every relative of a murder victim fantasizes about seeking revenge. But the vast majority of Americans are unwilling to kill, no matter how great their anger and outrage. A number of POMC [Parents of Murdered Children] have taken their own lives, however. One young mother went to the cemetery and committed suicide on her son's grave."[32]

The loss of a loved one by violent killing is a terrible and tragic loss; and so long as justice is done and the perpetrator is rendered harmless and even subjected to retribution for such a crime, I should think that the grief process could play itself out without feeling the need for more death. There are many survivors of capital crime who do not wish the execution of those who have killed a loved one. We can recognize the natural desire for revenge, but moral sensibilities will not demand more violence when what is most desired is that violence come to an end and peace be restored. Those victims of crime who announce their desire to pull the switch and act as the actual agent of execution do not strike me as persons psychologically prepared to receive peace by committing such an act, and that is meant to be a psychological observation independent of the view that it would be frightening if such an action did bring closure to grief, instill peace, and restore society to the equilibrium upset by the condemned person's criminal offense. It is justice and not more killing that will move society and individuals to the end of peace.

On Proportionality

Just execution theory will require that capital punishment be imposed as a proportionate punishment, an extreme penalty to fit an extreme crime. Three arguments can be made against the case that capital punishment is a proportionate punishment.

First, if crime is, from a moral point of view, an abuse of freedom, punishment should be directed at the moral personality that has, in committing a crime, abused its freedom to harm others. Fitting a proportionate response to the extreme crime of murder does not necessitate that the killer be killed any more than it necessitates that those who cause injury to others should suffer the same injury themselves—that we ought to blind those who cause blindness, or knock out the teeth of those who in a brawl knock others' teeth out, or rape those who rape. Criminal acts are from a moral point of view wrongful to the extent that they express an abuse of freedom, so that any abuse of freedom, from the slightest offense to the most grave, is to be dealt with proportionately by restricting freedom in accordance with the severity of the crime. The proportionate punishment for abusing freedom is to take freedom away, and this constitutes a moral justification for incarceration: it is retributive punishment that locates responsibility for crime in an individual's abuse of freedom and responds to that abuse by depriving the offender of freedom proportionate to the offense committed.

A consistent application of the proportionality requirement would require that the most serious restrictions on freedom attach to the most serious crimes. While capital punishment is often justified as the extreme penalty for the extreme crime, there are other factors in the American criminal justice system that subvert this view and challenge it. For the fact is that inconsistencies in the American criminal justice system would lead a reasonable observer to conclude that murder is not the most extreme crime in this society, since the average murderer is released after spending just over six years in prison.[33] Such a short restraint on freedom seems disproportionate to the severity of the crime, and once again should turn our thoughts toward reform of the justice administration system. How can the average murderer be released after only six years in prison, while a select few—the poor, the poorly defended, the uneducated, the minority—find themselves on death row condemned to death? Awareness of this inconsistency directs us to consider whether—and how—we observe proportionality in our American practice of the death penalty.

Related to this idea of proportional punishment, I would once again assert that capital punishment does not punish the moral personality so much as obliterate it; and it obliterates it by destroying the body. Capital punishment cannot be kept focused on the abuse of freedom committed by the moral personality, as proportionality requires—it necessarily focuses on the successful destruction of the body, which becomes the true objective of the execution itself. I say this because if the aim of punishment were the obliteration of the moral personality, that end could be accomplished short of execution. It could be done by, say, surgical lobotomy or some other mind-scrambling effort that would in effect destroy the moral personality and thereby permanently prevent any reappearance of the criminal offender. But that kind of response is not entertained for the simple reason that destruction of the moral personality is not the true object of capital punishment—the object is destruction of the body. Proportionality insists that those who abuse their freedom to harm others be punished, with the worst offenses receiving the worst punishments. By destroying the body and the good of life itself, the death penalty responds disproportionately to the abuse of freedom that any criminal act expresses.

Second, the proportionality criterion goes directly to the question of justice. For the sake of argument I have accepted throughout this discussion the appropriateness of retributive justice, the idea that retribution is appropriate as a defense of punishment and has a place in any theory of just execution. "A retributive theory of punishment," writes Jeffrie G. Murphy, "is one which characterizes punishment primarily in terms of the concepts of justice, rights, and desert—i.e., is concerned with the just punishment, the punishment the criminal deserves, the punishment society has a right to inflict (and the criminal has the right to expect)."[34] The idea of retribution—that punishment is an end in itself—has a role to play in a theory of just execution, for in its appeal to desert, it entails the idea that justice is served when more severe crimes receive a proportionately more severe punishment.

But retribution and the proportionality it entails do not provide adequate grounds for defending capital punishment on moral grounds. There is no objective standard by which punishments can be proportioned to fit a crime. In support of that claim I would once again remind my reader of the overwhelming evidence of a lack of proportionality in our use of the death penalty. Not only is there evidence that murder is not the most extreme crime in light of the average six-year prison term served by those convicted of murder, but we have noted how a discretionary justice system finds reasons to exempt from facing the death penalty the overwhelming majority—almost 99 percent—of those who have committed the crime of killing another human being. Estimates are that there are about a hundred thousand convicted murderers locked up in America's prisons, with another eight hundred thousand murderers living free in American society.[35] The three hundred persons sent to death row each year on the grounds that they are the ones who should receive the sentence proportionate to their crime are those who have proved unable to work the "discretionary" system of justice administration to their advantage, and their ability to do so may be tied to their ability to pay, since 90 percent of death row inmates could not afford a lawyer. There is no rational basis for holding that there is an objective standard by which punishments can be proportioned to fit crimes: our system is ad hoc and subject to rampant subjectivity, as I have argued. Kant made an objective appeal by demanding—and mandating—the death penalty for all who commit the crime of murder, but American society has explicitly rejected any such mandatory sentence for the crime of murder. And as much as Kant sought to meet an objectivity standard, he succeeded in exposing the price of such objectivity as so high few would willingly pay it.

Not only has there never been a rational connection between severity of crime and severity of punishment, but proportionality as practiced in the American justice system undermines the retributivist principle that persons should be punished because they deserve to be, with the more severe crime receiving the more severe punishment.

Retribution not only fails to provide a moral foundation for capital punishment, but it squeezes from our view other relevant notions of justice that might be preferable to it and that are deserving of wider societal debate. Among those notions would be "punitive restitution," where criminals make restitution to their victims or, where capital crimes are concerned, to the surviving families of victims. Lack of attention to victim compensation is a major flaw in contemporary retribution-based systems, but a restorative justice system, where restitution to victims is a major objective of punishment, could reshape the purpose and intent of punishment, perhaps even reviving interest in rehabilitation and turning departments of correction into departments worthy of the name. This much seems certain: execution necessarily confines justice to retribution, and restorative justice is summarily excluded from consideration. The question is not only whether proportionality can be served without resorting to state killing, but whether justice itself is broader than retribution. If it is, then executing human persons becomes a way of executing justice—in the sense of so restricting and confining it as to kill it.

Capital punishment cuts off any possibility of an offender making restitution of any sort to the surviving victims of the capital crime—and retributive justice ignores this dimension. This is not the place to explore restorative justice and victim restitution, though significant discussions are under way in the scholarly literature, and practical projects in various communities in the United States (even my own) are seeking to enact the restorative ideal. I mention restorative justice only to point out that such a notion can preserve proportionality while tying severity of punishment to severity of crime. Retributive state-sponsored execution eliminates the possibility of addressing the need for just restitution to surviving victims.

A proportionality tied to retributive justice fails to provide a positive justification for capital punishment and only succeeds in exposing the retribution model itself as a limited, even deficient, servant of justice.

Third, consideration must be given to the fact that proportionality is a notion influenced by cultural and historical differences. Just execution demands proportionality, but the history of the death penalty is not a history of proportionality. American law has until recently[36] restricted the death penalty to the crime of murder, this being the most grievous crime for which execution, the most serious sentence, is reserved. But this is a recent development, and this particular view of proportionality is not universally observed in the world today.

Consider the case of China. In 1996, China executed 4,370 persons, twice the number of the year before and more than all the other legal executions in the world. Many of those executed were put to death for nonviolent crimes such as embezzlement, fraud, and theft. Among those put to death were three men who had attempted—and failed—to steal value-added-tax receipts from a tax office, and purloiners of ballpoint pens and badminton rackets.[37]

Overlooking the history of past disproportionate death sentences in America—from the first execution demanded by law for the theft of a calf—America can now claim that proportionality is currently observed in that the death penalty is restricted to murder. But *no moral necessity attaches even to this restriction;* for example, Florida uses execution but Wisconsin does not, and internationally, China uses execution without this restriction, whereas England and France have abolished the death penalty entirely. Whoever uses the death penalty for whatever reason does so on the grounds that the death penalty is merited as a sentence proportionate to the crime. America may argue with China's notion of proportionality, but, by the same token, France could argue with America's. And France could do so because proportionality does not itself require death sentences even for the most severe crimes. Nonlethal means can satisfy the proportionality requirement that the most grave crimes be met with the most severe sentences.

Just execution theory demands that the death sentence satisfy a proportionality requirement. There is no objective standard to establish proportionality across legal jurisdictions or in response to a timeless and noncontingent moral truth, even that touted as truth at present in the United States, namely, restricting capital punishment to murder. There is no evidence from history to indicate that our current understanding of proportionality held sway as an obvious moral justification in the past, nor any reason to believe that it can in the future. American laws are already expanding the use of execution, pointing to the historical truth that a society cannot restrict use of the death penalty to some very specific crime without still allowing all kinds of discretion to affect the practice of fitting individuals to that "proportionate" sentence.

There is neither a moral nor a logical argument necessitating the conclusion that demanding the forfeiture of a person's life for a crime, even deliberate murder with malice, satisfies a proportionality requirement, not if the formal requirement of proportionality is that the most serious crimes be given the most serious punishments. Execution is not morally demanded, since there is clearly no moral obligation to kill human beings as punishment for breaking laws, even those involving the most serious violations. (Here the fact that the average murderer in the United States is released after serving a six-year sentence casts doubt even on the idea that murder is the "most serious" crime: first-time nonviolent drug offenders serve an average of six and a half years in federal prison.[38]) And there is no logical necessity to impose a death penalty as the most severe punishment if a moral presumption exists against the direct and intentional killing of persons and alternatives exist that can provide a fitting punishment proportionate to the crime.

Conclusion

Capital punishment is a legal and social policy issue, but because it involves the direct and deliberate killing of a human being, it is first of all a moral issue. Such a killing demands—and always demands—moral justification.

I have argued that the clear moral presumption against capital punishment explains why Americans seek a death penalty in only about three hundred of twenty-three-thousand homicide cases per year. It is in relation to this presumption against capital punishment that just execution emerges as a viable moral theory to explain the practice. In the reluctance to impose the death penalty on the vast majority of potentially eligible candidates for execution, the moral presumption against execution shows itself at work, but it is a presumption and not an absolute prohibition. Just execution as a proposed theory of nonabsolutist and moderate moral analysis has so developed that it will confirm that presumption and respect its weight. But being a presumption and not a prohibition, just execution is possible, and that possibility is created by strictly observing safeguards designed to prevent the presumption from being lifted lightly or without due attention to the demands for justice. In terms of just execution theory, capital punishment can be justified even if it cannot always be justified. On the theory, one could say that it has been justified in those cases where a citizen has been sent to death row. And the moral presumption against capital punishment would have to have been lifted successfully every time an execution takes place.

This theory provides a convenient explanation of the American practice of capital punishment, not only morally but in the way the evolution in American law corresponds to, and reflects, this moral understanding. This nonabsolutist approach to the question of state-sponsored execution reflects a pragmatism in the moral thinking of many if not most Americans, and it expresses suspicion of extreme perspectives, both the extreme of death penalty abolition and the extreme of mandatory execution.

But just execution raises problems for capital punishment. Just execution theory must be applied to the practice of capital punishment; the practice must be tested in light of the theory. My assessment of the capital punishment practice in light of the theory has not only called into question the moral justifiability of capital punishment in particular cases, but questioned whether this mode of killing can ever meet the moral test of the theory. The nine criteria that must all be satisfied if we are to lift the moral presumption against capital punishment set a reasonable but stringent standard that the practice of capital punishment fails to meet: each criterion provokes problems and difficulties. Testing the practice of state-sponsored execution against the just execution standard reveals that lifting the moral presumption against capital punishment is no easy task. In fact, just execution theory yields the conclusion that it is practically impossible to execute a person in conformity with the requirements of justice.

The framework of just execution has parallels in other theories, most notably just war and just abortion. Just war lays out various conditions that if lifted would allow a use of force in conformity with the constraints of justice. Just abortion theory lays out the various constraining conditions that would have to be satisfied in order to lift the moral presumption against abortion. Failure to satisfy these conditions would render abortion impermissible and prevent us from claiming that the evil involved in the killing of a developing form of human life is, in fact, necessary. Failure to satisfy the criteria prevents us from lifting the moral presumption, and without lifting that presumption, the presumption stays in place and governs moral meaning. It ought also to govern behavior.

The moral presumption against capital punishment is clear, even clearer than in abortion, for in abortion the moral issue of when in fetal development membership in the moral community is appropriately conferred is uncertain—at least scientifically uncertain. But no such uncertainty about personhood is at issue in the capital punishment debate. The moral status of the individual who faces execution is not in doubt. In fact, it is on condition that the moral status of persons condemned to death is not in question that we even consider the possibility of executing them as punishment for their crimes, for only persons who are responsible agents and can be held accountable for their crimes are deemed fit for the punishment of execution. Punishment in general—and capital punishment in particular—is directed toward human persons, who, as moral agents, are rights-bearing claimants who may lose certain rights due to an irresponsible use of freedom. But even criminal offenders possess by virtue of their status as persons a right to enjoy the good of life without that good being interfered with by others, so that when we say that a moral presumption against capital punishment exists, that presumption represents a clear and unqualified endorsement of the individual's status as a member of the moral community. If, in the abortion debate, doubts attend claims that a four-hour zygote or three-week embryo is possessed of full membership in the moral community, no such doubts attend the person facing execution. With moral status assured and beyond doubt, the moral presumption against depriving a person of the good of life is likewise firmly seated.

So, given the fact that the idea of punishing persons for wrongdoing requires recognition of their standing in the moral community, it is clear that the moral status of the capital criminal is not in question. Neither is the moral presumption against the state killing its own citizens through legalized execution. But in just execution theory, conditions attach. In this chapter I have laid out those conditions and critiqued them. What my critique has shown is that each of the nine criteria for lifting the presumption against capital punishment is problematic and hard to satisfy, not only in individual cases, but for the death penalty as a mode of justifiable homicide. Clearly some of the criteria, or some aspects of single criteria, can be satisfied in individual cases. There are cases where racial discrimination does not come into play, cases where juries are as reasoning and deliberate and free of emotional manipulation as can be attained, and cases where the actual execution comes off without a hitch and death ensues quickly and painlessly. Whether the criteria are satisfied in particular cases, or in general, becomes the focus of debate, and they serve to focus debate and identify the relevant hurdles that must be crossed if the moral presumption against execution is to be lifted justifiably. The criteria are not presented to settle the moral debate but to frame it.

My conclusion is that when we actually apply the criteria of just execution, we find ourselves with a mode of killing that cannot satisfy the requirements for lifting the moral presumption against capital punishment. While no doubt exists that specific criteria and some aspects of individual criteria can be satisfied in particular capital cases, the challenge of just execution theory is that all of the criteria—all nine—have to be satisfied. They must all be satisfied the same way the criteria for just war or just abortion must be satisfied. Certain criteria in just execution impose barriers that cannot be surmounted. Primary among them is last resort. A reasonable case cannot be made that execution is a last resort and that no comparable alternative to execution exists. Proportionality seems to me to fail as well, since destroying the body to punish the moral personality seems extreme and violative of a person's fundamental right to possess the good of life so long as any threat the person might pose to others has been neutralized; and the claim that capital punishment is objectively the most extreme penalty for the most extreme crime seems ludicrous in light of the history of capital punishment, even that in the United States where only a few murderers are executed and the vast majority of murderers—the average murderer—serve a shorter sentence than do those sentenced for nonviolent drug offenses. Lengthy waits for death and the prospect of botched executions fail the test prohibiting cruelty; the punishment continues to fall disproportionately on poor and minority and male persons; and everywhere—on every criterion—there is practical failure to meet the standard of justice. This failure robs the death penalty of moral justification.

So the question that confronts us is this: If just execution fails to justify capital punishment, not only in specific cases, but as a form of justifiable killing, have we abandoned a morally moderate and nonabsolutist theory and wound up advocating adoption of an absolutist stance?

My answer is both yes and no. The yes is drawn not from a religious or ideological commitment but from practical reason testing whether capital punishment can meet the demands of justice. To the extent that just execution theory prohibits execution killing, it does so in accordance with the same practical reason that would prohibit other kinds of actions categorically, such as killing the elderly because they are old, providing no life-sustaining treatment to premature newborns, planting bombs on airliners for political purposes, and so on. As practical reason prohibits such killings having denied them justification, it will likewise withhold moral authorization for capital punishment on the grounds that the death penalty has failed to meet the test of moral justification. Capital punishment ought therefore to be prohibited—absolutely.

But there is also a no. This conclusion is not an absolutist conclusion but a moral conclusion based on a model of moral moderation. This is a bit subtle, but my claim for saying no is that we have to shift our thinking at this point and place capital punishment in a broader moral context. The question is whether the state can ever claim moral authorization to kill its citizens. My case is that moral moderation would allow us to respond that it is morally permissible in certain situations and circumstances for the state to kill its own citizens, but only in light of a moral presumption that the state ought not ordinarily do so, and that doing so requires justification.

We can, then, devise a theory concerning the state's exercise of power to kill its own citizens in certain circumstances, as in using lethal force to protect innocent persons. It is in light of this nonabsolutist and morally moderate claim we must consider the question of capital punishment. If a morally moderate position would allow that in certain circumstances the state can morally justify killing its own citizens, the question is whether capital punishment constitutes an example of such a justified killing. Analysis has shown that capital punishment cannot meet the test of such justification. It is a form of morally impermissible killing directed at persons who are no longer posing a threat to others and who can face justice and proportionate punishment by means other than being put to death.

Drawing this conclusion does not absolutely prohibit the state from killing its own citizens if it can in other situations and circumstances justify doing so. The point is that capital punishment is not a form of state killing that can pass the moral test. One can subscribe to the morally moderate position that the state ought not kill its own citizens but can justify doing so in certain circumstances, then determine that capital punishment is not a form of killing that would ever pass moral muster as a particular instance of such justified killing.

To reach this conclusion does not make one an ideological absolutist but a moderate moral practitioner who finds capital punishment morally impermissible as a result of determining that the execution practice fails to overcome the moral presumption that already stands as a practical barrier to its use. In a comparable vein, it is possible to hold to the morally moderate position on abortion that some abortions are permissible and others are not, and come to the practical conclusion that there are *kinds* of abortions that are not and will not be justifiable due to the failure of the practice to pass the moral test of the just abortion theory. Sex-selection abortions are not unknown—they are, in fact, common today in India—but by applying just abortion theory we can discern that this particular form of abortion killing is, as a form of killing, unjustifiable and thus morally impermissible. Similarly, on the analogy of "well poisoning," which has always been prohibited in just war theory, the use of strategic nuclear weapons is not morally justifiable because of the disproportionate and uncontrollable effects of contamination and poisoning on noncombatants—including future generations.

My case is that capital punishment constitutes a killing of persons by the state that fails to satisfy the conditions the state must satisfy—and conceivably can satisfy with respect to other situations and circumstances—to kill one of its citizens for just cause, with due authority, proportionality, and so on. When killings take place where these criteria are not met, the state cannot claim moral justification. So it is possible that the state can justifiably kill its own citizens just as it is also conceivable that certain abortions and certain uses of force are morally permissible. But capital punishment is not one of those particular forms of "the state killing its own citizens" that satisfies the relevant moral requirements any more than abortion for reason of sex selection is justifiable. Capital punishment, then, is morally akin to sex-selection abortion: it is a form of killing that appeals to a test of moral justification but it fails to meet that test in a categorical way. Other cases and kinds of cases where the state uses lethal force against a citizen are open to examination and evaluation and could, conceivably, pass the moral test that capital punishment fails.

With the moral presumption against capital punishment still in place, we must conclude that capital punishment lacks warrants for moral justification. There is not even a compelling case to make that would support the contention that we should accept the death penalty as a necessary evil. *It is, rather, an unnecessary evil.* The way capital punishment is practiced provides no reason to consider it anything but unnecessary. If we cannot claim it as a necessary evil—and we cannot—then we must conclude that it is disallowed—morally. Capital punishment is an immoral form of killing.

9

Symbol, Power, and the Death of God

The analysis of the death penalty has yielded a clear conclusion: reasons advanced in support of capital punishment are inadequate to justify lifting the presumption against it. The death penalty as a practice fails to meet the standards of justice imposed by a theory of just execution. Therefore the death penalty is neither moral nor just.

The fact that a majority of Americans approve the practice of capital punishment and find in it nothing morally objectionable presents, then, the question raised in the opening pages of this study: Why should so many support a practice that fails to meet the requirements of justice and morality? The obvious answer is that the death penalty is not ordinarily subjected to moral scrutiny and moral justification, for the practice is taken for granted.

Quick reflection on the question of moral meaning goes to an obvious place: the death penalty seems a fitting act of retributive justice. It is the extreme penalty for the extreme crime. If justice requires delivering what is due, then it is justice—and many would argue morality itself—that stands behind this reckoning of just execution: those who take life unjustly should in the name of justice forfeit life themselves.

Moral justification for the death penalty may be within reach theoretically, but the appeal to retributive justice does not address the actual practice of execution. For, as the analysis in these pages has shown, the practice of execution falls short of the demands of justice. It falls short in the face of an imperfect criminal justice system. It falls short in the face of actual injustices committed in the process of deciding through a wildly arbitrary system of execution selection who will and will not pay the ultimate penalty for the ultimate crime. The moral appeal to retributive justice fails to explain how in the face of imperfection and injustice *the practice of execution* can continue to lay claim to moral justification.

My conclusion is that the ultimate sanctions for capital punishment are not moral. If they were, coming to understand that the practice of execution falls short of the demands of justice would necessarily lead to calls for a moratorium on executions, and, in light of evidence of inherent injustice, actual abolition.[1] The ultimate sanctions for the death penalty are to be located elsewhere, in other sources or springs for action.

I have already suggested that the deeper sources of popular justification for capital punishment lie in such matters as public frustration with crime and doubt that the criminal justice system is adequate to the task of meting out justice and protecting citizens. A related source of justification resides in the fear that such mistrust engenders. For not only is crime feared, but that fear affects how the criminal justice system is perceived, and the suspicion grows that that system is inadequate to provide protection and ensure the public safety. Fear can incite the desire to go beyond containing, restraining, and disempowering the object of fear to wanting the object of fear eradicated and eliminated.

Fear and frustration do not generate a strong and positive argument in support of the death penalty as a morally worthy project commanding universal assent. They do, however, go a long way toward explaining why so many support the death penalty today. And since protecting society from those who threaten it is a morally worthy end, it is at least a consistent argument to say that by killing them, that end will be secured with certainty, at least as regards those individual offenders actually put to death. A dead criminal can no longer hurt anyone.

Another source of support for capital punishment, one I have not discussed at any length, concerns the death penalty as symbol. The case can be made that the deeper significance or symbolic power of capital punishment is that it has come to signify society's resolve to protect itself in the face of those who would threaten the lives and safety of citizens. To be sure, acting to ensure public safety is a good and morally worthy end. In light of the criminal justice system's failure to reassure an anxious public, coupled with the reality that criminal offenders pose a constant and never-ending threat to the public safety, the death penalty presents itself as a symbol of an effective and absolute power to eliminate anxiety and end threats to the safety of persons.

The question we must ask, beyond the moral analysis considered up to this point, is what the death penalty actually means as a symbol. Is it an effective metaphor for justice, or does it draw its power as symbol from another symbolic locus, another center of meaning and value?

The symbolic appeal that capital punishment makes in its claim to be just is simple enough to understand, for if justice means returning to offenders their just deserts, then the death penalty returns the desert of an extreme penalty for an extreme crime—"a life for a life." But a problem arises. The death penalty is an instrument of state policy and action, and its symbolic power goes deeper than association with retributive justice; in fact, since it can be used as an instrument of state repression, its deeper symbolic value must be said to rest in values beyond any requirements of justice.

The heart of the matter at the level of symbol is that the death penalty represents a rare instance of legitimated killing—like just war, tyrannicide, and self-defense. The death penalty as symbol transforms moral meaning and authorizes such killing, and does so in the face of our ordinary moral prohibitions against such killing; ordinarily prohibited killings of members of the moral community become permitted acts. The authorization may be sought in the name of justice, but justice can be effected by other means; and the power to execute, once claimed, can be—and has been—used to effect ends that have nothing to do with serving justice.

Capital punishment is a symbol as well as a concrete expression of state power. It is a symbol of power independent of justice; subtract justice from any execution and what is left is power. And it is not simply power, but a claim to power. To discern the difference between power and a claim to power, we must enter the crawl spaces of motivation and intentionality and discern the depth of human desire for power and security. For in making the case that the death penalty symbolizes power, I want to say that it symbolizes the power we seek to face the fundamental insecurity of existence, especially as that insecurity is presented to us in the face of those we most fear.

I have already claimed that the death penalty as symbol presents us with the possibility of an absolute safety, which then offers us the hope of reducing our fear absolutely. The death penalty does not work this magic by appealing to universal moral principles but by holding up individuals in the particularities of their offenses and authorizing their elimination. And in that act of elimination, which effects a reduction in our fear, we confront the attractive but terrifying realization that the power to rid ourselves of insecurity by actually killing those who have harmed us and threatened us is in our hands.

We grasp at that power because we desire it, but then, in anxiety at possessing it, use it only sparingly. We authorize use of the death penalty in only enough cases to maintain the illusion that by having this power we can act to counter the threats we see posed by whoever comes to personify and embody our fear. And where we locate and personify our fear is the same place human beings have always located and personified it—in the stranger.

We cannot crush our condition of insecurity, so we resort to crushing particular individuals who symbolize our insecurity and arouse our fear—those who necessarily confront us as strangers. We execute the uneducated, the poor, the minority member, even the ugly, and those who present themselves before the legal system as powerless. We kill the stranger, the person who embodies a presence we fear. The threat posed to our security by such as these can be addressed rationally by alternatives to execution, but those we condemn to execution confront us with deeper threats to our security. For in such as these we experience the anxiety of life, and in legitimating the killing of the stranger who confronts us as poor, uneducated, or mentally defective we seek to act symbolically against a threat that goes beyond the particularities of his or her crime. Capital punishment provides an effective means to kill the symbol of our fear in the stranger; and it authorizes us to act to counter, overpower, and then rid ourselves of the sources of our fear under the cover story that what we are doing is delivering justice.

In the second chapter of this book I told the story of Willie Darden. Willie Darden was convicted of murder and executed, and this book has attempted to discern the moral meaning of such a death as he suffered. Because we examined Darden's story in the context of opening up a moral investigation, we accepted Willie Darden as a man, a human being and a member of the moral community. But now let us consider that Willie Darden was also a symbol, for if Willie Darden did not receive justice as a man, it is likely that on the analysis I am offering now, he was killed as a symbol.

Willie Darden appeared before his accusers and prosecutors as a poor black man unable to exert power to defend himself. He appeared as a stranger to those who convicted him and demanded his death. He was tried not as a fellow citizen deserving of competent legal representation and protection from unjust prosecution, but as a symbol of all that threatened the security of the community. No physical evidence tying him to the crime was entered, and evidence corroborating his innocence was later to be denied a hearing. Thus the conclusion to be drawn on the level of symbol analysis is this: that he was, as symbol, a threat to the public sense of security. In judging him deserving of death for a crime it was not proven he committed, he was judged a fit sacrifice in the quest for power that sought to eliminate the threat he posed as stranger—a poor man, a black man, unable to defend himself and unworthy of being defended by others.

On the level of symbol, the question of Willie Darden's guilt or innocence for a terrible crime is not and never will be the critical issue. If it were, evidence connecting him to the crime would have been required, and evidence corroborating his alibi would have been allowed to come once again before the system of justice for evaluation, which did not happen. On the level of symbol, what put Willie Darden in the electric chair was a jury's judgment that conformed to those who asked that he be killed because he was an animal. The meaning of his death was a matter of symbol, not justice. The death penalty effected its symbolic work—but only in his case. Darden's death did not eliminate crime. It did not even eliminate any other killing of white persons by poor black males. Darden's death provoked more questions about justice than it settled, so its symbolic meaning must be sought in the realm of power rather than justice: his death ought to be understood as a symbol of what society can do when strangers threaten.

The death penalty is a symbol of a great and absolute power, and it is this symbolic meaning of the death penalty that helps explain why the system of capital punishment persists in the face of clear evidence of its injustice. I wish now to explore how absolute power over life and death symbolized by state-sponsored execution connects with the symbol system of religion, for religion deals with questions of meaning, with the issue of life and death, and with all variety of symbols, even symbols of absoluteness, and it is well known that sanctions for the death penalty exist in the realm of religious symbol. Although the focus of this inquiry has been on the moral warrants for execution, religion provides a powerful guide for action, as it presents another basis for assessing the moral meaning of the death penalty.

Religious Sanctions of Violence

Although it is well known that capital punishment was sanctioned by the society out of which the Hebrew Scriptures grew—thirteen classes of capital offense are specified in the Mosaic law—another one of the world's early religious texts takes pains to counsel rulers against resorting to execution.[2] In the Chinese Taoist text, the *Tao Te Ching*, which may originate as early as the sixth century B.C.E., we hear these words:

> What then is the use of trying to intimidate [the people] with the death-penalty? And even supposing people were generally frightened of death and did not regard it as an everyday thing, which of us would dare to seize them and slay them? There is the Lord of Slaughter always ready for this task, and to do it in his stead is like thrusting oneself into the master-carpenter's place and doing his chipping for him. Now "he who tries to do the master-carpenter's chipping for him is lucky if he does not cut his hand."[3]

Taoism scholar Holmes Welch tells the story of a fourteenth-century emperor of China who read this passage and "reflected that while every morning in the capital ten men were executed, by evening there were a hundred others who had committed the same crimes. Therefore he withdrew the death penalty and soon 'his heart was relieved.'"[4]

In the Pentateuch of the Hebrew Scriptures death is sanctioned as punishment for a wide variety of ethical and religious offenses. The book of Deuteronomy makes clear that the purpose of punishment was deterrence, for in light of an execution, "All the people shall hear, and fear, and not act presumptuously again" (Deut. 17:13; see also 13:11; 19:20; 21:21). Execution is also prescribed as a means of purging evil from the midst of the community (Deut. 13:5). The crime of murder is construed not only as a moral and societal offense, but as a religious offense, for murder offends God and imputes bloodguilt to the community. Execution expiates the sin and enacts the community's redeeming response. (This is the imputation of bloodguilt that even Kant, as we saw earlier, would reference in his support of the death penalty.)

A certain pragmatism can be seen at work in the Hebrew Scriptures' sanctioning of execution, since community-sponsored execution would have taken blood revenge against a killer out of the hands of individual clans, placed it in a wider community authority, and thus contributed to maintaining a balance of power between clans. Furthermore, the execution of those who refused to obey judicial decisions was clearly aimed at maintaining good social order. But such pragmatic concerns were not the heart of the matter. The death penalty was a religiously grounded act in the self-consciousness of the covenanting community of Israel. The death penalty was prescribed by religious law and imposed for religious purposes. Offenses that violated Israel's covenant with God merited death, not only those that directed offense to Yahweh directly, as in apostasy, blasphemy, or profanation of the Sabbath, but also those that undermined the people as a covenanting people of God (false witness, adultery, sorcery) or that stained the holiness of the "realm of priests" (bestiality, incest, harlotry). The thirteen classes of capital offense identified by Mosaic law covered thirty-six specific capital crimes. Of those thirty-six crimes, eighteen call for death by stoning, ten by burning, two by decapitation, and six by strangulation. These capital crimes were not simply moral offenses—and who could read such a list today and discern in every one of these acts a moral offense against the human community deserving of death? These were religiously construed offenses that were, in the covenanting religious community of Israel, offenses before God.

It is beyond dispute that the Hebrew Scriptures present the death penalty as a divinely ordained sanction for dozens of crimes. It is also beyond dispute, and shocking to realize, that this sanction will continue to provide justification for support of the death penalty even into our own time, with a "pick-and-choose" hermeneutic being applied to extract from the ancient Mosaic law contemporary justifications for violence. Dr. Mel White, a gay clergyman who serves as dean of the Cathedral of Hope in Dallas, Texas, told in my hearing of his experience on a live radio program in the Pacific Northwest when a listener phoned in, quoted the Leviticus 20:13 passage that proscribes male homosexuality as a capital offense, then told White that because God's law explicitly demands it, all homosexuals should be put to death. There is no doubt that much if not most of the energy behind hatred of gay and lesbian persons is religiously inspired, and stories like this remind us that any overruling of morality's requirement of respect for persons by such religious fervor is exceedingly dangerous.

Scripture contains opposition to, as well as endorsement of, execution practice, but that opposition is insufficient to overcome the appearance that execution carries the weight of divine support. Internal opposition can be extracted from, say, the story of the first murderer, Cain (Gen. 4:1–16). What is significant about this story is that God judges Cain directly and not through any human agency of criminal justice. And God, when judging directly, does not demand death but rather imposes exile—a living death perhaps, but not a death that destroys the divinely created goodness of the body. "Whoever kills Cain," God says in Genesis 4:15b, "will suffer a vengeance sevenfold," so that God can be said not only to oppose killing Cain in vengeance for his crime, but will direct vengeance toward those who interfere with God's justice.

Likewise, the Sinai commandment "You shall not kill" (Exod. 20:13; Deut. 5:17) has often been appealed to in religious opposition to the death penalty, but it is likely that this commandment was thought not to apply to all the authorizations for execution to be found in the Mosaic law. It is *after* receiving this commandment on Sinai that Moses will, in the very next chapter, say, "Whoever strikes his father or his mother shall be put to death" (Exod. 21:15). Saying this so soon after receiving the divine prohibition on killing provokes no cognitive dissonance. Moses does not engage the question of how executing disrespectful children might—or might not—conform to the killing prohibition enunciated in the Decalogue. Clearly, no inconsistency was discerned. The "You shall not kill" commandment is clearly not a general and all-encompassing directive; it targets nonprescribed and malicious killing, the kind of killing of persons we associate with murder. As biblical scholar Lloyd R. Bailey puts the matter, the commandment against killing "forbids premeditated, malicious violence that is not sanctioned by divine decree as mediated by the stipulations of Israel's covenant."[5]

A justified killing is not murder, so killings authorized by God, being justified, were exempted from the prohibition. Since God recognized no inconsistency between the command "You shall not kill" and the command that thirty-six crimes should be designated capital crimes deserving of death, the people of Israel ought not to be expected to discern any inconsistency either. The enunciation of a prohibition on killing—the Fifth Commandment—simply did not apply to divinely specified capital offenses, so that God can be said to have sanctioned the death penalty as a legitimate exception. And in their covenant with

God, the people of Israel acknowledge the legitimacy of these killings as divinely directed, decreed, authorized, and legitimated.

Yet despite this divine sanctioning, the practice of capital punishment never became a common religious practice in Judaism. As increasingly stringent conditions for charging and prosecuting capital offenses grew within the covenanting community, opposition to the practice of execution arose, even to the point that the religion of Judaism, rather than endorsing the practice of execution by taking the Mosaic law literally, actually opened the law governing capital offenses to interpretation—and disputation. The history of the death penalty among the people of Israel has led scholars to believe that these codified directives of Mosaic law cannot be assumed to represent actual or usual judicial practice. In fact, some scholars urge the view that by comparing this codification of capital offenses to actual practice, the Scriptures are serving less as a moral guide than as a reminder to the people of Israel that they are a covenanting community with responsibilities as covenant partners. The various religious offenses that merit death before Yahweh thus constitute symbolic reminders of this covenantal bond and its life-and-death seriousness rather than reports of sociological insight concerning justice administration in the community. Thus does scholar Gerald Blidstein comment, "Jewish law abolished capital punishment in fact not by denying its conceptual moral validity but rather by allowing it ONLY this conceptual validity."[6]

Various rabbinic materials further the discussion of Judaism's understanding of the death penalty. As certain rabbis will offer the view that the death penalty offends contemporary sensibilities and ill accords with the moral law, other rabbis will caution against overruling biblical action guides on such grounds, for the religious decree ought always to overrule fluctuating moral interpretations. But a tendency to oppose the death penalty appears in Judaism. Rabbis came to acknowledge societal abuse in imposing the death penalty, and opposition to the death penalty was pronounced by the time of the Talmud. The Mishnah *Makkot* 1.10 illustrates this opposition. In one death penalty discussion, a rabbi irked by the rare use of execution mentions that a Sanhedrin that executes only once every seven years is destructive. This comment leads Rabbi Tarfon and Rabbi Akiba to say, "'If we were in the Sanhedrin, no man would ever have been executed." Scholar Edna Erez comments on this passage from the Mishnah, which is clearly the most important rabbinic discussion about capital punishment:

> These Rabbis are advocating the abolition of the death penalty despite the Bible sanctioning such punishment in a number of instances. They evidently believed that biblical law was intended as a solemn warning to the extreme seriousness of crime but that the courts were justified in circumventing the law so that it becomes a dead letter. The statement [of Rabbis Tarfon and Akiba cited above] . . . which concludes the passage is the stock argument of the antiabolitionists even today.[7]

It is clear that widespread reluctance to impose the death penalty emerged in the developing religion of Judaism, reflecting deeper theological and ethical opposition, even to the point where Judaism, it has been said, moved "toward the complete abolition of the death penalty."[8]

Christianity's involvement with the death penalty has been long-standing and somewhat complex, but there is no doubt that support for the death penalty is to be found throughout the tradition, including, as in Judaism, classical sources. Augustine lent it support in the name of law and the rule of rational justice, believing it to be an exception to the commandment not to kill; Aquinas defended it as an instrument necessary to preserve the common good; Luther and Calvin championed its use, as do many Christians today. Current Catholic teaching is opposed to the death penalty, though possible exceptions for "grave cause" are still officially countenanced. Mainline Protestant Christian churches are on record as opposing the death penalty, though this opposition seems not to have affected attitudes toward the death penalty in the American culture or even among the majority of church members. Christianity has known a tradition of opposition that appears as early as the fourth-century Christian apologist and pacifist Lactantius, who held contra Augustine that no exception to the Fifth Commandment prohibition on killing should be allowed:

> When God forbids killing, he is not only ordering us to avoid armed robbery, which is contrary even to public law, but he is forbidding what men regard as ethical. Thus, it is not right for a just man to serve in the army since justice itself is his form of service. Nor is it right for a just man to charge someone with a capital crime. It does not matter whether you kill a man with the sword or with a word, since it is killing itself that is prohibited. And so there is no exception to this command of God. Killing a human being, whom God willed to be inviolable, is always wrong.[9]

This absolutist interpretation of the Fifth Commandment has never dominated Christian theology and ethics, but the tradition of opposition to the death penalty has always had support from significant voices. In the twentieth century, Swiss Protestant theologian Karl Barth expressed a view typical of this opposition:

> If what we are to attest in the sphere of human punishment is not a self-conceived, imaginary and lifeless justice, but a righteousness of the true God who has acted and revealed Himself in Jesus Christ, capital punishment will surely be the very last thing to enter our heads.[10]

The Christian church has never demanded as a test of faith a particular viewpoint on the death penalty, nor made a particular view a condition of membership in the church. There have always been Christians who support the death penalty and those who oppose it. Supporters have relied on explicit scriptural warrants, beginning usually with the Genesis notion that "whoever sheds the blood of a human, by a human shall that person's blood be shed" (Gen. 9:6). Christian death penalty supporters seeking scriptural justification have then proceeded to appeal to Romans 13, where Paul speaks of the legitimacy of government and the need of "every person"—including Christians—to submit to the government authorities. What is most notable about the use of this passage to support the death penalty is that the death penalty is not even mentioned. There is certainly no mention of any obligation the state has to execute criminal offenders, as some interpreters are always willing to argue. Romans 13 asserts the state's punitive function and affirms its validity. It does not explicitly endorse bloodshed or any particular method of punishment, but it does mention "the power of the sword": "But if you do what is wrong, you should be afraid, for the authority does not bear the sword in vain!" (Rom. 13:4). Many Christians who support the death penalty have found religiously sanctioned legitimation for the death penalty in this verse. But it can be argued against this interpretation that the reference to the "power of the sword" is clearly symbolic, a metaphor for the penal and punitive authority of the state, which is the topic of the passage; and it may make pointed reference to military power.

Paul recognizes state authority and its symbol—the "sword." But it is deadly whimsy to infer that by such recognition he is also acknowledging the death penalty as a legitimated and divinely authorized instrument in the orchestra of state power—perhaps his deep meditations on the cross and the unjust execution of Jesus restrained him.[11] In any event, Christians who support the death penalty by appeal to Romans 13 overinterpret Paul, extracting legitimation for the practice of state-sponsored execution from the text to conform state use of the death penalty to Christian values and beliefs.

Christians who oppose the death penalty likewise appeal to various scriptural sources to support their views, including the Fifth Commandment itself, which, as noted above, sufficed for Lactantius. But Christian opponents of the death penalty have made other kinds of interpretive moves, including appeal to the spirit of love and mercy so central to the gospel,[12] even to the statement attributed to Jesus in Matthew 5:38 that repudiates the ethic of retribution so often used to support the death penalty: "You have heard that it was said, 'An eye for an eye and a tooth for a tooth.' But I say to you, Do not resist an evildoer. But if anyone strikes you on the right cheek, turn the other also."

That this renunciation of retribution is applicable to the death penalty can be seen from the scriptural presentation of Jesus asking God's forgiveness for those who were participants in his own execution. Jesus adds that they do not know what they are doing. What they did "not know" can only be the meaning of their act as moral and religious violation. Jesus is certainly not taking the occasion of his own crucifixion to lend support to the idea that the state has a legitimate right to do as it was doing. Rather, by his words, Jesus condemns this execution act, and his condemnation is clear from the fact that he asks God to forgive his executioners. The only reason that would make such a request sensible is that the executioners have been judged and condemned for their offense, and forgiveness is required. Jesus' condemnation is offered in words consistent with his more general teaching concerning the repudiation of retribution; and so committed is Jesus to this ethic of nonretribution that he is able to express it one last time—even as his own death agony begins. The implication is that if those who have brought him to the cross understood the meaning of their actions, they would not be doing what they were doing, for what they were doing was morally and religiously wrong.

The lack of understanding on the part of those willing to support and carry out an execution is also at issue in another story directly related to Jesus and the death penalty. In John 8, Jesus interferes with an execution that was about to get under way. He steps in to prevent the lawful stoning of an adulterous woman.

The crime at issue was, according to Mosaic law, punishable by death by stoning. Jesus interferes not because the punishment about to take place is illicit, for clearly it is not. Jesus stops a legal killing, rather, by simply reminding those with stones in their hands that they too do not know what they are doing. When Jesus says, "Let anyone among you who is without sin be the first to throw a stone at her" (John 8:7), he reminds them that undertaking an execution in observance of divine law requires a perfect conformity to God's will that those holding stones lack.[13] They come to understand that they lack such perfection when they are asked to proceed as if they were God—"without sin." Jesus sought to disqualify these prospective executioners from claiming a perfection they lacked and exercising an absolutism that belongs to God alone. Their killing of the adulteress could have constituted an exercise of God-like power, for the executioners would have committed an absolute act that yielded an absolute consequence as they held her absolutely responsible and thus absolutely accountable.

Jesus' point was simpler than the language I must use to express it: those with stones had no valid claim on such absolutism. They were in no moral or religious position to hold another absolutely responsible and absolutely accountable, not so long as they stood before this condemned woman in their own condition of finitude and fallibility. Jesus exposed their claim of execution power as a pretense to a God-like power, the implication being that only a perfect justice—God's justice—could require that this woman's life be made forfeit for her misdeeds. Jesus awakened the executioners to their pretense of power and perfection, their absolutist act annulled by a recognition of their quite ordinary fallibility, which, in Jesus' eyes and finally their own, undercut the foundation for claiming absolute and obliterative power over another person's life—even if legally authorized.

Beyond these two specific Jesus-centered engagements with the death penalty, there looms a larger theological perspective in the New Testament that, if taken seriously, could be said to undo further the harsh and retributive aspects of Mosaic law. And that is simply the Pauline announcement of freedom from the law, so prominent a theme in the Pauline revolution. Freedom from the law could be applied to the death penalty the same way it was applied to the other aspects of the Mosaic law—regulations on cleanliness, restrictions on diet, even circumcision itself: "For in Jesus Christ," writes St. Paul, "neither circumcision nor uncircumcision is of any avail, but faith working through love" (Gal. 5:6). Such freedom from the law as "faith working through love" effected provides, it could be argued, sufficient authorization for the Christian to overrule scriptural warrants justifying the death penalty found in Mosaic law.

Religion and religious practitioners have often justified the death penalty as a legitimate and morally authorized practice because religious authority has sanctioned it. The ethical appeal of the position is to a "divine command" ethic, the idea that an Ultimate Arbiter of moral meaning—God—has revealed to humanity what is expected in the realm of human action. Accordingly, our moral duty is to obey what this Ultimate Arbiter prescribes. Finding religious sanction for the use of the death penalty settles the question of moral meaning for many people. Questions about moral permissibility are answered by human agents claiming authorization to carry out the divine will.

It is not inconsequential that no single view on the death penalty commands universal allegiance from people who identify themselves as religious. Neither is it inconsequential that opposition to the death penalty emerges from within religious traditions themselves, even those with strong traditions of support. I have noted such opposition in Taoism, and have pointed out how such opposition was articulated by rabbis in Judaism, even by Jesus himself if his actions as presented in the Gospel stories are any indication of his attitudes or those of the communities that produced the Gospel stories.

Standing back from the internal debates over moral meaning as it is religiously grounded in the faith traditions of Judaism and Christianity, we can assert that religion can be—and has been—used as a primary locus of power for legitimating violence. Religion, in other words, has played an important role in sacralizing—as well as delimiting—coercion and violence against persons, and this dialectic can be seen both in religious support—and in religious opposition—to the death penalty. Religious sacralization of violence—violence as an aspect of God's justice—renders the absolute action undertaken in execution a direct expression of the divine. There is, I admit, a deep consistency in this view.

Although I will not explore further the general question of the religious legitimation of violence—this is a broad topic that others have addressed with insight[14]—I do wish to take on the question of what I am calling the absolutism of the death penalty. For despite the fact that many of those who support the death penalty do so on the grounds that it is divinely authorized, there is still a theological problem to be examined. The problem is a twist on the classic issue of theodicy: If God is both all-powerful and good, how can God allow evil to exist?

Support of the death penalty on religious grounds raises the theodicy question because execution is accepted as action that God endorses and entrusts to fallible human agents. The troubling issue is not the traditional theodicy problem that evil is present in a divinely created world. The problem is God's active legitimation of evil and acceptance of known wrongdoing. For a religious endorsement of the death penalty would locate the source of the death penalty's legitimation in a God possessing (presumably) absolute moral knowledge. As the ultimate arbiter of justice, God would be held to evaluate the meaning and justice of human acts with absolute moral certitude regarding that meaning; and in the divine call for execution, God, the author of life, would be held to possess the power and moral certitude to cancel justly any capital offender's subscription to life, thus demanding certain lives in punishment for specified misdeeds. Since this demand for death issues from an infallible God, no mistakes are even possible. Taking back the life would satisfy God's justice perfectly, for the punishment is consistently imposed in light of a perfect evaluation of moral (and religious) meaning.

But the problem that arises is this: Why should a God possessing such perfection in moral knowledge and understanding ignore the fact that such perfection as God possesses cannot translate into perfect human justice? Human justice is beset with fallibility and an imperfect moral knowledge. Human beings make mistakes. They wrongly accuse, condemn, and execute, and fallible human beings can claim to understand no human act—not even a crime—as God might understand it in light of God's perfect assessment of moral meaning. We do not know—despite our willingness to make judgments—how to assess the moral meaning of a crime with absolute certitude, yet by acting to deprive persons of life, we hold individuals absolutely accountable for crimes—and sometimes mistakenly so. Why would a God concerned about justice in a matter of life and death be willing to delegate an absolute power over life and death to such fallible and morally benighted creatures?

Could it be that God does not realize that human beings make mistakes, even when deputized with a divine power? Could it be that God does not fathom the depth of human fallibility? To assert this "solution" would be to undermine any claim of God's omniscience, and radically to challenge God's intelligence and capacity for simple moral insight.

Could it be that God does not care whether justice is done in accord with the standard of perfection that would necessarily attach to God's capacity for moral knowledge and insight? It could be argued that deviations from that standard of perfection are not of interest to God, since God does not intervene to stop such injustices, and allows lethal practices to continue because God has no choice but to work justice through human agency, such as it is. This is the more plausible answer, and it is this view that I think lies behind the claim one hears that human beings, not being infallible, must do the best they can and seek to do justice with the best that is in them, even if perfection cannot be realized. There is, in this view, a practicality that allows Christian evangelical scholar John Jefferson Davis to say, "It is important not to exaggerate the problems of the [justice] system, and not to require perfection before the administration of criminal sanctions is possible."[15] Not requiring perfection is, of course, reasonable, but only if that recognition affects the administration of justice. Action must take imperfection into account. And action may require nothing beyond the reasonable effort to administer justice holding open the possibility that in the human arena of action, where errors and uncertainty are always possible, irrevocable and absolutist acts must be avoided. Recognizing that errors are possible requires that room be created for correction of error. The issue is whether such a view of justice and the ambiguities of existence can ever apply in capital cases. For capital cases proceed toward execution as if all ambiguities have been resolved and a justice that is beyond error—final and irrevocable—can be administered.

Bringing a classical theism into the question of the death penalty allows us to consider that the power to kill exercised in capital punishment is not a self-consciously ambiguous and finite power, but an absolute power that closes off any opportunity to redress injustice. An absolute power such as God would possess were God to execute offenders directly would be the irrevocable power over life and death that God would exercise without any injustice ever turning up after the fact. In carrying out the death penalty criminal justice systems claim such power and exercise it. The theodicy question relevant here is this: Would God delegate such power to beings such as we are and experience satisfaction that justice—an absolute, irrevocable, even divine justice—is accomplished whenever human beings take it upon themselves to require a death penalty in the name of justice?

A God willing to make this move might be idly optimistic and possessed of a style that avoids micromanagement, but the more reasonable interpretation, given all that classically attaches to God, is that such a God is simply indifferent to what human beings do. Thus does Camus's Meursault, facing a beheading for a murder—was it for murder or because he did not cry at his mother's funeral?— open himself "to the gentle indifference of the world," or, as another, more meta-physically charged translation put it, the "benign indifference of the universe."[16] Thus does this sense of divine indifference to human fallibility present itself in another execution practice, provoking the question reported by Elie Wiesel in his Shoah memoir, *Night*. When a young boy beloved by all was hanged by the SS for possible complicity in sabotage—and he may have been guilty of the crime for which he was hanged—those who witnessed the agonizing half-hour stran-gulation said: "Where is God now?" Wiesel comments that within himself this answer came: "Where is He—He is hanging here on the gallows."[17] Absolute power. Divine indifference. That is what the question confronts.

To say that God possesses perfect moral understanding yet is aware that fal-lible human beings through flawed justice systems have assumed power to dis-pense an absolute and irrevocable penalty in defiance of their fallibility is to en-counter a God either powerless or indifferent. In either case, the God possessed of certitude in matters of moral meaning, the God who cares about justice and who could be expected to deplore the injustice of unjust execution, is undone, eviscerated, weak, even dead. This leads to the most critical theological conclu-sion to be drawn from an analysis of the death penalty as a symbol of power.

For the power in question is an absolute and divine power. It is irrevocable and beyond correction even though exercised in the realm of ambiguity, contin-gency, finite knowledge, and fallible moral understanding. Human appropria-tion of such power, and God's deputizing of human beings to exercise this power knowing that it cannot be exercised consistently with God's perfect justice, nec-essarily leads us to conclude that the religious meaning of the death penalty is that God is dead. God is dead because human beings have usurped a divine power. If human beings can do God's work as God would do it—perfectly— then God is emptied of meaning. Only by refusing such absolute power as exe-cution requires do we continue to maintain our status as fallible beings exercis-ing justice in light of ambiguity and finitude. To deny the possibility of correcting errors in human actions—inevitable errors—is to act absolutely; and inasmuch as execution is action that excludes any such correction, it discounts the possi-bility of error, and, theologically speaking, as an absolute action, announces the death of God.

The death penalty can be a symbol of God's perfect justice, and many sup-port the death penalty on religious grounds, holding that when the state executes, it is enacting that perfect justice. Possessing the power to execute can be explained by appealing to God's deputizing of agents to kill in God's name, in an autho-rized act of dispensing infinite and absolute justice in the name of the Absolute, which is no doubt how Romans 13 came to play such a pivotal role in the Christian defense of the power of the state to execute. The problem, just to be clear on this point, is that the authorities cannot exercise this power with infinite wisdom or in accordance with infallible justice. Only by allowing God to kill directly could that end be accomplished.[18]

Killing in the name of God, then, constitutes the human usurpation of a power that appropriately belongs to God alone; and the human claim to this power has the necessary effect of displacing God, thus returning the symbol of the death penalty back to power and away from justice. The death penalty is, even theologically, a symbol of power, not justice. It is a symbol of absolute power, not divine justice. It is ultimately a symbol of the death of God, for where the death penalty is, God has been necessarily displaced.[19]

The Guilty Jesus

I have been arguing that the death penalty is a symbol of power rather than justice, and I have been examining some of the implications of thinking about the symbol of the death penalty theologically. I cannot conclude this discussion without considering Jesus and the cross. Jesus of Nazareth was actually a victim of the absolutist action I have been referring to, a victim of state-sponsored execution, yet the symbol of his death, the cross, is not appropriated by Christians as a sign of theological horror at the human usurpation of absolute power and the attendant displacement of God. Many Christian followers of Jesus understand the cross as a symbol of redemption and look to that symbol for comfort and salvation. And that symbol encapsulates a central Christian theological meaning, namely, that humanity—limited, finite, and sinful humanity—has been reconciled to God through the death Jesus suffered on a cross.

The cross is a Christian symbol, but it denotes a historical event. I wish to consider the cross first as a symbol grounded in history, then as a signifier of theological meaning. Our understanding of the history of the cross ought to affect the symbolic meaning we abstract from it—and so it has in the tradition of Christian theological interpretation. But if our understanding of the history supporting the symbol is flawed and in need of revision, Christian theological thinking ought to adapt in light of the history that undergirds the Christian affirmation of God and the divine activity in history—and in a crucified Christ. My case is that the cross as history challenges many of the traditional modes of theological interpretation that attach to it. Furthermore, the cross as metaphysical symbol authorizes alterations in theological understanding so that what Jesus' death means requires reconsideration of the execution itself.

The Cross as History

Confronting the cross historically yields sparse material for theological reflection, and so reflection will be necessarily limited, authorizing only tentative remarks. The reason for this is that we do not know very much about Jesus of Nazareth and his death. The texts as we have them do not suffice to produce for the modern reader anything resembling historical knowledge or certitude. The Gospels as documents present a witness to the faith commitments of the early Christians and their communities. They even reveal a political agenda important in the early church. They do not, from the historian's point of view, however, provide an uncontested historical record of the details of Jesus' life or death.

That said, let me proceed to say something about the cross as history—the cross on which Jesus died.

In his study of the crucifixion, biblical scholar and historian John Dominic Crossan concludes with these words: "I cannot find any detailed historical information about the crucifixion of Jesus. Every item we looked at was prophecy historicized rather than history recalled." What is presented in the Gospels, rather, is a story showing Jesus fulfilling messianic prophecy as told by authors and communities committed to the claim that Jesus was the Messiah. That claim guides the narrative and directs it away from history and into faith. But not completely. Crossan then mentions what he considers a "glaring exception" in the Gospel story of prophecy fulfilled: "The one time the narrative passion broke away from its base in the prophetic passion . . . was to assert Jewish responsibility [for Jesus' death] and Roman innocence." Crossan goes on to comment, "These motifs were neither prophecy nor history but Christian propaganda, a daring act of public relations faith in the destiny of Christianity not within Judaism, but within the Roman Empire."[20]

We know and can accept as historical fact that Jesus was executed and died on a cross. Crossan reminds us, however, that much of what is in the Gospel story recounting that death has been altered by the writers and communities of faith who give witness to their faith in the Gospel accounts. And the Gospels reveal an anti-Jewish attitude that could be said not only to locate blame for Jesus' death on the Jews but to blunt Roman responsibility for it. Thus the Gospel narrative of Jesus' passion and death—"Christian propaganda," as Crossan calls it—limits and even obscures what can be known about the death historically.

Having said this, I think it is important to note that even if we accept Crossan's conclusion without question, we can still make some firm "historical claims" based on the Gospel narratives. We know that Jesus died, and we know that the Gospel stories blame the death on the Jewish authorities. But the third thing we know and can assert with confidence is this important fact: The Jews did not kill Jesus. The Gospels impute "innocence" to Rome, as Crossan notes, but this is a historical fiction. As historian and biblical theologian Ellis Rivkin writes, confirming the widely accepted scholarly perspective I have used Crossan to articulate, "It was not the Jewish people who crucified Jesus, it was not the Roman people—it was the imperial system, a system which victimized the Jews, victimized the Romans, and victimized the Spirit of God."[21] As much historical fact as we can wring out of the Gospels necessitates the view that Jesus did not die at the hands of the Jews but of the Roman authorities. Crucifixion was a Roman execution method. And he did not die because Jewish authorities found him guilty of religious offense. Investigating the specific charge of blasphemy that the Gospels claim was the specific religious offense that brought Jesus originally before the Sanhedrin for judgment and condemnation, legal scholar Leonard W. Levy clarifies the historical challenge to the Gospel story in this blunt language:

> Jesus had not blasphemed in the opinion of the Sanhedrin. His blasphemy did not exist. It was simply a symbol of the Jewish rejection of Jesus, and was the only capital charge the evangelists could put in the mouths of Jesus' Jewish opponents. The Sanhedrin trial itself never happened. It was the creation of Mark, imitated by Matthew, but rejected by Luke and especially by John. . . . None of the Gospels is reliable as history and none purports to be. They all propagate faith in Jesus.[22]

The Gospel stories are constructed, then, not as eyewitness accounts but as theological documents that clearly had a practical and political function. Levy writes: "Their pro-Roman stance was intended to protect the early churches from the Romans, by severing those churches from their Jewish origins. The safety of the early churches depended on their identification with a pacifistic Savior who never opposed Rome and who had been crucified at Jewish instigation."[23] The Jesus who appears in the Gospels is not political and presents no threat to Rome even though his was the death of a political subversive, and the "pacifist Jesus" shows forth in the Gospels to blunt any suppression of the Christian community by Rome. In other words, the Gospels portray Jesus as having been put to death not by Rome, not really, but by the Jews, who rejected claims made by the Christian community that Jesus was the Messiah. The story of Jesus' execution is presented as an unjust and conspiratorial killing instigated by the Jews, the real culprits, with Rome washing its hands of the affair and letting the Jews have their way. Rome thus comes across as relatively innocent and the Jews deeply guilty of what was viewed in the early church as an unjust execution.

The Gospels are riddled with anti-Jewish sentiment, and nowhere more so than in the Passion narratives. The anti-Jewishness that permeates the narratives obscures from us—from history itself—what I want to claim as the fourth historical fact about Jesus' death that we can claim with certainty. And that is the fact I have already alluded to—that Jesus was condemned to death for offense against Rome and was executed by the Romans in the Roman manner. The offense in all likelihood was sedition. Having been judged guilty of a capital offense as a political undesirable, Jesus paid the penalty for posing a threat to the established order.

A fifth fact to be extracted from the historical record is that because Jesus was accused, sentenced, and then executed by the Roman system that claimed legal jurisdiction over such capital cases as his, Jesus stands in the history of criminal justice administration as guilty. He was guilty of a capital offense before the legal authorities who claimed jurisdiction over his case. They claimed the authority to judge him and to dispose of his case as the law allowed. Having the power of execution, they used it. Having found Jesus guilty of capital offense and thus meriting death, the judging authority saw that Jesus was condemned, crucifixion being his just desert. As a matter of historical reconstruction, with so many story lines distorted and details lost, what we can say with historical certainty is that the criminal justice system Jesus faced executed him and did so because it found him guilty. Jesus was not innocent before the law, but a guilty man condemned by proper legal authority to suffer execution.

What we can conclude from looking at the cross historically is that if there was something terrible in Jesus' death, it was not that the Jews conspired to kill him or were in any way involved in his execution. As Levy said, there was no trial before the Jewish authorities, no crime of blasphemy on the Sanhedrin docket. Rome killed Jesus. The Gospel distortion of this sliver of historical fact unleashed a terrible destructive energy against the Jewish people that has tragically persisted into our own time, a distortion of the Gospel message itself.

If there was something terrible in the fact that Jesus died, it is not to be found in the "fact" that Jesus was an innocent man unjustly condemned. We do not know that he was innocent of any crime against the state, but can, on the basis of his condemnation, reasonably infer his guilt under Roman law. The Jesus we encounter in history is a guilty Jesus; if, in fact, what Jesus was advocating was a realm of God based on the rule of love and justice rather than Roman power, such an affirmation simply underscores his actual guilt.

If there was something terrible in Jesus' death, all we can do is point to the simplest fact of all—that he was executed. If we want to condemn the execution of Jesus as an evil act, all we can base our condemnation on, historically, is that he died a terrible death and that what was terrible about that death is that he was actually put to death by a state that claimed power to execute him. And if it is true that two thieves were crucified with him, they died deaths that were just as terrible and for the same reason—because they were executed. It is in the fact of Jesus' execution that we must locate condemnation for his execution, if condemnation of that death is in our hearts—and it may not be, as I shall indicate in the next section.

I have argued in this book that execution is a symbol of power, not justice. The cross could be considered a symbol of justice, in the same way many people today think of the electric chair or the lethal injection gurney as a symbol of justice. But if, on the other hand, the cross is a symbol of power, Jesus' death is really no different from any other execution at any other time in history justified for any other reason. If the reasons for executing a person matter, then justice raises its head, and Jesus, like every other person condemned to death, could be said to have received such justice as the state is able to deliver. But if the issue is power, then Jesus suffered the same death that any other person suffers when subjected to such power as the state will claim in order to kill an individual for whatever crime the state specifies—be it murder or rape or theft or political trouble-making, or sedition.[24]

Historically, the cross represents a particularly unpleasant method employed by the Roman state in the time of Jesus to execute the state's will, but that is not to equate the will of the state with justice. Who among today's staunchest death penalty supporters could know anything about the history of the Roman Empire and its rather liberal execution policy, especially in its territories, and claim that justice rather than power was what sustained that policy? The power to execute is secured by the state claiming the power to impute an absolute responsibility to an individual offender. What justice demands when such absolutes are in play is action fitting the absolute attribution of responsibility. By killing the offender and rendering what is due, justice is served in an absolute and perfect—perfectly fitting—way, that is, by means of a just and fitting execution. But if perfection cannot be had in the evaluation of the offender's offense, any action that delivers an absolute justice does so by pretense and illusion. When certain of the Gospels record that Jesus cried out that his executioners did not know what they were doing, his words were an accusation not only against his executioners, but against all who claim such power.

The cross, then, is a symbol of a state power to execute that is necessarily an absolute power. It is also a power that ultimately contradicts itself by legitimating the killing of those who ought to be protected from unjust killing—the innocent. And in that the absolute power is posited in the state, and not God, the cross could be considered from the point of view of history as a human pretense to absolute power which displaces God and announces that God is dead.

The Cross as Symbol

Christians affirm the cross as a central symbol of faith, and they consider the death of Jesus to have been a terrible thing. Why that particular execution was more terrible than any other is not clear—in fact, Jesus may very well have been guilty of the crime for which he was executed, more guilty of the capital crime of sedition than Willie Darden was of the capital crime of murder. If Jesus' death was a terrible thing, it is not because he can be seen as innocent and certainly not because he was the victim of a Jewish conspiracy—we have reason to believe he was not. It was, as I claimed, simply because he was executed. But many Christians support the death penalty. The question, then, is this: Was Jesus' execution evil or not? If it was wrong, in what sense was it wrong?

The answer to this question is well known. Christian theology has taken the cross—this instrument of Roman justice and absolute power—and so transformed its meaning that the cross as a historical event is all but removed from view—and is clearly removed from moral consciousness. Christian theology invests the cross with theological and metaphysical meaning. The rugged and splintering crossbeam that probably made Jesus tremble and buckle at the knees when he first shouldered it has become a symbol.

And what a symbol.

It symbolizes human suffering and divine passion. It symbolizes sacrifice and obedience unto death; it symbolizes expiation and redemption and atonement—and salvation itself. It does not serve as a symbol for the small salvations that show up in the Gospel story. I refer specifically to the disciple Peter, who, in the Passion narratives, kept his distance from Jesus and whom Jesus refused to identify as one of his followers.[25] By that dissociation, Jesus "saved" Peter as concretely as one person can save another. That concrete act of salvation is not caught up in the symbolic power of the cross. The cross, rather, is transformed to serve as the act that redeems all of humanity and saves the whole world.

The cross as symbol has become so abstracted from the cross on which Jesus died that Christians who think Jesus' death was a terrible thing can continue to deplore that evil while at the same time supporting "in principle" the death penalty. How can Christians deplore the crucifixion of Jesus, yet turn around and lend the death penalty their support, as if there were no contradiction? My answer to this question is simple: They do not really deplore the meaning of the death penalty. They do not even deplore Jesus' execution, if truth be told. This assertion can be defended by a brief consideration of certain theological meanings that attach to the cross.

Christian theology has given positive meaning to the cross, investing it as a symbol of salvation. In this symbolic investiture, the meaning of the cross has become essentially metaphysical, disconnected from the arena of justice dispensation. Atonement theologies, for instance, assert that the cross provided a mysterious means of human salvation from the power of sin and death (1 Cor. 1:17 f.; Gal. 2:19; 6:14), so that as much as it is a sign of Christ's obedience to God and a demonstration of Christ's voluntary humiliation, it is also a sign of victory over the powers of spiritual oppression. Traditional Christian atonement theologies hold that in Adam's fall all of humanity was made prisoner to Satan, sin and bondage unto death. Jesus' death provides a redeeming sacrifice that liberates humanity. As the Christ, Jesus submits to the cross to make expiation for human sin before God, to repair humanity's alienation from God "by his own blood" (Rom. 3:25; 1 Pet. 1:18 ff.). In light of the cross, traditional Christian atonement theologies hold that by his death Christ effected a reconciliation of the world to God so that God would no longer count sin against humanity (2 Cor. 5:19).

The cross, then, stands as a multivalenced symbol of expiation, sacrifice, reconciliation, atonement, and redemption that restores humanity to right relation with God. It signals humanity's redemption from sin and the power of death. The lamb sacrificed in this atonement-expiation theology must be innocent and undeserving of death. Incarnate of God, meaning, as Paul put it, that God was "in" him reconciling the world, the Christ accepts this death as the consequence of human sinfulness and presents his sacrifice to God in expiation for human sin. God accepts this expiation by blood so that humanity's salvation can thus be effected. The innocent Christ takes on an undeserved punishment, and the cross becomes a symbol for the redemption of all of humanity.

In atonement theologies the logic of sacrifice and expiation governs the symbol of the cross. God imposes this divine logic and requires that it be played out, even to the point of requiring Jesus as the Christ to accept an unjust death. Though it is not always put in such blunt language, the theology that upholds this sacrifice-expiation-redemption requires Jesus' death, unjust though it may be. If it is unjust in human terms, unjust because of Jesus' innocence, it is clearly "necessary" in the divine logic and the divine justice.

The divine justice that accepts the sacrifice of blood in Christ's atoning work of expiation for sin is essentially retributive. The divine logic of atonement requires a sacrificial death, which Jesus provides as the Christ. As John Jefferson Davis explains this symbolization of the death penalty as it applied to Jesus:

> The necessity of the death of Christ on the cross is grounded on the fundamental moral fact that in the sight of God certain actions (sin and crime) are *inherently worthy of punishment*. The moral scales of the universe must be righted. The concept of retributive justice is rooted in the very heart of God's character and the gospel itself. The good news is not that God has disregarded

standards of justice, but that he himself has satisfied those standards for us and taken our rightful punishment upon himself in the person of his Son. Capital punishment is actually the application on the human plane of the principle of retributive justice demonstrated by God himself in the cross of Jesus Christ.[26]

What I want to say about this theology is that it is abstract and thoroughly metaphysical, even if its roots go back to blood-sacrifice expiation theology and ritual practices familiar to Paul and the evangelists. In this theologizing of the cross, the guilty Jesus cannot and does not appear. Jesus is subsumed by the Christ and presents himself for sacrifice as an innocent undeserving not only of execution but of death itself, since death is a consequence of sin and the Christ as incarnate divinity is sinless. Jesus as guilty before the law is transformed through Christian atonement theology into a metaphysical innocent who suffers unjust death and by that death effects the salvation of the whole world. It is no wonder that capital punishment as an issue can receive no hearing in this presentation of the cross's symbolic meaning. If the execution of Jesus saves me, and not only me but potentially everybody, the call to reclaim a theological meaning for the cross relevant to capital punishment seems trivial, almost ridiculous.

Given the positive theological consequences that flow from Jesus' death on a cross, including the triumph over death itself in the resurrection theology that follows, it is hard for many Christians not to accept this death as so beneficial that the execution behind it comes to be regarded as "an acceptable loss." If, in accordance with a mysterious but divine logic, the cross is necessary to effect reconciliation with God, the cross cannot really be the evil act an opponent of capital punishment would want to claim for Jesus' execution or any other execution. Christian theology so transforms the meaning of this execution death theologically and metaphysically that the execution is rendered a good thing—a bad thing that God has made good. The qualification is added, of course, that only God has sufficient power to effect such a transformation, but the point is that the transvaluation of the cross to salvific symbol is accomplished, and Christian theology grasps this positive meaning. The evil of the execution is suppressed by the glorious redemption of humanity which the cross was instrumental in effecting. This may account for the fact that certain Christians will continue to endorse the death penalty, not seeing this instrument in the state's arsenal of power as being truly evil, for even the evil of Jesus' cross is obscured by the glorious fact that by that cross humanity's reconciliation with God is effected, the cosmos is redeemed, the world is saved, and, not incidentally, so am I.

The cross has been transformed from a symbol of the state's power to obliterate human life—in the name of justice—into the burnished icons of salvation worn around Christian necks, placed on worship altars, and displayed in places of Christian worship for aesthetic enhancement and symbolic reminding. The power of this symbol to remind directs attention to the abstract theology of salvation rather than to the brutality of the cross and its destructive power. It seems not to direct reflection toward the theological meaning of the death penalty but to the grace of God and the belief that by the acceptable sacrifice—the acceptable loss—of Jesus' death, redemption was effected and salvation was made possible.

My purpose here is to describe the symbol of the cross as it has come to possess meaning in a Christian theological picture. My aim is not to attack this picture; I prefer to leave it to Jesus' own words and actions in the Gospels to do that. The Gospels present a Jesus whose God was a God of love and mercy, not a God willing to support human beings in their execution practices. In the Gospel story of the woman about to be stoned to death for adultery, Jesus shows his theology of execution by intervening to prevent it, reminding the attackers that their justice is imperfect because they are imperfect.

Jesus speaks elsewhere to express his execution theology. Let me point out once again that on the cross Jesus asks forgiveness for his executioners. In this statement is revealed the true evil of the death penalty theologically considered. Jesus on the cross does not say, "I forgive you," for he recognizes that the offense being committed by this execution is not ultimately directed at him. It is directed at God. God therefore is the appropriate party to forgive the execution wrongdoing. Only God can forgive the executioner, according to Jesus on the cross, for the death penalty is directed not only at a miscreant found guilty of a crime as Jesus was, but at God, who, because humans have seized the power to execute, is displaced by human authority and symbolically killed. Jesus, therefore, asks for the forgiveness for his executioners that God alone seems to have the power to grant. That many of those who follow Jesus religiously may fail to appreciate that by his death the death penalty itself was being put on trial theologically gives new meaning and added poignance to the curious expression recorded in Scripture, now not so curious, that his executioners "know not what they do."

Expiation theologizing transforms the cross into a divine instrument of blessing, healing, and restoration of relationships. The cross as cross, however, is no such symbol, and Jesus, as I have argued in this chapter, clearly opposes picturing God as the source of retributive justice. Casting the cross as yielding a positive redemptive benefit rather than as a symbol of political terrorism, moral horror, and theological destruction distorts the clear condemnation of execution that the Gospels show Jesus expressing and enacting. This construction of the cross as a positive boon to humanity requires an extraordinary leap into abstraction and metaphysical meaning. The Jesus confronting the death penalty, the guilty Jesus, has been abstracted from history so that he stands before his judges as an innocent. But what must be remembered is that in this abstracting process, the innocence that attaches to Jesus is all metaphysically concocted, as is the atonement theology that requires the lamb to be innocent and pure so that the sacrifice will be acceptable to God.

I have opened this discussion in the interests of trying to revivify the cross as a symbol of the death penalty even though this is hardly what it means to Christians and despite the fact that this is the plainest, clearest, and most grounded meaning that could conceivably attach to it. The mystery is that the meaning of the cross as death penalty is not appropriated or experienced by many who claim to understand the symbol, who use it and practice their faith in relation to it. The mystery is that the cross seems not to denote the death penalty to many Christians and forges no connection to execution as it is practiced today. For the cross still possesses power to symbolize the human penchant to be rid of undesirables and legal offenders and to do so with legally authorized violence. It is as a dangerous symbol of death, of legalized killing and unjust death, even the death of God, that this symbol needs to be reclaimed, not as a symbol of salvation.

Seen as a symbol of the death penalty, the cross points toward our fallibility and our tendency to refuse to recognize our fallibility, covering it by legalizing our claim to exercise God-like power. As an accusation and indictment of persons who stand historically unredeemed from such behavior, its accusatory power is as relevant today as ever it was in Jesus' day. But many do not see this, including many Christians who continue to think that the death penalty can be divorced from Jesus' salvific death, and that salvation can be had from a crucified Christ without that crucifixion in any way challenging their support for use of the execution power.

The tendency of Christians to cover up the cross as death penalty symbol has been achieved by the self-deceptive act of transforming Jesus' death from a moral horror into a salvific event that saves me and my loved ones and potentially all the world. My theological accusation is that this process has divinized Jesus at the expense of his humanity, thus pointing to a heretical Docetism that has always affected Christian theologizing about the person and work of Christ.

The cross as a symbol of capital punishment provokes a new theological starting place for theology, directing theological reflection away from the idea of universal salvation toward the need of human beings to condemn universally the execution practice that, as the Gospels show Jesus saying, requires forgiveness and requires that forgiveness first of all from God. New theological directions can be opened by focusing not on the claim that Jesus' death saved humanity, but on the question, What would have happened if we had refused to execute Jesus? What would that have meant theologically? What then?

Some Christians would undoubtedly say that without that death, that execution, we would have no claim on salvation, that the redemptive work of Christ would not have been effected, and that we would be lost. But could not a case be made that because we crucified him, we demonstrated just how lost we were— and are? Could it not be the case that because we crucified him and continue to execute others we show not that we are saved but that salvation has eluded us? A theology of the cross that begins with a condemnation of the cross leads us to consider revision of central theological concepts, for could our salvation have been effected just as easily—more easily and certainly more visibly—by saying no to Jesus' execution, and to every execution? I accept the claim that only God possesses sufficient power to transform the moral and theological horror of an execution into a positive, life-affirming salvific event, but saying no to executions—to Jesus' execution and to all executions that, for Christians, have meaning in light of his—could have effected a different kind of salvation, the kind that does not rely on an inscrutable metaphysics generated out of models Jesus himself is shown in the Gospels rejecting—models of retributive justice, and of appeasing a wrathful God with innocent blood.

The challenge of the cross as symbol is not to see the metaphysics beyond it but the physics—the ordinary reality of fear and fainting, of pain and blood, of a profound human cruelty and willingness to obliterate life. Were we the kind of beings who would not crucify the best among us, we might not need such a grand leap into metaphysics to create meaning and justification for such a death as this death was. The cross is a hope for many, but I hold that it is, theologically, an accusation. It points to human injustice. It points to the usurpation of divine power which to claim and to use in the name of justice is to displace God. And while it may be regarded as a symbol of salvation, its deeper meaning, obscured by theological metaphysics, may be this—that we should not do such things, that we should refuse to exercise such a power even if we can claim it, grasp it, and use it. Could the message of the cross not be something plain and simple—that we should not have done to him what we did, and that as we should not have done to him what we did, we should not do such things to others? "Were you there when they crucified my Lord?" the old hymn asks. Yes. And we did not protest, and that is why "Sometimes it causes us to tremble, tremble . . . "

The cross as metaphysical abstraction obstructs the clarity of both moral and theological vision, preventing many Christians from seeing that what Jesus went through people still go through today. That we did not stop his execution could be a starting place for considering that in that failure is the motive for stopping this from happening to others. By aligning ourselves with Jesus' own condemnation of execution and the vision of God on which Jesus based that condemnation, do we not participate in atoning for his death, not in the realm of abstraction, but in the realm of history where God is with us? Would a church united in its condemnation of execution not be pointing toward a hope for salvation by asserting a claim that to be human is a grand and deep mystery, and that no one ought to assume that any life is worthless and disposable, even those guilty of serious crimes and heinous moral violations? Redemption in such a view would be turned from a divine demand for innocent blood to this thought: that until all are saved none of us is saved. By reclaiming the cross as cross, a broader effort at theological reclamation could begin—but it requires a no to the cross and to all forms of execution, even if they are not so bloody and cruel, even if they appear antiseptic and a swab of alcohol is applied before injecting a needle of death.

The cross is a symbol of an action we undertake toward one another. It is quite possible that its meaning ought not to be abstract but rough and plain, and that that meaning ought to have weight for us, a weight comparable to that of the crossbeam that felled him, the story goes, bringing him to his knees. And that meaning is dimly this: that we ought not do this. That it was done to him is no reason it should be done to others in his name—just the opposite would seem the plainer meaning. It ought not be done. Not to Jesus, or Willie Darden—not even to Ted Bundy or Timothy McVeigh. Jesus' death was so horrific to his followers that to justify it, to find meaning in it, his death was sublimated into a theological abstraction that makes everything right. Christians need to consider in this refashioning of a theology of the cross that human salvation could have been effected less metaphysically, more concretely, had we not killed him. Expiation theology blinds us to other options for theological thinking by requiring a shedding of innocent blood to appease a divine wrath and satisfy a divine retributive justice. But what this obscures is another possibility for theological meaning, one we seem not to want to attend to, which is simply this: that the killing of Jesus was a death God did not want. Were we the kinds of beings who did not do this to one another, we would not be the kinds of beings that required such an elaborate justification for this one death that, truth be told, however guilty Jesus was, ought not to have occurred and cannot be justified.

The death penalty is a moral evil and a theological horror that traditions of Christian theologizing prevent us from seeing. And because we can justify it, see it as a necessary and even a good thing, we cannot see this horror. But I think Jesus saw it, as does any person condemned to death. I cannot believe that, confronted with the cross on his day of swift execution, his heart leaped at the thought of saving humanity, of atoning for humanity's sin with his blood. He died surrounded by only a few who loved him, as do those who face execution today. He died asking for God's forgiveness, but also condemning all that was happening to him. Too many who follow him, even today, grasp at the forgiveness and accept it, ignoring the condemnation the forgiveness presupposes. Sharing in the condemnation might have prevented that death and the innumerable deaths of others that can be traced to trying to locate blame for this death anywhere other than in where it belongs—in the human heart that calls for Jesus' blood one day, Willie Darden's another, Timothy McVeigh's on yet another.

Execution ought, from a theological point of view, to be condemned, the condemnation serving as the source of our theologizing. As it was, that execution outside the walls of Jerusalem two thousand years ago changed everything. Saying no to it—to that killing and every other one like it—has a similar potential. For what might be transformed by that no is something more important than a theological system that takes an evil and makes it good. What might be transformed by this no is the human heart.

Notes

1. Popular Support for the Death Penalty

1. Albert Camus, "Reflections on the Guillotine," in *Resistance, Rebellion, and Death*, trans. and introduction by Justin O'Brien (New York: Modern Library, 1963). The statistics have been gleaned from Kevin Drawbaugh, "Halt to Illinois Execution Not Seen as Turning Point," *Reuters News Service*, January 16, 1996; and Bruce Tomaso, "Texas' Deadly Ritual," *Dallas Morning News*, October 1, 1995.

2. Dr. Jack Kevorkian observes that condemned persons could help the living by allowing the state to harvest their organs at execution and that condemned prisoners support this because they are seeking some kind of meaning in their deaths. The moral queasiness that quickly surfaces springs from concern over the violation of a physician's professional ethic to "do no harm." A physician willing to become the practical agent of execution by harvesting organs in usable form would be forced to perform vivisection. The American Medical Association's code of ethics, which prohibits physician assistance in execution, has taken no stand on the morality of execution itself.

3. See my *Life/Choice: The Theory of Just Abortion* (Cleveland: The Pilgrim Press, 1994).

2. Who Was Willie Darden?

1. Robert W. Lee, "Deserving to Die," *The New American*, August 13, 1990; reprinted in *The Death Penalty: Opposing Viewpoints*, 2d ed., ed. Carol Wekesser (San Diego: Greenhaven Press, 1991), 97–104.

2. See *Truth Seeker* 121, 5 (1994); quoted in *The Death Penalty: Opposing Viewpoints*, 3d ed., ed. Paul A. Winters (San Diego: Greenhaven, 1997), 136.

3. Lee, "Deserving to Die," 100.

4. Ibid., 100–101. Emphasis mine.

5. The details of Darden's case presented in this section are taken from various press stories, including John Nordheimer, "Defense Say Florida Is Hasty in Moving to Execute Convict," *New York Times*, March 10, 1988, 20; and David Behrens, "Question of Time and Fairness," *Newsday*, February 22, 1988, 4 ff. Also valuable is Joseph B. Ingle, *Last Rights: Thirteen Fatal Encounters with the State's Justice* (Nashville: Abingdon, 1990), 254–68.

6. Ingle, *Last Rights*, 258.

7. Ibid., 261.

8. Quoted in Tony Mauro, "Blackmun: No Longer a Cog in the Machinery of Death," *Connecticut Law Tribune* (March 7, 1994): 16. Also quoted in Ingle, 262.

9. Quoted in Ingle, *Last Rights*, 266.

3. Just Means and Ends, or "Just Killing"?

1. Commutative and distributive justice were notions advanced by Thomas Aquinas in the *Summa Theologica*, 2, II, q. 61, art. 1, trans. T. Gilby, O.P., Blackfriars edition (New York: McGraw-Hill, 1975), 37: 87–101.

2. Robert C. Solomon, *A Passion for Justice: Emotions and Origins of the Social Contract* (Lanham, Md.: Rowman and Littlefield, 1995), 3.

3. Social justice means society has a duty to ensure that all persons have an opportunity to participate fully in the life of society.

4. See chapter 5 for a critique of Mill's death penalty position.

5. John Stuart Mill, "Capital Punishment, 21 April 1868," *Public and Parliamentary Speeches, November 1850–November 1868*, ed. John M. Robson and Bruce Kinzer (Toronto: University of Toronto Press, Routledge, 1988), 271.

6. For example, the American Bar Association resolved on February 3, 1997, that a moratorium be placed on the death penalty in the United States, yet little notice has been given to this.

7. *The Los Angeles Times* reported (October 4, 1995), in the wake of the O. J. Simpson criminal trial, that 52 percent of respondents nationwide considered the U.S. court system to be unsound; only 33 percent expressed confidence in the jury system.

8. U.S. Department of Justice, Bureau of Justice Statistics, for persons executed in 1995 <http://sun.soci.niu.edu/~critcrim/dp/cp95>, 2.

9. Gacy was executed May 10, 1994. During his lethal injection one of the drugs clogged the tube leading into his arm, stopping the flowing. The witnesses were screened from view, a new tube was inserted, and the execution resumed. For summaries of 19 botched executions since 1976, see Michael Radelet <http://sun.soci.niu.ed . . . crim/dp/dppapers/mike2>.

10. On March 25, 1997, Pedro Medina was executed in Florida with witnesses horrified to see flames erupting from his head as the execution commenced. A similar incident had occurred on May 4, 1990, when a fire erupted from Jesse Joseph Tafero's skull and three electric jolts were required to stop his breathing.

11. For example, as noted by Andrei Sakharov, the Darden case attracted international attention. In Pennsylvania, the case of Mumia Abu-Jamal, a convicted murderer whose guilt is widely doubted, has also received media attention. See also International Concerned Family and Friends of Mumia Abu-Jamal <http://www.Mumia.org>.

12. See *Sentencing for Life: Americans Embrace Alternatives to the Death Penalty*, 6, Death Penalty Information Center (April 1993). Quoted in Staff Report by the Subcommittee on Civil and Constitutional Rights, Committee on the Judiciary, 103d Cong., 1st sess., "Innocence and the Death Penalty: Assessing the Danger of Mistaken Executions," issued October 21, 1993, 2. Hereafter cited as Staff Report.

13. This statistic is from NAACP Legal Defense Fund <http://sun.soci.niu.ed . . . rim/dp/do.breakdown.96>.

14. Michael L. Radelet, Hugo Adam Bedau, and Constance E. Putnam, *In Spite of Innocence: Erroneous Convictions in Capital Cases* (Boston: Northeastern University Press, 1992).

15. Stephen Markman, "Innocents on Death Row?" *National Review*, September 12, 1994, argues against this claim by examining the case of James Adams, one of the 23 wrongful executions claimed by Radelet, Bedau, and Putnam, *In Spite of Innocence.*

16. For the story of James Richardson, who was released from death row on the basis of evidentiary findings of innocence, see my article "Casting the First Stone: Capital Punishment Is Still a Moral Problem," *Christianity and Crisis* 50, 1 (February 5, 1990): 11–16.

17. Staff Report, 2. Since 1930, 48 persons have been released from prison after serving time on death row. In 44 cases, inmates were acquitted, pardoned, or released after charges were dropped. In four cases, inmates pleaded to lesser offenses. In the remaining case, the inmate was declared innocent by a parole board.

4. The Right to Life, Liberty, and Security

1. Edwin Good, "Capital Punishment and Its Alternatives in Ancient Near Eastern Law," *Stanford Law Review* 19 (May 1967): 947–67.

2. Ibid., 951.

3. Ibid., 952–53.

4. Ibid., 947–77.

5. Norman Krivosha, Robert Copple, and Michael McDonough, "A Historical and Philosophical Look at the Death Penalty: Does It Serve Society's Needs?" *Creighton Law Review* 16 (1982–83): 1–46. See also John Jefferson Davis, *Evangelical Ethics: Issues Facing the Church Today*, 2d ed. (Phillipsburg, N.J.: P & R Publishers, 1993), 177.

6. See Francis A. Allen, "Capital Punishment," in *International Encyclopedia of the Social Sciences*, ed. David Sills (New York: Macmillan, 1968), 2:290–94.

7. Harry Potter, *Hanging in Judgment: Religion and the Death Penalty in England* (New York: Continuum, 1993), 213 n. 6. See also Francesco Compagnoni, "Capital Punishment and Torture in the Tradition of the Roman Catholic Church," *Concilium* 120 (1978): 39–53.

8. Krivosha, Copple, and McDonough, "Death Penalty," 12.

9. Ibid., 22.

10. Ibid., 27.

11. Ibid., 28.

12. Charshee Lawrence-McIntyre, *Criminalizing a Race: Free Blacks during Slavery* (Queens, N.Y.: Kayode, 1993). Gerald Horne, "America's Justice System Discriminates against Blacks," quoted in *Race Relations*, ed. Paul A. Winters (San Diego: Greenhaven Press, 1996), 135.

13. Legal Defense and Education Fund (LDF) attorneys from the NAACP have argued in several legal challenges to capital punishment that racial discrimination affects the way the death sentence is imposed. The Baldus study shows that of 2,000 cases in Georgia, black defendants had a significantly higher likelihood of receiving a death sentence than whites. Even though the U.S. Supreme Court did not refer explicitly to racial bias in its 1972 *Furman v. Georgia* decision, which struck down the death penalty, its decision did mention that racial minorities were disproportionately affected by the way the death penalty was administered. Then in 1987, the Supreme Court handed down its decision in *McCleskey v. Kemp*, declaring that the death penalty should *not* be ruled unconstitutional because of racial discrimination. Justice Lewis Powell Jr. accepted the validity of the Baldus study but held that the broad pattern of discrimination was insufficient to prove *actual* discrimination in McCleskey's case. The discretion provided prosecutors and juries would lead to inevitable, albeit occasional, disparities. A defendant, however, has "to prove that the decision makers in his case acted with discriminatory purpose."

14. Moral thought is always constructed in relation to an affirmation of the good. On the one hand, postmodern attempts to take up a position outside such an affirmation are impoverished to the extent that they eschew this pursuit of a vision of goodness; on the other hand, their claims to freedom from such a vision continue the modernist impulse. Enlightenment views are inescapable and prevalent in how we go about shaping moral arguments and positions.

15. Christina Hoff Sommers and Fred Sommers, *Vice and Virtue in Everyday Life: Introductory Readings in Ethics* (San Diego: Harcourt Brace College Publishers, 1993): 203–9.

16. Ibid., 206.

17. Ibid., 203.

18. See Ruth Benedict, "Anthropology and the Abnormal," *Journal of General Psychology* 10 (1934): 59–82. The Star Trek prime directive of noninterference with other cultures has been thoroughly appropriated by younger persons, and this is the positive aspect of Benedict's discussion of relativism. What is often absent from teaching about the goodness of diversity is the common moral vision of goodness that supports sociological diversity and provides a basis for critique of morally offensive actions. John Hospers in *Human Conduct* (New York: Harcourt Brace Jovanovich, 1961) offers one of the most cogent defenses of sociological versus ethical relativism and is the warrant for my claim that ethical or moral relativism is philosophically incoherent.

19. Preston Williams, "Human Rights Thinking in Relation to African Nation-States: Some Suggestions in Response to Simeon O. Ilesanmi," *Journal of Religious Ethics* 23.2 (fall 1995): 324: "Not origins [of the idea] but what it means to be human qua human is the key [to establishing a claim to a universal human right]."

20. Naomi Hirakawa, "Amnesty Call for Abolition of the Death Penalty," *Japan Times Weekly International Edition*, May 15, 1995, 3.

21. See exception regarding extreme gravity in *Catechism of the Catholic Church* 2266, 604. The exception seems tricky to apply.

22. All references and quotations in text are to John Locke, *Two Treatises of Government: A Critical Edition*, 2d ed., ed. Peter Laslett (Cambridge: Cambridge University Press, 1967). References are to the *Second Treatise*, chapter and section, plus page number in the Cambridge text.

23. See Brian Calvert, "Locke on Punishment and the Death Penalty," *Philosophy* 68, no. 263 (January 1993): 219; and A. John Simmons, "Locke on the Death Penalty," *Philosophy* 69, no. 270 (October 1994): 477.

24. Hugo Adam Bedau, "Capital Punishment," in *Matters of Life and Death: New Introductory Essays in Moral Philosophy*, 2d ed., ed. Tom Regan (New York: Random House, 1986), 180–81.

25. Harry Potter, *Hanging in Judgment*, 6. The Bloody Code in use before the nineteenth century explicitly justifies the practice—applied to children as young as eight—as a means of deterrence.

5. A Service to the Greater Good

1. See, for example, Richard B. Brandt, *Morality, Rights and Utilitarianism* (Cambridge: Cambridge University Press, 1992), 9.

2. See, for example, s.v. *utilitarianism*, *Dictionary of Philosophy and Religion: Eastern and Western Thought*, ed. W. L. Reese (Atlantic Highlands, N.J.: Humanities Press, 1980).

3. See, for example, Bernard Williams, *Morality: An Introduction to Ethics* (Cambridge: Cambridge University Press, 1972), 97; and J. J. C. Smart and Bernard Williams, *Utilitarianism: For and Against* (Cambridge: Cambridge University Press, 1973), 7.

4. Although critics of utilitarianism point out that utilitarian calculation can permit actions that are not benevolent—the deliberate infliction of pain or suffering is allowable if a net savings results—defenders of utilitarianism such as John Stuart Mill have argued the opposite case, namely, that by advancing the welfare of all, utilitarianism encourages an attitude of general benevolence. See Tom Sorell, *Moral Theory and Capital Punishment* (Oxford: Basil Blackwell, 1987), 64.

5. Hugo Adam Bedau, "Bentham's Utilitarian Critique of the Death Penalty," *Journal of Criminal Law and Criminology* 74, no. 3 (1983): 1033–65.

6. Ibid. Bedau notes that Bentham identified that the utilitarian-based justifications for punishment ought to be "general Prevention" of crime (ibid., 1038), with punishment itself being a harm or evil. Bentham thought that alternative punishments met the general utilitarian objectives without the disutility of destroying a citizen life. Bentham fails to explain why some of the factors he raises to weigh in his utilitarian calculus have the particular weight he assigns them. He also faces the general utilitarian problem as to what "total happiness of the community" means.

7. Bentham excluded sexual acts between consenting adults from the category of crime.

8. See Jeremy Bentham, "Capital Punishment Examined," *The Works of Jeremy Bentham*, vol. 1, ed. John Bowring (New York: Russell & Russell, 1962), 444–50.

9. Speech 92, "Capital Punishment," in John Stuart Mill, *Public and Parliamentary Speeches: November 1850–November 1868*, ed. John M. Robson and Bruce Kinzer (Toronto: University of Toronto Press, Routledge, 1988), 266–272. Page numbers in parentheses in this section of the above text make reference to this edition of the text of Mill's speech.

10. Michel Foucault, *Discipline and Punishment: The Birth of the Prison* (New York: Pantheon, 1977), 46.

11. Statistics cited from Carol Ann Campbell, "A TV Guide for Kids," *The Record*, September 15, 1996, A1. Campbell also claims that homicide rates doubled in the fifteen-year period after television was introduced into American culture.

12. Albert Camus, "Reflections on the Guillotine," 143. The murder rate in Florida rose 12 percent after the state resumed executions.

13. I owe this point to Michael Raposa.

14. Thomas Sowell and John J. DiIulio Jr., "The Death Penalty Is a Deterrent," reprinted in *The Death Penalty: Opposing Viewpoints*, 3d ed., ed. Paul A. Winters (San Diego: Greenhaven Press, 1997), 104. Sowell and DiIulio claim that deterrence cannot work when so small a number of persons are put to death in comparison to the number of murders that could be made eligible for execution.

15. For an extended discussion of this kind of covering of moral wrongdoing with justifications, see my book *Self-Deception and the Common Life* (New York: Peter Lang, 1986).

16. Recent numbers are 23,000 homicides per year, but only 300 death sentences. Actual execution rates are smaller. In the 19-year period between 1977 and 1995, 5,237 persons were under sentence of death, and 313 executions were carried out (171 whites, 120 blacks, 19 Hispanics, 2 Native Americans, and 1 Asian), or 19 per year on average. See the National Archive of Criminal Justice Data as reported by the U.S. Justice Bureau of Justice Statistics, <http://sun.soci.niu.edu/~critcrim/dp/dp95>.

17. Opponents of the death penalty could support executions if they were pretend events. Knowing that they were pretend events, however, would render Mill's deterrent effect inefficacious.

18. Americans who honor the war dead do so on the grounds that they have sacrificed life for a higher good, namely, the preservation of freedom. This means that the greatest evil that could befall Americans is the loss of freedom. If Americans also hold that aggravated murder is the worst crime, then not death but loss of freedom (imprisonment) ought to be the fitting response to this scheme of valuation.

19. Mill reminds us that life imprisonment is a harsh punishment, the harshness of which ought not be downplayed. But Tom Sorell, *Moral Theory and Capital Punishment*, notes that a faked execution would yield relevant benefits in a way that is even more humane than execution (87–89).

6. A Just Retribution for Murder

1. Immanuel Kant, *Foundations of the Metaphysics of Morals*, trans. and introduction by Lewis White Beck (Indianapolis: Bobbs-Merrill, 1959), 39. The categorical imperative is "act only according to that maxim by which you can at the same time will that it should become a universal law." Page citations in text refer to this work.

2. Ibid., 40.

3. Sorell, *Moral Theory and Capital Punishment*, 138.

4. Cesare Beccaria, *On Crime and Punishments*, trans. Henry Paolucci (Indianapolis: Bobbs-Merrill, 1963). Beccaria's work influenced the cause of penal reform in several European states.

5. Sorrell, *Moral Theory and Capital Punishment*, 143–44.

6. See Roger J. Sullivan, *Immanuel Kant's Moral Theory* (Cambridge: Cambridge University Press, 1989), 244 n. 23.

7. The Court in *Woodson*, addressing Mill's concerns, held that particularized consideration must be given to relevant aspects of a convicted defendant's character and record.

8. Kant, *Metaphysical Elements of Justice*, 132. "Like for like" reciprocal punishment, Kant held, cannot be obtained in crimes such as rape, pederasty, or bestiality. Thus, rapists and pederasts are to be castrated, and those who practice bestiality are to be expelled or exiled from society (132–33).

9. Extralegal execution of children is widespread (Amnesty International in 1993 cited 35 countries with violating human rights by executing and torturing children extralegally); legal execution of juveniles, while not common, is practiced. The U.S. Supreme Court has upheld the execution of juveniles 16 years old and older. Governor Pete Wilson of California has supported state legislation to impose the death sentence on eligible 13- and 14-year-olds. The Commonwealth of Virginia has debated lowering the minimum execution age to 15. Between 1976 and 1993, nine men who were juveniles at the time of their crimes were executed. In *Penry v. Lynaugh* (1989), the

Supreme Court ruled that it is not cruel and unusual punishment to execute criminals who are mentally retarded.

10. John Kemp, *The Philosophy of Kant* (London: Oxford University Press, 1968), 89.

11. Kant, *Lectures on Ethics*, 214.

12. See Richard Taylor, *Good and Evil: A New Direction* (London: Collier Macmillan, 1970), for a harsh criticism of Kant.

13. Although abstract, Kant's theory that punishment is right action is easily graspable by reasonable persons: our duty is to punish criminal offenders in proportion to their crimes. Kant moves toward *absolutism* (a refusal to make exceptions) in conformity to an equality principle that shows insensitivity to situation, circumstance, and consequence. The U.S. legal system's complexity reflects that not all murders are the same and that justice is done by giving consideration to such factors as age, maturity, motive, and the like. Kant's categorical imperative that punishment must follow crime and fit the crime proportionately would simplify our legal system, for example, by demanding more consistency across jurisdictions. But it would not deliver justice in accordance with a principle of fairness.

14. Robert Johnson, *Death Work: A Study of the Modern Execution Process* (Pacific Grove, Calif.: Brooks/Cole Publishing, 1990): 54.

15. Ibid., 57.

16. Ibid.

17. Ibid.

18. Death row inmate James Richardson was subjected to such terror before he was released because convincing evidence proved his innocence. See my article, "Casting the First Stone: Capital Punishment Is Still a Moral Problem," 11–16.

19. When John Spenkelink was executed, a physician checked his heart three times, and found it to be beating after the first two surges of electricity. Attention was given only to the body as a third and final application was called for; Spenkelink was never asked if by this punishment he had learned his lesson. Any sophisticated phenomenological treatment of execution (which itself is hardly sophisticated) would reveal that the body and not the moral personality is the center of execution punishment. If this is so, then destroying the body violates Kant's demand that the moral personality not be subjected to punishment as a means to any end but be treated as an end in itself.

20. Prison officials were so concerned about a suicide threat that Spenkelink's mother, on her last visit to her son, was subjected to a strip search, including vaginal and rectal probing. The dehumanization involved in execution seems difficult to restrict only to the condemned individual.

7. A Theory of Just Execution

1. To oversimplify Western ethics tradition, duty-based or deontological ethics is associated with Kant, virtue ethics with Aristotle (and sometimes Plato), and natural law ethics with Cicero and Aquinas. I leave aside the historical development of the natural law tradition and believe that my comments about natural law broadly conceived are defensible as a moral philosophy. The best kind of moral philosophy is synthetic, and I look to Cicero for guidance because Cicero thought virtue, duty, and natural law all play a role in how we live morally and think about the moral life. Cicero was the first to devise a "just war" perspective, which Augustine imported into the Catholic moral tradition.

2. In applying this kind of theory to the abortion issue, any appeal to rights was avoided because rights is what created the abortion impasse that I was seeking to overcome. See my *Life/Choice: The Theory of Just Abortion.*

3. See my *Life/Choice*, 15–30.

4. Ibid., 31–54. I first worked out this argument in "Abortion and the Conflict of Moral Presumptions," *Papers of the Craigville Theological Colloquy VI: Human Beginnings: Deciding about Life in the Presence of God* (Craigville, Mass.: Craigville Conference Center, 1989), 20–23.

5. Some U.S. states, even those in which the death penalty is legal, cannot attribute even one death to capital punishment.

6. This is not tendentious reasoning. The moral presumption with respect to just war theory is against the use of force; with respect to abortion, against abortion; with respect to withholding treatment for severely handicapped newborns, against withholding treatment; and with respect to capital punishment, against execution. These are all consistent with the presumption that the good of life ought to be neither directly attacked nor destroyed. But as a nonabsolutist perspective, the presumption-exception model considers cases in which this presumption may be overturned.

7. W. Fitzhugh Brundage, *Lynching in the New South: Georgia and Virginia, 1880–1930* (Urbana: University of Illinois Press, 1993), 258–59. Lynchings occurred in 1954 and into the 1960s.

8. *Trop v. Dulles,* 356 U.S. 86, 101 (1958).

9. Mohamed S. El-Awa, *Punishment in Islamic Law: A Comparative Study* (Indianapolis: American Trust Publications, 1982), 10–12.

10. Locke, *Second Treatise on Civil Government,* IX, 125: 369.

11. Paul Winter, *The Death Penalty: Opposing Viewpoints,* 3d ed. (San Diego: Greenhaven Press, 1997), 178.

12. For a helpful critical discussion of the "sanctity of life" position, see Robert Holyer, "Capital Punishment and the Sanctity of Life," *International Philosophical Quarterly* 34, no. 4 (December 1994): 485–97.

8. Just Execution: Testing Practice against Theory

1. Murder is also the least repeated felony crime. See Ginny Carrol, "Society: Justice: Staying Clean: Life after Death Row," *Newsweek,* May 6, 1991, 56–57.

2. This view finds broad support. See my *Self-Deception and the Common Life* (New York: Peter Lang, 1986), 195–228.

3. For a helpful discussion of punishment as "connecting to correct values," see Robert Nozick, *Philosophical Explanations* (Cambridge: Harvard University Press, 1981): 363–93.

4. Kant, *Lectures on Ethics* (Indianapolis: Hackett Publishers, 1980), 214.

5. See C. Haney, "On the Selection of Capital Juries: The Biasing Effects of the Death Qualification Process," *Law and Human Behavior* 8 (1984): 121–32.

6. Valerie Hans, "Death by Jury," in *Challenging Capital Punishment: Legal and Social Science Approaches,* ed. Kenneth Haas and James Inciardi (Newbury Park, Calif.: Sage Publications, 1988), 149. The U.S. Supreme Court held in *Spaziano v. Florida* (1984) that no constitutional violation attaches to the complete exclusion of juries in a penalty phase. Judges who impose death sentences do so at a higher rate than juries. Thus jurors' perception that legal authority figures support the death penalty is not unfounded, and some jurors may seek to please such an authority figure by their vote for death.

7. Hans, "Death by Jury," 167.

8. Patrick Langan, "No Racism in the Justice System," *The Public Interest* 117, no. 3 (fall 1994): 48–52.

9. Stephen B. Bright, "Challenging Racism in the Infliction of the Death Penalty," *Guild Practitioner* 51, no. 4 (fall 1994): 120–28.

10. David C. Baldus, George Wordsworth, and Charles A. Pulaski Jr., *Equal Justice and the Death Penalty* (Boston: Northeastern University Press, 1990).

11. See remarks of Henry B. Gonzalez, *Congressional Record,* June 30, 1995, E1386–87. Jill Smolowe in "Law: Race and the Death Penalty," *Time,* April 29, 1991, 68–69, puts the number of white victims at 86 percent.

12. Smolowe, "Law," 68–69. Smolowe's uncited source is Watt Espy, who has documented over 16,000 legal executions in the United States since 1619 and who expects the number to climb over 22,000 when his work is completed. See Russell F. Canan, "Burning at the Wire," in *Facing*

the Death Penalty: Essays on Cruel and Unusual Punishment, ed. Michael Radelet (Philadelphia: Temple University Press, 1989), 67.

13. The Columbus, Georgia, statistics are from William Greider, "George Bush Sings the Executioner's Song," *Rolling Stone,* September 19, 1991, 37–38. Other statistics here are from *Hearings on the Death Sentence: United States, House Committee on the Judiciary,* July 10, 1991, 3.

14. Benjamin R. Civiletti, "Opinion: Death Penalty: Black and White," *Christian Science Monitor,* May 29, 1990, 18.

15. See Gonzalez, *Congressional Record,* E1386–87.

16. For references to some of these controlled studies, see Phoebe Ellsworth, "Unpleasant Facts: The Supreme Court's Response to Empirical Research on Capital Punishment," in *Challenging Capital Punishment,* ed. Hass and Inciardi, 188.

17. This information was entered by Carol Moseley-Braun; see *Congressional Record,* June 22, 1995, S8957–58.

18. Roberta Francis, "Battered Women and Child Custody Litigation Hearing," U.S. House Committee on the Judiciary, August 6, 1992, 48. Of the 33 women on death row in 1990, 14 had killed a husband or lover.

19. Frank H. Julian, "Gender and Crime: Different Sex, Different Treatment?" in *Female Criminality: The State of the Art,* ed. Concetta C. Culliver (New York: Garland Publishing, 1993), 358.

20. Ibid.

21. Smolowe, "Law," 68–69.

22. Gonzalez, *Congressional Record,* E1386–87.

23. 136 U.S. 436 (1890) at 447.

24. Russell Canan, "Burning at the Wire," 68.

25. *Amnesty International Report on Torture* (New York: Farrar, Straus & Giroux, 1975), 35. Quoted in Johnson, *Death Work,* 124.

26. Edward Peters, *Torture* (Oxford: Basil Blackwell, 1985), 4 n. 2. Quoted in Johnson, *Death Work,* 122.

27. The Barber story was published in *The Tennessean,* June 23, 1997, 1A. Much of my information comes from a conversation with Joe Ingle.

28. Johnson, *Death Work,* 126.

29. This is as of January 31, 1996. For NAACP Legal Defense Fund documents, see <http://sun.soci.niu.ed . . . rim/dp/dp.breakdown.96>.

30. Isidore Zimmerman with F. Bond, *Punishment without Crime* (New York: Clarkson N. Potter, 1964), 97. Quoted in Johnson, *Death Work,* 123.

31. My theory of just abortion is that just abortions do not subvert the value of life. Note that the reveling so typical of capital punishment is not present when abortions are performed. Just abortion has a tragic dimension to it, and the experience of that tragic dimension is the affective aspect of the criterion of nonsubversion of the value of life. Capital punishment does not seem to instill this tragic sense, and the actual presence of satisfaction (if not joy for some) in an execution is prima facie evidence that the value of life has been subverted by that execution for those caught up in such an experience.

32. Eric Schlosser, "A Grief like No Other," *Atlantic Monthly,* September 1997, 69.

33. Ibid., 75.

34. Jeffrie G. Murphy in "Cruel and Unusual Punishments," in *1979 Proceedings of the Royal Institute of Philosophy on Law and Morality,* quoted in J. L. Mackie, "Retributivism: A Test Case for Ethical Objectivity," in *Philosophy of Law,* 5th ed., ed. Joel Feinberg and Hyman Gross (Belmont, Calif.: Wadsworth, 1995), 678.

35. Schlosser, "A Grief like No Other," 75.

36. The 1995 federal crime bill increased the number of capital crimes to around sixty.

37. Trevor Marshallsea, "Amnesty Condemns China's Execution Record, " *AAP Newsfeed,* August 26, 1997.

38. Steven R. Donziger, ed., *The Real War on Crime: The Report of the National Criminal Justice Commission* (New York: HarperCollins, 1996), 55.

9. Symbol, Power, and the Death of God

1. A call for a moratorium and abolition should come not only from ideological abolitionists but also from death penalty advocates whose support of the death penalty as a moral practice is contingent on justice being served.

2. The particular capital offenses listed in the first five books of the Hebrew Scriptures (Torah) are detailed in Lloyd R. Bailey, *Capital Punishment: What the Bible Says* (Nashville: Abingdon Press, 1987), 19–22. Other capital offenses (such as treason, 1 Kings 2:13–25) were added by the monarchs.

3. Arthur Waley, *The Way and Its Power: A Study of the Tao Te Ching and Its Place in Chinese Thought* (New York: Grove Press: 1958), 234.

4. Holmes Welch, *Taoism: The Parting of the Way* (Boston: Beacon Press, 1957, 1965), 28.

5. Bailey, *Capital Punishment,* 48.

6. Gerald J. Blidstein, "Capital Punishment—the Classical Jewish Discussion," *Judaism* 14 (1965): 164.

7. Edna Erez, "Thou Shalt Not Execute: Hebrew Law Perspective on Capital Punishment," *Criminology* 19:1 (May 1981): 37.

8. *Encyclopedia Judaica,* vol. 5, 147, quoted in Lloyd R. Bailey, *Capital Punishment: What the Bible Says,* 94.

9. Lactantius, *Divinae Institutiones,* VI.xx.15, as translated in Louis J. Swift, *The Early Fathers on War and Military Service* (Wilmington, Del.: M. Glazier, 1983), 62 f.

10. Karl Barth, *Church Dogmatics,* III/pt. 4 (Edinburgh: T. & T. Clark, 1961), 443.

11. Paul understood that the Romans inflicted the death penalty, and one might argue that this understanding was assumed. The Greek term *macharia* ("sword," Rom. 13) refers specifically to the superior provincial magistrates who had the power to inflict the death penalty. Paul's reluctance to discuss this issue in light of his theology of the cross is significant. The story in Acts 25:11 is from the author of Luke-Acts. If Paul had acknowledged the state's authority to execute, Paul would logically be forced to admit Jesus' guilt before the Roman law. I do not have any evidence that Paul believed that Jesus in any way merited the execution he received.

12. Historically reliable artifacts of what Jesus really said or meant are hotly contested. I am skeptical that the received and transmitted tradition is a series of accurate quotations. The debate is irrelevant to my present purposes because I want to engage that tradition (the texts of the Gospels whether as history or interpretation or both).

13. Many biblical scholars consider this story to be non-Johannine in origin because the oldest, most reliable Greek manuscripts do not include it. The counterargument is that its preservation may very well indicate an authentic oral tradition that preserved an actual incident. The issue for our purposes is whether acting to interfere with and prevent an execution seems consistent with Jesus' broader moral and religious stance—and I think such a conclusion is clear.

14. See Christopher G. Wellison and John Bartowski, "Religion and the Legitimation of Violence: Conservative Protestantism and Corporal Punishment," in *The Web of Violence: From Interpersonal to Global,* ed. Jennifer Turpin and Lester R. Kurtz (Urbana: University of Illinois Press, 1997), 45–68.

15. Davis, *Evangelical Ethics,* 186.

16. Albert Camus, *The Stranger,* trans. Matthew Ward (New York: Vintage Press, 1989), 122.

17. Elie Wiesel, *Night,* trans. Stella Rodway (New York: Bantam Books, 1960, 1982), 62.

18. Life imprisonment would satisfy this end. The punishment would be in conformity to the demands of justice, and the ability to correct error is left open. To argue that God will effect a direct punishment does not preclude death by natural causes as fulfilling such a divinely intended end.

19. It could be argued that God fully understands that human beings can only deliver fallible justice but that God has relinquished this authority to impose an absolute and irrevocable punishment to human beings on the theory that "acceptable losses" must be viewed in a bigger context—the total good and evil produced. God, being omniscient and incapable of calculation errors in weighing good and evil, could then be said to justify wrongful executions on the utilitarian theory that in the divine and perfect calculus, the good of the execution practice finally—eschatologically—outweighs the evil and maximizes the utility of divine justice. What an extraordinary solution to the problem of theodicy!

20. John Dominic Crossan, *Who Killed Jesus?: Exposing the Roots of Anti-Semitism in the Gospel Story of the Death of Jesus* (San Francisco: HarperSanFrancisco, 1995), 159.

21. Ellis Rivkin, *What Crucified Jesus? The Political Execution of a Charismatic* (Nashville: Abingdon, 1984), 24.

22. Leonard W. Levy, *Blasphemy: Verbal Offense against the Sacred, from Moses to Salmon Rushdie* (Chapel Hill: University of North Carolina Press, 1993), 29.

23. Ibid.

24. Analyzed through the lens of history beyond Christian propagandizing of Jewish complicity in Jesus' death, the cross symbolizes imperial (even absolute) Roman power. This absoluteness appears when the death penalty is imposed beyond the reach of human correction and with fallibility in both the guilty and the innocent. That the innocent will be killed is an inevitable consequence of human fallibility, and this fact cancels any claim the death penalty can make to serving justice. Only the bald power claims of the state can support this contradiction. Jesus found himself in just this situation, along with everyone who faces death. What criminal justice system is so infallible that it can impute an absolute guilt to an individual and thus demand forfeiture of a life as just punishment, doing so secure in the knowledge that no error has been made, that no one else is implicated in the guilt, that no factors that might mitigate this absolute guilt are discernible or ever could be made available, that no grievance of injustice could have merit, now or ever, even in the future?

25. Pilate had no interest in killing Jesus' disciples. The Gospel narratives, however, present Peter as being afraid to be associated with Jesus, and I assume Peter feared for his life by the association—my reference to his lowercase salvation experience.

26. Davis, *Evangelical Ethics*, 185.

Index

abortion, 2, 4–9, 89, 91, 138, 141. *See also* just abortion theory
absolutism, 6–8, 26, 29, 33, 43–48, 88, 90, 92–93, 95, 98, 103–4, 106–7, 109, 117, 137, 140, 143, 144, 146, 150, 152–57, 161–62
acceptable losses, 64, 66, 77–78, 164–65
Amnesty International, 36–38, 41, 43, 45–48, 115, 127
animal rights, 82, 91
appeals process, 2, 5, 9–11, 17, 22, 24–25, 27–28, 108, 110, 116, 128, 139; average length, 25; reversals, 27
Aquinas, Thomas, 32, 150, 171, 176
Arkansas: executions in, 25, 101; race bias in death sentencing, 123
assisted suicide, 2. *See also* suicide
Augustine, 32, 150

Bailey, Lloyd R., 148, 179
Baldus, David, 122, 173, 177
Barber, Terry, 127, 128, 178
Barth, Karl, 150
Bass, Christine, 12–14
Beccaria, Cesare, 32, 76, 175
Bedau, Hugo Adam, 28, 47, 50, 172, 174
Benedict, Ruth, 37, 173
Bentham, Jeremy, 32, 50–51, 67, 174
Biko, Steve, 115
Bildstein, Gerald, 149, 179

Blackmun, Harry, 16
bloodguilt, 73, 81, 147, 163, 168
Bonhoeffer, Dietrich, 115
botched executions, 25, 85, 102, 109, 126–27, 139
Bundy, Ted, 168

Cain, 148
California, expenditures for executions, 9
Calvin, John, 32, 150
Camus, Albert, 1, 2, 6, 8, 56, 156, 171, 174, 179
capital punishment, 2, 4–9, 19, 32, 45, 63, 88, 91–94, 96, 97, 99, 102–7, 109, 112–13, 115–18, 121–22, 125, 128–35, 137–45, 150, 164, 166, 178–79; as attack on body, 84–86, 133–34, 139; self-deception of belief in effectiveness, 6, 24, 58, 115, 116, 175
castration, 81
categorical imperative, 70, 72–73, 75, 77–78, 81, 175
cheating, 20
China, 2, 97, 115, 136, 146
Cicero, 176
class discrimination: in applying criminal justice, 33, 34; in capital cases, 100–101, 125, 133, 134, 139; in Willie Darden case, 17

codes. *See* legal codes
Coker v. Georgia, 111
consequentialism, 48, 49, 52, 64, 66–67, 69, 71, 103–4, 112. *See also* utilitarianism
conservatives, 94
cost of execution, 9, 17
Council of Toledo, 32
cross/crucifixion, 7, 32, 97, 102, 151–52, 157–68
Crossan, John Dominic, 158–59, 180
cruelty, 54, 62–63, 67, 101–2, 106, 109, 126, 127, 131, 139, 167

Darden, Willie, 9–19, 21–22, 24, 26, 65, 120, 145–46, 162, 168–69, 171–72; class discrimination in Darden case, 17; prosecutorial misconduct in Darden case, 15; as symbol, 145–46
Davis, John Jefferson, 155, 163, 173, 180
death of God, 156–57, 161, 166
death penalty: approval ratings, 1; delays, 25; high cost, 9–17; hypocrisy of, 130; as illusion of worst punishment, 60, 62–63, 68, 144, 161; mistakes, 18, 24, 25, 27–29, 33, 36, 51, 64–66, 77, 79, 95, 154–56, 166; opponents, 2, 22–23, 29–30, 106, 112, 149–51, 164; release from death row, 28; reluctance to execute, 58–60, 92–93, 106–7, 115–16, 144; reversals, 27; supporters, 1, 2, 4, 8, 22–23, 29–30, 67, 92, 93, 106, 112, 117, 130, 142, 150–51, 164. *See also* capital punishment; deterrence; discrimination; just deserts; just execution; rights; retributive justice; wrongful execution
Death Penalty Information Center, 125
dehumanization, 85–86, 120, 128, 145
deontological ethics, 69, 71, 112. *See also* Kant
deterrence, 3, 22, 40, 45, 48, 51–58,

60–63, 65, 67, 69, 72, 88, 102, 120, 147, 174; psychic numbing, 56–57; psychological arousal, 53–56, 61–65, 102
Deuteronomy, 31, 47, 148. *See also* legal codes
DiIulio, John J., 58, 175
diminished capacity, 82, 92, 100–101, 108, 111
discrimination, 101, 121–22, 124–26. *See also* class discrimination; gender/sex discrimination; race discrimination
divine command, 153
docetism, 166

effeminacy, abolishment of death penalty as, 60–63
England: capital crimes in, 32, 47, 52; death penalty abolished, 136
Erez, Edna, 149, 179
euthanasia, 2, 54
execution. *See* botched executions; capital punishment; cost of execution; death penalty; practice, execution as
"eye for an eye," 3, 131, 151

fairness, 20–22, 26, 28, 30, 34, 64, 80, 99–101, 108, 112, 120–23, 121–26. *See also* justice; procedural fairness
feminist critique, 124
Fifth Amendment, 107
Fifth Commandment, 148, 150–51
Florida: and execution of Willie Darden, 16–17; expenditures for executions, 9; malfunctioning electric chair, 25; mistreatment of death-row prisoners, 86; race bias in death sentencing, 123
Foucault, Michel, 55, 174
France, death penalty abolished, 136
Francis, Willie, 126–27
Frank, Daniell, 32, 97
Franklin, Benjamin, 32

Furman v. Georgia, v, 34, 80, 110, 125, 173

Gacey, John Wayne, 25, 172
gender/sex discrimination, 33, 34, 80, 100–101, 121–22, 124–25, 139, 178
General Accounting Office, 123
Georgia, race bias in death sentencing, 122–23
Godfrey v. Georgia, 111
Golden Rule, 81
Gonzales, Henry, 126, 177–78
Good, Edwin, 31, 172
goods of life, 7, 19–20, 22, 89–94, 103–4, 114, 120, 134, 138–39
Graham, Robert, 16
Gregg v. Georgia, 110, 119

habeas corpus, 2
Hatch, Orrin, vi, 103, 110, 130
Henry VIII, 32
Hitler, Adolf, 94, 113
homicides, 2, 5, 58–59, 137, 169
homosexuality, 148
human rights. *See* rights
Hume, David, 32

incarceration, 9, 62–64, 68, 116–17, 121, 129, 133, 137, 139; average sentence for murder, 133, 137, 139
India, sex-selection abortions in, 141
Ingle, Joseph B., vi, 128, 171
In re Kemmler, 126

Japan, death penalty in, 38
Jesus, vi, 7, 115, 150–53, 157–68, 179, 180
Johnson, Robert, 85, 176, 178
juridical rights. *See* rights
just abortion theory, 5, 6, 95, 138–39, 141, 178
jus talionis, 72, 81, 84

just deserts, 9, 10, 134, 143, 160
just execution theory, 4–6, 89, 92–93, 98–101, 103–7, 109–14, 118, 121–23, 125–29, 131–32, 134–40, 142
justice, 1, 5, 6, 9–11, 18–23, 26–27, 28–29, 30, 33–34, 38, 44, 47, 59–60, 63, 68, 72–77, 82–84, 91–92, 95–96, 99–102, 104–6, 108–14, 116–18, 120, 124, 126, 128–29, 132–35, 137–40, 142–46, 150, 152, 154–57, 159–61, 163–65, 167; commutative justice, 20; distributive justice, 20, 101, 108; ends of justice, 19–21, 23, 30, 144; restorative justice, 65, 135; social justice, 20. *See also* fairness; restitution; retributive justice
just war theory, 5, 95, 138, 139, 141, 143

Kant, Immanuel, 3, 4, 69–86, 96–100, 105, 112, 118, 120, 126, 134–35, 147, 175–77
Kemp, John, 82
Kevorkian, Dr. Jack, 171

Lactantius, 32, 150–51
Langan, Patrick, 121, 177
Lawrence-McIntyre, Charshee C., 33, 173
Lee, Robert W., 9–11, 17–18, 171
legal codes: Covenant, 31; Deuteronomy, 31; Hammurabi, 31, 35; Hittite, 31; Holiness, 32; Priestly, 31
lethal injection, 25, 54–55, 110, 126, 127, 168
Levy, Leonard W., 159, 180
lobotomy, 133
Locke, John, 39–49, 69, 83–84, 96, 98, 99, 144
Lockett v. Ohio, 111
Luther, Martin, 32, 150
lynching, 95–96, 113

Martinez, Robert, 16
Marx, Karl, 32
McCleskey v. Kemp, 173
McVeigh, Timothy, 168–69
Mill, John Stuart, 3, 4, 23, 50–69, 71, 77, 79, 96, 98, 102, 172, 174
Mishnah, 149
moral imagination, 26, 64, 66
moral presumption, 5, 6, 89–95, 103–4, 137–42. *See also* presumption against execution
moral relativism, 37, 38, 90, 94, 97, 113, 116
moratorium on executions, v, 143, 179
Mosaic law, 146–49, 152–53; Decalogue, 148
Murphy, Jeffrie G., 134, 178

natural law, 43, 89–90
natural rights. *See* rights
Nazi Germany, policy on execution, 45, 46
North Carolina, mandatory death sentencing, 80. *See also Woodson v. North Carolina*

Origen, 32

Paine, Thomas, 32
Parents of Murdered Children (POMC), 132
paternalism, 124
Paul, 151, 153, 163–64
Peter, 162
Potter, Harry, 173–74
power, 3, 6, 7, 17, 37, 45–46, 67, 95, 113, 115, 117, 127–29, 131, 143–46, 153, 156–57, 161, 163–64
practical reason, 17, 19, 67, 113–14, 120, 130, 140
practice, execution as, v, 4–6, 23, 31, 35, 46, 57, 65, 86–88, 98, 114, 133, 137–38, 141–42, 165–66

presumption against execution, 5, 6, 92–95, 97, 101–7, 111–14, 118, 127, 131, 137–39, 141–42
procedural fairness, 19, 22–24, 26, 29–30, 44, 121, 126. *See also* fairness
proportional justice/punishment, 42–44, 61–63, 67–68, 72, 74, 77–78, 81, 84, 94, 96–97, 100, 102, 105, 110–11, 118, 125, 132–37, 139–40
prosecutorial discretion, 125–26, 134
Putnam, Constance, 28, 172

Qur'an, 97

race discrimination, vi, 3, 17, 22, 24–25, 33–34, 80–81, 100–101, 111, 115, 121–25, 139, 177; race of victim, 122–23
Radelet, Michael, 28, 172
religion, 7, 81, 96, 97, 146–49, 152–54, 156, 159, 165, 179; Christianity, 7, 150–51, 153–54, 158–59, 162–66, 168; Judaism, 149–50, 153
restitution, justice as, 65, 135
retributive justice, 2, 3–4, 22, 40, 42–43, 69, 71–75, 77, 81, 83–84, 87–88, 99–100, 104, 118, 129, 132–35, 142, 144, 151, 163, 165, 167–68, 178
rights, 40–42, 44, 74, 138–39; human rights, 3, 26, 36–39, 41, 43, 45–47, 88, 89, 97, 112; juridical rights, 71, 74–76; natural rights, 5, 36–37, 39–43, 45, 47–48, 117; right not to be executed, 88
Rivkin, Ellis, 159, 180
Roman Catholic Church, 39, 150
Roman Empire, and execution of Jesus, 158–62
Rousseau, Jean-Jacques, 32

sacrifice: execution as, 145; of Jesus, 162–66

self-defense, 35, 40, 42, 44–45, 48, 83–84, 91–92, 98–99, 116–18, 124, 143–44
Simpson, O. J., 59, 60, 126, 172
Socrates, 115
Solomon, Robert, 20, 172
Sorrell, Tom, 175
South Africa, death penalty in, 123–24
Sowell, Thomas, 58, 175
Sparks, Sam, 14
Spenkelink, John, 86, 176
standard of decency, 33, 96–97
Steffen, Lloyd, 171–72, 175–77
suicide, 69, 128, 132. *See also* assisted suicide
symbol: cross as symbol of power, 161–68; death penalty as, 6–8; 143–46, 149, 156–57; executioner as, 34

Talmud, 149
Taoism, 146, 153
Tao Te Ching, 146
terrorism, 45–46, 78, 95, 140, 165
Tertullian, 32
Texas: executions in, 60; expenditures for capital cases, 9; race bias in death sentencing, 123; support for death penalty, 1
theodicy, 154–55
theological sublimation, 7, 168
Tocqueville, Alexis de, 94
torture, 46, 68, 73, 102, 105, 110, 126–28, 178
Trop v. Dulles, 177

Turman, Helen, 12–15
Turman, James, 12–14, 18

United Nations, 36–38, 127
universalism, 37–38, 43, 70, 72–75, 78–79, 81–82, 112, 143
utilitarianism, 36, 40, 47–53, 56–68, 77, 78, 83, 131, 174; act, 49–50; rule, 49–50

vengeance, 83, 99–100, 108, 118–20, 132
victims of crime, 1, 25, 49, 56, 74–75, 93, 96, 100, 104–5, 110–11, 114, 122–23, 131–32, 135
vigilantism, 95, 113
violence, 1, 7, 39, 43, 46, 53–57, 67, 85, 88, 93, 130–32, 153, 166, 179
vision of goodness, 35, 89–90, 113
Voltaire, 32

Welch, Holmes, 146
White, Mel, 147
Wiesel, Elie, 156, 179
Williams, Preston, 38, 173
Wisconsin, abolishment of death penalty, 33, 136
women executed, 80, 124, 125
Woodson v. North Carolina, 80, 110, 175
wrongful execution, 26–29, 64–67, 77, 128

Yerdley, George, 32

Zimmerman, Isidore, 128, 178